NATURAL FINGERING

NATURAL FINGERING

A TOPOGRAPHICAL APPROACH

TO PIANISM

Jon Verbalis

OXFORD
UNIVERSITY PRESS

OXFORD
UNIVERSITY PRESS

Oxford University Press, Inc., publishes works that further
Oxford University's objective of excellence
in research, scholarship, and education.

Oxford   New York
Auckland   Cape Town   Dar es Salaam   Hong Kong   Karachi
Kuala Lumpur   Madrid   Melbourne   Mexico City   Nairobi
New Delhi   Shanghai   Taipei   Toronto

With offices in
Argentina   Austria   Brazil   Chile   Czech Republic   France   Greece
Guatemala   Hungary   Italy   Japan   Poland   Portugal   Singapore
South Korea   Switzerland   Thailand   Turkey   Ukraine   Vietnam

Published by Oxford University Press, Inc.
198 Madison Avenue, New York, New York 10016
www.oup.com

Oxford is a registered trademark of Oxford University Press

Library of Congress Cataloging-in-Publication Data
Verbalis, Jon.
   Natural fingering : a topograpihcal approach to pianism / Jon Verbalis.
      p. cm.
   Includes bibliographical references and index.
   ISBN 978 0 19-518184-5 (hardcover : alk. paper) — ISBN 978-0-19-978163-8
(pbk. : alk. paper) 1. Piano—Fingering. I. Title.
   MT232.V47 2012
   786.2'19368—dc23   2011031324

1 3 5 7 9 8 6 4 2

Printed in the United States of America

to Sara Bershtel

It was at a piano teachers' forum, in New York City nearly four decades ago, that a very well-known and respected colleague asked his simply put question: "What about the fourth finger?" The hall fell deadly silent, with not one of the nearly one hundred piano teachers present daring to utter so much as a word in response. Somehow the moderator of the session, an esteemed pedagogue and nationally known in her own right, managed to finesse us all from the obvious awkwardness of the moment on to a new question—though without comment on that sincere but provocative inquiry. It was an unforgettable moment for me as a young teacher, a remarkably singular occasion.

What about the fourth finger? Chopin bemoaned his, while Schumann fatefully tried to strengthen his; Claudio Arrau recommended avoiding it, but Arthur Rubinstein ultimately did not hold it to be a problem. The matter was apparently of such stubborn and pervasive concern throughout the profession that the great Moriz Rosenthal bitingly remarked: "The deep, almost pious seriousness with which so many pianists set to work on their choice of program and playing is very often derived from a weakness of the fourth finger." Is it possible that Mother Nature could have gotten it so very wrong?

The reader will find much herein about the "problem" of the fourth finger and, in the process, will glean a great deal about what else underlies that which persistently plagues pianists. But Natural Fingering chiefly concerns the correlating of the hand's extraordinary functional design to the keyboard's fixed topographical symmetry. It is about enlisting this remarkable black-and-white-key organization in the service of the pianist's playing mechanism as it journeys throughout the keyboard space it inhabits. It is about the quest for fingering solutions that can rightly be called "natural."

C.P.E. Bach first called for such a "natural fingering" and hinted broadly at the solution. But Chopin really got it, intuiting symmetrical inversion and positing what I have termed his "fundamental pattern" as its conceptual core. And Charles (Carl) Eschmann-Dumur took it further, figured it all out and systematically documented it. Moritz Moszkowski championed his discovery in turn.

Several enthusiastically ran with the ball, among them Rudolf Ganz, the notable Swiss pianist to whom Ravel dedicated his "Scarbo" (Gaspard de la Nuit). Eventually the great Heinrich Neuhaus passionately pleaded for an abandonment of "beloved C" and the formulation of a pianistic pedagogy founded on Chopin's pattern in its stead. Sviatoslav Richter, his most famous student, later proclaimed: "Symmetry! Everything has to be symmetrical."

More recently, in a 2009 Clavier Companion interview, the phenomenal pianist Marc-André Hamelin espoused the virtues of the keyboard's mirrored topography and endorsed employment of symmetrical inversion "for equal development of the hands. . . . Many teachers aren't aware of this," he went on to say, "but it's a very useful tool, probably one of the most useful in the acquisition of a good piano technique. Luckily . . . my father imparted it to me." Hamelin's father, an amateur pianist, had encountered this concept in Ganz's published exercises.

But then there is Irving Berlin and his "funny, shifting piano" that travelled with him wherever he went. Mary Ellin Barrett, his daughter, tells us about "that special piano . . . the brown transposing upright piano . . . the old one with the knob that moved the keyboard, at which at odd hours of the day and night, my father worked. . . . Though he played only in the key of F-sharp, the black-note key that fell easily under his fingers, he needed to hear different keys. . . . One pull of the knob, and as he continued to play in F-sharp, out the notes would come . . . in whatever key was right for singing that particular song." F-sharp, not "beloved C"!

What ever has been going on? And what is it that has yet to be brought to the fore in our pianistic and pedagogical thinking? The "red thread" in all this is the liberating insight that the keyboard's topographical symmetry holds the potential to contribute mightily to pianists' comfort. It further signals a broadly applicable approach to fingering that comports with this amazing design and a search for a compatible pedagogy, one that takes this into account from the start.

I hold here that pattern rarely trumps topography. I also hold that the pianist's entire playing mechanism is perfectly suited to negotiating the entirety of keyboard space, even in the face of the most demanding, most complex repertoire. With this I invite the reader to challenge conventional thinking and join all those who have dared to dislodge "precepts" seemingly cast in stone.

J. V.
New York
April 2011

ACKNOWLEDGMENTS

Natural Fingering is in most respects a distillation of many decades of thought, study and experience. The *I Ching* instructs us that "when the student is ready the teacher will come." Each of us is the "student" of course, and our "teacher" can come in the form of a person, an experience or a challenge. Challenges in turn may also include a person—who is a teacher or student in the usual sense, for example—a technical, performance or musical problem as well as a provocative idea: someone or something that is the antithesis of any existing *status quo*.

Bearing this in mind, I must first of all express my deepest gratitude to *all* these teachers. And I sincerely thank all my students, now far too numerous to acknowledge individually, who from the very first have given me the opportunity to grow in and through my work.

From conception to publication, it is fair to say that *Natural Fingering* has had its own evolution for the better part of the last decade. As a practicum it has always been subject to improvement, further experimentation and refinement. What it holds must ever bear the constant test of broad practical application and conceptual communication. There are therefore many others—more than a few of whom I can count as students, colleagues *and* friends—who are deserving of special thanks for their ongoing support and encouragement, in deed as well as heartening word.

I think it is not a stretch to say that *Natural Fingering* would not have come into being without the enthusiasm and expertise of Sara Bershtel. It must be a rare circumstance indeed that a writer of such a tome as this has the extremely good fortune to have ever available the steady, patient and reliable guidance of one so well versed in the making of books who also knows his work firsthand. Sara's commitment has been an inspiration every step of the way, from start to finish, so it is entirely fitting that *Natural Fingering* is dedicated to her. And to Sara's husband Richard Brick I also remain deeply grateful: suffice it to say that he came to the rescue at a critical time, enabling my writing and back-up research to proceed without undue interruption or difficulty. Friends like Richard and Sara are most definitely, as it is said, pure gold.

To Jane Llewellyn Smith I owe a debt of supreme gratitude; she has been my "right hand" throughout the process. It is to her I must credit the patient—even tedious— work of producing the multitude of text examples, fundamental forms, and repertoire excerpts supporting the concepts presented and expanded on within the text. Given the lack of previously existing models, this was a most difficult and challenging task in far too many respects. But the results (some have called them "elegant") are testimony to her expertise, perseverance and dedication. Jane and I also have a very long professional association, and it has been no small comfort to have her, another "insider," take on all that I have brought to her as well. She is not only among my dearest of friends but an expert and gracious hostess; the many long weekends at her lovely Orient home made our productive work together not only possible but thoroughly pleasant.

My sincere appreciation goes to others as well. Tony Manzella prepared the text examples for the initial proposal, and Marie Bannister was most helpful with her suggestions for select chapters of the first draft. Ruth Golub has believed in *Natural Fingering*'s worth from the bottom of her heart and has always been there for helpful suggestions; I have found her judgment to be of the first order and indispensable. Others to whom I owe thanks include Dr. Paul R. Cooper, Rolla Eisner, Bunny Gable, and Sylvia Seid.

Several colleagues have generously given of their time and expertise in the process of manuscript research or revision. Sandra P. Rosenblum, whose positive, encouraging comments and most helpful suggestions on the earlier chapters and the Bach and Chopin excerpts in particular, contributed significantly to a better revision of my first draft. Beatrice Allen, Corey Hamm, Tomoko Harada, Burton Hatheway, Henry Sheng and Joseph Smith were generous in directing me to, or supplying me with, relevant articles and other information or resources of potential value. Our discussions were enjoyable as well as valuable. And a very special note of gratitude must go to Ann Barnes Halper and Katalin Szekeres Stapelfeldt (both of late) as well as Sarah Halper Krogius. Their gifts of certain texts that are rare and difficult, if not impossible, to obtain—especially what I have come to call my "Horace Middleton Collection"—contributed not insignificantly to the argument for a natural fingering.

A special word must go to Karen Dearborn, director of the Dance Program at Muhlenberg College: for the past ten years it has been my good fortune to serve as dance musician/pianist for this superb program, and *Natural Fingering*'s realization parallels this period. Karen is an extraordinary teacher, and her classes in particular have been informative, inspiring and stimulating in a way that has served my writing and research well. Such an "out of the piano studio" context helped to further clarify, reinforce and validate a great many of the biomechanical and kinesiological principles that I had long sought to bring to the discussion of piano playing generally, and as they relate to pianists' fingering specifically.

I also want to thank the staff of the New York Public Library (Lincoln Center Library of the Performing Arts) and the Pierpont Morgan Library in New York City as well as the Bibliotèque national de France (Music Department) and Bibliotèque Polonaise in Paris.

And last, but certainly not least, I am deeply indebted to my team at Oxford University Press. The project began during Kim Robinson's tenure as senior music editor and was then taken up by her successor and current senior editor, Suzanne Ryan, for the better part of its completion. I thank Kim and Suzanne for their foresight and unwavering support in bringing *Natural Fingering* to the shelves. Suzanne has been uncompromising in her goal of making it the "best book possible," and working with her has been most gratifying in every respect.

Todd Waldman fortuitously came on board in time for the prepublication and publication stages, and it is to him we owe the solution of publishing it as a hybrid book—of posting supplementary material for the printed text online. Todd has demonstrated a deep commitment to *Natural Fingering* over and over, in all the ways an author of such a work could wish. My association with him has been ever assuring as well as productive.

Norm Hirschy has been with this from the start, advising on matters of production as well as reproduction. When I finally met him he enthusiastically announced that I could be certain he would build a terrific website for *Natural Fingering*. I had no doubt that he would—and he did.

And to my production editor, Erica Woods Tucker, and all the reviewers I also owe many thanks. As a university press, Oxford adheres to a system of manuscript peer review at progressive stages from proposal to final submission, and the excellent outside reviewers have contributed in no small measure to whatever success *Natural Fingering* will enjoy. Their attention to its copious detail, and equally their enthusiastic endorsement of its content and intent, was a source of great encouragement throughout my writing and ongoing research. The reviewers' pointed but constructive criticism was invaluable and contributed greatly to the successive revisions that led to a better book.

CONTENTS

I shall build upon nature, for a natural fingering. . . .

Carl Philipp Emanuel Bach

It is the familiar that usually eludes us in life. What is before our nose is what we see last.

William Barrett

ABOUT THE COMPANION WEBSITE

www.oup.com/us/naturalfingering

To accompany *Natural Fingering*, we have created a password-protected website where readers can access copious excerpts from the extant repertoire with natural fingering solutions, extended discussions on relevant topics and a comprehensive manual of the fundamental forms with symmetrically adjusted fingerings.

You may access the site with username Music1 and password Book5983.

NATURAL FINGERING

INTRODUCTION

Everything is a matter of knowing good fingering.
—Frederic Chopin

The science of fingering has not kept pace with the changes and developments of the science of technique.
—Thomas Fielden

BOTH OF THESE STATEMENTS, their words a hundred years apart, remain as true now as ever. Since then, numerous treatises on technique have contributed immensely to the understanding and advancement of pianism, and its pedagogy has been enormously enriched by them. But in matters of fingering—this everyday tool of pianists at all levels—there has been an amazing dearth of comprehensive and cohesive guidance, an enormous gap in the methodology and literature toward a practical and healthy pianism.

It is generally appreciated that the evolution of the piano as we know it today was neither steady nor swift. And that the road to the magnificent instrument we now enjoy was littered with its own "carnage," so to speak (in the physiological sense, an apt metaphor), and with baggage no longer useful or appropriate to the journey. Mostly this is accepted—more than 250 years later—as the understandable, if unfortunate, result of what was only a very gradual transformation of approaches to keyboard technique. The pace of technological innovation has historically always proved much faster than any commensurate adaptation, and a certain cognitive lag impedes our progress to this day. Ideas no longer valid or necessary have remained operative—even "below the surface," if you will.

It has been an extraordinary evolution, and what was once adequate or appropriate for the earlier instruments is no longer sufficient for the vastly extended dynamics of the modern piano, with its newfound potential to accommodate an enormous range of individual expression. And that has exerted its own influence in matters of fingering.

Because the keyboard, as we have now come to know it, only gradually increased in range, horizontal movements were understandably not of such immediate concern at first. Black and white keys in their respective planes require movements forward and backward, and absent these, a "neutralizing" assignment to complementary fingers of appropriately varying lengths. The equal-tempered octave continues to be directly calibrated to the span of the average hand,[1] still setting forth certain fixed parameters for a practical organization of the keys: octaves, four-part chords, and tonic-to-tonic scale/arpeggio divisions still follow from this. But as the potential of the instrument itself grew in dynamic and dramatic power, the application of a more powerful vertical force was ultimately required.

Further experimentation and serious attempts at further innovation did not cease with the dawning, or the passing, of the piano's Golden Age. Nonetheless, our present keyboard has remained the great "constant." But this very constancy has contributed much to an innocent underestimation of the adaptability required of the modern pianist of every musical epoch.

We have come to take the keyboard so for granted, in both visual and tactile senses, that we do not seem to feel there is anything more to discover. Accustomed as we are to the keyboard, it would seem to have no more "secrets" to yield. And so, too much of current methodology remains either an unadorned recycling of ideas that have long outlived their novelty and relevance or can be fairly described as creative presentations of "old wine in new bottles"—however imaginative, attractive and entertaining. The pedagogical superstructure is now top-heavy, unwieldy and overwhelming—just what happens when essential underpinnings are neglected, underestimated and overlooked. Or long in need of repair or replacement.

In the singular matter of fingering, this is manifest at a most basic level: the generally unquestioned acceptance of scale and arpeggio fingerings that are now enshrined as "standard," with all-white-key C major as archetype and pedagogical model. But it is similarly telling that the "everyday" thumb-hand pivoting movements receive relatively only the most minuscule attention in the technical manuals and treatises, if at all, rarely deserving even so much as a mention or reference (one need only scan their indexes to see that this is so). In fact, many prefer instead to deny their validity as appropriate keyboard actions, even while they are unable at the same time to otherwise demonstrate a legato connection without the aid of the damper pedal at slower to moderately fast tempi. Recommendations to avoid the fourth finger if at all possible do nothing to shed light on the issues surrounding it, or those, similarly, for the fifth finger. Avoidance of a problem has never brought about its solution.

That evolving compositional styles also bear a great role in all this must likewise be remarked. Along with technological innovation, they too have pushed the envelope as to what pianists of a later day must acquire as merely a serviceable technique. Such an unceasing stretching and straining of the accustomed boundaries has always placed continual strains on pianists and pianism. But the current *fashion* of an era—the prevailing aesthetic, often at odds with more appropriately relevant considerations of the particular performing style and sentiment of an earlier period—may take its toll on the performer as well.

It most often happens that only a limiting, debilitating, or even paralyzing physiological state—in other words, a crisis—forces closer examination of playing mechanism use (rather than tone quality, which is both harbinger and ultimate arbiter). Yet the possibility that fingering choices themselves may be a root cause of such problems is severely underestimated. And the fact that one cannot embark upon any healthy reeducation of the pianist's playing mechanism, and that it cannot be sustained for any significant length of time, without an in-depth appraisal of accustomed habits of fingering—most of them reflexive and no longer conscious—has been given scant attention. The search for a resolution of troublesome fingering matters is rarely relegated to the physiological, even less so to the kinesiological.

Otto Ortmann, and considerably later József Gát, seriously attempted to differentiate the fingers to some extent in terms of individual physiological attributes and affinities. And Thomas Fielden called for a fundamental reappraisal of long-held fingering concepts on the basis of the keyboard's topography and the fourth finger as preferred black-key pivot. But only E. Robert Schmitz managed to elevate the discussion to include a full confluence of the physiological, kinesiological and topographical—all the while, curiously, avoiding a meaningful survey of the thumb-hand pivoting action!

Nonetheless, comprehensive principles of fingering, to the extent they are even considered as such, are otherwise deemed "fixed." That is, their basic rationales are taken to have been long settled during the history of the modern piano's evolution, with its great roster of performing giants and hundreds of years of an astounding repertoire that is vast, rich and varied. Surely, the argument goes, there is nothing more to it. Challenges not easily or neatly met by these commonly held precepts, few that they are, must therefore be solely a matter of the "individual hand" or some ill-defined and elusive "art of fingering"—or even demonstrative of a lack of talent or natural affinity for the instrument.

But therein lies the inherent absurdity of the "every hand is different" argument. If that is so—and in certain *specific* ways it is indeed so—what then is the justification for slavishly adhering to the fingering of any particular edition, as many do? Why are the standard fingerings for the fundamental forms nonetheless prescribed for every hand? Why not, then, just teach the scales and arpeggios theoretically and let each hand find its own way in these as well?

This of course is exactly what the untrained (even if talented) pianist does at first. But such contradictions surely fly in the face of any and all sincere attempts over these last few hundred years to unlock the keyboard's mysteries and organize its tones in a meaningful and practical manner. This, after all, is what any rational approach to fingering is all about.

The search for optimally suitable fingering is as old as the keyboard itself, and the early keyboard players wrote much about fingering for their instruments. Some even advocated use of the thumb, an extraordinary proposition at a time when fragile instruments called for a restrained touch. J. S. Bach is generally credited with successfully advancing this then-revolutionary innovation, moreover elevating it to preeminence as the "principal finger."[2] And among the most famous and influential of those attempting to formulate principles, rules and guidelines in regard to keyboard fingering was his son Carl Philipp Emanuel.

In C.P.E. Bach's *Essay on the True Art of Playing Keyboard Instruments*, he sought to firmly establish that the thumb should be assigned to a white key and that the third is the finger of choice for a black-key "pivot." As for the scales, it is noteworthy that he conceded that there were fewer fingering options as the number of black keys increased, since there were then fewer white keys available to the thumb. Most significantly, certain fingering alternatives advanced for those scales having a paucity of black keys nonetheless reflected his recognition of the chief problem inherent in scales for more than one octave in movement away from the torso: the most advantageous assignment of the fourth finger for thumb-under pivoting. But he did not include fingerings for the harmonic minor forms.

C.P.E. Bach and other contemporaries took monumental steps toward establishing principles and guidelines for fingering. But it was not until the nineteenth century that many of them became widely and seriously debated—and ultimately disavowed. In regard to the scale fingerings, for example, what we now know as the "standard" fingerings were established and generally adopted during that period.[3] Of the post-Classical "transitional" luminaries, Johann (Jan) Nepomuk Hummel's thinking on pianistic and pedagogical matters must be considered the most modern and influential of its time. His monumental *A Complete Theoretical and Practical Course of*

Instructions on the Art of Playing the Piano Forte was published in 1828, first in German and then with subsequent translations in English and French. Chopin considered Hummel the most "knowledgeable" in fingering matters[4] and customarily included his compositions in his own teaching repertoire.

C.P.E. Bach had already observed that the three "long" (second, third and fourth) fingers best complemented the group of three "short" black keys and rightly suspected that they held the key to successful fingering solutions. And Chopin's thinking on the "pivot" was generally in concurrence with that of C.P.E. Bach and others of his time; he too felt that the third finger, the longest, should be the pivot finger of choice. This is certainly not surprising given his well-known personal complaint of a "weak" fourth finger. But it was revolutionary in at least one fundamental respect. He considered those scales with an abundance of black keys to be the most *pianistic,* that is, the most naturally suited to the hand *and* keyboard. Chopin argued that they should constitute the *basis* for determining appropriate fingerings, as well as further serving the hand's optimal *orientation* to the keyboard.

Although his *Projet de méthode* addresses the fingerings for the major scales only and provides little or no definite instruction for left-hand (LH) fingerings, it is nonetheless suggestive of a wealth of intriguing ideas. Noting that the B major scale assigns the thumb to the white keys and the three long fingers to the three shorter black keys, he therefore designated it as *the* scale that is the most natural to the hand. He instructed that it should be taught first, rather than the C major scale, which "has no pivot"—no doubt referring to the absence of a black key that would best enable the necessary pivoting action in extending a scale *beyond the range of an octave*.

Amazingly however, what Chopin neglected to observe, or at least to fully appreciate and highlight, was another most distinguishing feature of the B major scale: the unavoidable *black key pivot of the fourth to the thumb* (RH: A-sharp to B and LH: F-sharp to E).[5] Apart from the advantage of long fingers on short keys, this is the other distinguishing, determining factor behind his elevation of B major as the exemplar of a scale that is most natural and most demonstrably "pianistic." All of the other scales of five black keys (the enharmonic major scales of the Circle of Fifths)—including their parallel *and* relative minors, for that matter—are similarly distinguished and likewise most pianistic.

Chopin's unfinished sketch for his *méthode*,[6] though extremely insightful, was not comprehensive and, for the most part, bore little fruit in its day beyond his circle of devoted students.[7] But what I have called his Fundamental Pattern will be shown to be the most revolutionary insight of all. Chopin, with his customary brilliance, intuited this as excerpted from the D-flat scale for the LH (F-G♭-A♭-B♭-C) and the B major scale for the RH (E-F♯-G♯-A♯-B), scales of five flats and sharps respectively (see Chapter 1, Examples 1.1 and 1.2). Heinrich Neuhaus, one of the twentieth century's greatest pianists and pedagogues, was ultimately to consider this symmetrical pattern to be at the very core of a successful pianism and pianistic pedagogy, passionately pleading for a reappraisal and reversal of a long-entrenched pedagogy rooted in C major. But he rendered it as E-F♯-G♯-A♯-B♯, though noting that the "B sharp can also be replaced by a B natural."[8] Now a whole-tone rather than diatonic pattern, it is spelled enharmonically as F♭-G♭-A♭-B♭-C (see Chapter 1, notes 1 and 3).

With the continuing technological development of the piano and the construction of larger concert halls to accommodate an ever-growing *bourgeois* listening public, the piano achieved a new level of popularity. It was, musically speaking, the symbol of the nineteenth-century Romantic hero, the individual—whether poet, artist or other "revolutionary"—who, as misfit or outcast, stood his ground vis-à-vis society and the establishment. The piano concerto expressed this relationship metaphorically: it is the piano that stands in the foreground, at once alone yet in necessary dialogue, collaboration and even conflict with the orchestra. As the piano became more and more popular, an instrument reserved not solely for professionals and "geniuses" but attractive to amateurs as well, piano "methods" and other pedagogical regimens multiplied, along with the quest for better means of pianism and piano artistry.

The ongoing evolution of a compositional style of increased complexity and unparalleled technical demand further stimulated the need to revisit traditional approaches to the keyboard. The climate was ripe to question the prevalent approach to piano technique, one theretofore based on a relatively uncritical transfer of earlier principles of keyboard playing, appropriate for the older keyboard instruments but not the still-evolving modern piano. Established approaches to matters of fingering, even those of the scales, were not exempt from this new spirit of reevaluation and reconsideration.

But strangely, the highly chromatic musical language of the time instead favored general acceptance of the C major fingering sequence for its (arguably) perceived advantage in facilitating transposition. In an important sense, this fit very nicely with the iconoclasm of a more "modern" approach to fingering: whereas previously the thumbs were reserved for the white keys, they were now readily placed on the black keys.

Indeed, the "singing" ability of the thumbs, especially the role of alternating thumbs in taking on melodic lines in the piano's middle register, became one of the hallmarks of nineteenth-century piano technique. To encourage ease with this rather innovative technique, pianists were simply urged to transfer those scales having white-key tonics (using the C scale as model) from the white-key plane to the black-key plane; Liszt played an influential role in this. That *all* scales should ultimately be practiced with the C major fingering, thumbs on tonic, soon became *de rigueur* for the training of advanced pianists. C major remained firmly established as the foundation and ideal model for scale study.

Except in regard to compositional key choice, it cannot be said that the keyboard's topography was consciously enlisted as an agent in the resolution of fingering matters. Pattern remained king. And Chopin's own persuasive arguments and compositional practice notwithstanding, all-white-key C major has prevailed as the basis of piano pedagogy to this day.

Since Liszt's time, the search for alternative scale fingerings has been a persistent one, albeit sporadic. Teachers and pianists as diverse and renowned as Francis Taylor (a student of Clara Schumann), Theodore Wiehmayer, Rudolf Ganz, Ernst Bacon, Powell Everhart, Stanley Fletcher and, most recently, Penelope Roskell have argued for and offered alternatives to the standard, conventional fingerings.[9]

Toward the end of the nineteenth century, two particularly significant contributions began pointing to the fourth finger as the most important black-key pivot. Charles (Carl) Eschmann-Dumur further explored and expounded on the keyboard's symmetrical organization, with revolutionary implications. In his *Exercises techniques pour Piano,* he developed an original approach to the note/finger grouping of scales. He appears to have been the first to observe that major scales of equal sharps and flats are, in fact, mirror images of each other as to interval and black-key, white-key sequence when regrouped and compared contrariwise.[10] In the following, the four- and three-note patterns of the descending scale with three flats (three black keys) exactly mirrors the ascending scale with three sharps (three black keys), and vice versa. The fingering patterns are appropriately mirroring as well:

Left Hand / Right Hand

<u>**3 2 1 4 3 2 1**</u>   <u>**1 2 3 4   1 2 3**</u>

E♭ FG A♭ B♭ CD   DEF♯ G♯   ABC♯

C♯ DE F♯ G♯ AB   FGA♭ B♭   CDE♭

Most important for our purposes, these mirror images represent consistent and systematic employment of the fourth finger as black-key pivot. Similar groupings for all major scales, thumbs assigned to white keys and fourth to a black key, reveal symmetrical relationships that likewise mirror as to topography (black and white keys), interval *and* fingering!

Moritz Moszkowski, in his *Écoles des Gammes et des Double Notes*, reiterated these observations in his presentation of scales in thirds and sixths, and he also offered alternatives to the conventional fingerings for the harmonic minor scales by consistently applying the fourth finger to a black key (thumbs on white keys). Alberto Jonás[11] refers to these contributions in volume two of his seven-volume compendium *Master School of Modern Piano Playing & Virtuosity* (1922). Although he also included the standard fingerings, Jonás strongly advocated and argued for these alternatives.

Even as Eschmann-Dumur and Moszkowski were experimenting with alternative approaches to scale fingerings that were already "standardized" at the time, the overall climate was also ripe for questioning the then-prevailing approaches to piano playing. Teachers such as Ludwig Deppe, Elisabeth Caland, Frederic Horace Clark, Rudolph Maria Breithaupt, Marie Jaëll, Friedrich Adolf Steinhausen, William Townsend and Tobias Matthay, among others, did much to encourage independent thinking from a more rational, scientific standpoint.

Otto Ortmann, in his preeminent *The Physiological Mechanics of Piano Technique* (1929), would later designate the fourth finger as the center of axis for the forearm and thus suggest a fuller appreciation of the role of the fourth finger as pivot. In *The Riddle of the Pianist's Finger* (1936), Arnold Schultz concurred. Though not employing the more inclusive term "topography," Ortmann does address black and white key formulations to some extent in his comparatively brief considerations of fingering.[12] But most remarkable, his entire movement analysis of scale playing is based on that of C major—and of the right hand only![13]

It was Thomas Fielden who, in *The Science of Pianoforte Technique* (1927, 1934), most loudly decried the lack of progress in putting fingering matters on more solid ground: again, "The science of fingering has not kept pace with the changes and developments of the science of technique."[14] He appears to be the first to have introduced the term *topography* in relation to fingering, and he pointedly admonished that "a sound knowledge of this is essential if many technical problems are to be mastered." In regard to scale fingering he succinctly advises: "All scale fingerings should follow the pattern of alternate groupings of fingers 1, 2, 3, 4; 1, 2, 3 with *the rule that the*

4th finger in either hand should (except, of course, in the scale of C) *always be on a black note.*" Further, this rule "ensures that the 4th finger should be used in its natural and most comfortable position." In identifying the fourth finger as the important black-key pivot, Fielden logically infers that it is the four-finger/note group that determines the superior fingering; indeed, this is reflected in his ordering of fingering sequence in the preceding "rule." He did not address the coordinated pivoting action of the thumb and fourth finger per se. But he did state unequivocally that "the thumb goes under the fourth always after a black note, and not after a white note, a fact which experiment will show to be most important in the matter of comfort and ease."[15] Fielden does note the symmetrical mirroring of the major scales.

In *The Capture of Inspiration* (1935), his brilliant, complex, but little-known and mostly misunderstood and underestimated work, E. Robert Schmitz too proposed that the conventional scale and arpeggio fingerings, widely in use then as now, be reconsidered from the standpoint of keyboard "topography" and be made compatible with it. He set about to elevate topographical considerations to the role of indispensable ally in the specific problem of fingering.

Schmitz contemplated alternatives to the standard fingerings in light of just one "guiding" principle: that short (thumb and fifth) fingers should be on long (white) keys and long (second, third and fourth) fingers on short (black) keys *whenever possible*. This application thereby "neutralized" the otherwise varying finger and key lengths to maximize the action of the keys as levers. He charted some newly proposed scale and arpeggio fingerings primarily on the basis of his belief that the third finger, being the longest, should be the finger of choice for a black key, with the thumb, as always, best reserved for a white key. Schmitz referenced Chopin's *méthode* and included a facsimile of a page from his manuscript. Although advocating Chopin's pattern as the most natural accommodation of the (right) hand to the keyboard—and the basis of a "natural position of the hand" at the keyboard[16]—Schmitz did not, most curiously, credit him with that very pattern. But it is extremely noteworthy that he included a facsimile page of Chopin's manuscript,[17] one year before Cortot's celebrated acquisition of the *Projet de méthode* manuscript in 1936 and his subsequent publication of its translation with commentary.[18] And Schmitz does go on to confirm this central link in his thinking by informing us that from "other manuscripts by Chopin we see that the use of short fingers on white keys and long fingers on black keys was also sensed by him."

Other pianists and teachers also began to seek fingering solutions based on a more heightened awareness and knowledge of anatomy, physiology and kinesiology—as opposed to mere "preference"—in a determined effort to address their overall dissatisfaction with the standard fingerings and their limitations when practically applied to the repertoire. However, a more encompassing, thoroughly consistent and rational approach, one that embraces the keyboard's topography and its remarkable symmetry, remained elusive.

When referred to at all, the topography of the piano keyboard is usually considered in terms of its biplanar construction and orderly arrangement of black and white keys, whether or not its symmetry is fully understood or appreciated.[19] But the designation properly refers to *all* its physical characteristics:

1. Relative key length, width, depth and height; varying differences in key resistance due to leverage at specific points of contact, as well as the length and thickness

(girth) of the strings; even the tactile quality of its key surface materials (ivory/plastic and ebony)

2. "Biplanar" construction (white-key and black-key horizontal planes)
3. Dimensions as reflected in the vertical and horizontal spatial continuum that are traversed in movement from key to key and plane to plane

The term *topology* is more specifically applied when quantifying the spatial distances encompassed within an overall topography or a particular topographical organization or relationship, such as interval and keyboard range. *The parameters and scope of movement at the keyboard follow from both its topography and its topology.*

I first became acquainted with the concept of a physical accommodation of the pianist's playing mechanism to keyboard topography in my undergraduate years. Through my studies with Alice Pashkus, I was extremely fortunate to have received a thorough understanding and practice of the "Fundamental Principles of Training" (Appendix 9) and their compounds as proposed by E. Robert Schmitz, with whom she had studied and whose work informed much of her own unique approach, in *The Capture of Inspiration*. At the time, I also received from her a copy this seminal work, which proved an invaluable resource during those studies with her and has remained so to this day. Schmitz, Debussy's friend, assistant and colleague, is best known as the author of the authoritative treatise *The Piano Works of Claude Debussy*. He contributed greatly as performer and pedagogue, and even as impresario.[20]

At the time of my introduction to Schmitz's fingering concepts, however, I was not unfamiliar with Chopin's Fundamental Pattern. In fact, it had long served as one of my most useful technical "tools" from my early teens, although I was unaware of any connection to Chopin's pedagogical thinking—a good example of its somewhat "mainstream" survival. Anne Vanko Liva,[21] my teacher at the time, likewise presented it to me as the most natural accommodation of the hand to the keys: long fingers on short keys and short fingers on long keys. The unique advantage of this obviously singular arrangement was, of course, immediately apparent to me. Many basic patterns—single and double notes, repeated and trilled—and their variants were applied to it on the road to greater finger "independence" and control. I did not then fully grasp the topographical implications of Chopin's pattern or its potential as a core basis for keyboard fingering. But that it was emblematic of a fundamental principle of fingering was certainly clear to me. The stage was set for more in-depth thinking along those lines, and I was ready to seriously consider Schmitz's proposals.

At the time, though, I was of two minds in regard to his topographically adjusted fingerings for the scales. I found them intriguing on a theoretical level, but I did not find his revisions appealing or convincing on a practical one. Lacking in certain consistencies, the standard fingerings nonetheless appeared to follow a logic that I was quite comfortable with after so many years of practicing and teaching them. Moreover, Schmitz's preference for the third finger for a black-key pivot did not convincingly address what I increasingly came to see as the central difficulty: *the pivoting action of the fourth finger and thumb on adjacent or consecutive white keys, particularly in movement away from the torso.*

The results of Schmitz's search for alternative fingerings were often inconsistent as well. He studiously avoided the fourth on a black key except when inescapable (such as note groups of three adjacent black keys or arpeggios with more than one black key). Thus, like Chopin, he failed to fully discern just what else it was that made scales such as B major or arpeggios such as G-sharp minor most comfortable, or more "pianistic": the fourth finger as pivot on a black key followed by the thumb on a white key.

The standard fingerings also seemed to benefit greatly from certain *adjustments* advocated by Schmitz (including horizontal upper arm movements to and from black keys—"in" and "out"—and lateral movements at the wrist for finger/arm alignment.[22] I could therefore see no significant advantage in learning a new set of scale and arpeggio fingerings at the time. In addition, professional groups and music schools expected, even required, scales and arpeggios to be performed with these conventional fingerings. For students not to do so would likely be deemed a gross deficiency in their training; it seemed to be needlessly iconoclastic to train them otherwise.

Nonetheless, I began to seriously reconsider my overall approach to fingering and experiment further from a topographical standpoint, eventually arriving at what I came to call "topographical fingering." Though continuing to adhere to the standard fingerings for scales and arpeggios, my approach to passage work became increasingly topographically based as I searched for the most advantageous fingering, including fingerings for the scales and arpeggios found therein. I consequently found myself constantly reworking the "nontopographical" fingerings that seemed to be all too frequently encountered in available editions and that I now found to be, comparatively speaking, unsatisfactory.

Although long committed to engaging my students in the process of discovering the best fingering options, I soon realized that they required a set of comprehensive principles if they were to proceed more independently along topographical lines. I began to experiment with the fingerings for these fundamental forms, now consistently assigning the fourth finger as pivot on black keys and maintaining the thumb on white. From this I discovered that just *one* principle, **fourth on black and thumb on white,** can be applied effectively and systematically to all thirty-six diatonic scales in all their forms, major and minor. Moreover, in searching for arpeggio fingerings that avoided *unnecessary* lateral stretches—an important *qualifying* principle for extended seventh patterns, for example—I discovered something most amazing: *all* arpeggio fingerings having one or more black keys may likewise be gleaned from this single guiding principle. Fielden had it right!

But going further, my analysis revealed that there were *only five "topographical"—black and white key—possibilities for **all** scales and arpeggios* at their core. The consistent application of just this one guiding principle, **fourth on black and thumb on white,** revealed an organization of scale and arpeggio fingering that is truly amazing in its logic, ease of execution and consistency.

I immediately began to embark wholeheartedly on implementing this topographical approach with my advanced students. The results and their reactions were remarkable. In spite of many years of "working *in*" the conventional fingerings, the shift to the topographical was immediate and illuminating. All marveled at the elimination of former difficulties and at the evenness and clarity of articulation that resulted from a mere change of fingering. And *all* responded with the very same words: "It's so rational!" Those who had previously resisted practicing scales and arpeggios now approached it with newfound interest and enthusiasm. Most important, and most satisfying to me, was that my students could now be enthusiastically engaged in the fingering process with an insight and enjoyment that formerly eluded them.

The next challenge was to do the same for my less-experienced students. What followed were some of the most interesting and stimulating "chapters" of my teaching experience.

One of the arguments for the standard approach is the supposed ease with which the C scale fingering sequence can be transferred to a new tonal center, and therefore a new key. However, for *both* hands this really works only for C, G, D, A and E major and their parallel minors. Proceeding from C major and introducing the sharps (black keys) one by one certainly has the advantage of a certain logic, visual clarity, and theoretical consistency—but *only for those keys,* that is, C, G, D, A and E. Whereas the *fingering* patterns of these keys are obviously symmetrical contrariwise, there is little or no topographical symmetry. Except for E, which is topographically correct for both hands, they are not as physically comfortable for the LH *beyond one octave when the fourth must pivot on a white key* (a comparison with their RH counterparts is revealing in this regard).

But since the standard fingerings offered a relatively simple means of introducing the scales, I decided to continue teaching them to students at the elementary and intermediate levels. As they progressed, however, I began concentrating on those keys, mostly the major flat and enharmonic (D♭/C♯, G♭/F♯ C♭/B) keys, for which the fingerings have always been topographically correct, saving for last those keys still requiring topographical resolutions. As for C major, I now assigned it only in order to introduce or reinforce the theoretical construction of scales relative to the Circle of Fifths.

At this stage of my experimentation, I noticed something surprising: those younger students who had the strongest physical sense of the keyboard (the "naturals," as we usually refer to them) had the most difficulty with the standard, *non*topographical solutions. They inadvertently lapsed into topographical fingerings, especially when extending the scales more than one octave in the left hand descending. I had already noticed that my older, more accomplished students, despite their many years of training in the conventional fingerings, would inevitably lurch into topographical fingerings, exclaiming with frustration at these "slips": "I don't know why my finger keeps wanting to go there!" I then began to realize that it was time for me to make the big leap and find a way to introduce these topographical fingerings as close to day one as possible.

For now, suffice to say that young people are absolutely amenable to topographical fingerings at a very early stage. And as Part IV will show, the theoretical advantage of beginning with C major does not have to be relinquished. The discussion therein also includes suggestions, strategies and guidelines for reeducating ("retooling," if you will) students of many years' experience as well as for introducing scales and the basic concepts of topographical fingering to students in the formative stages.

Over the many years in which topographical considerations have been paramount in my approach to a "natural" fingering, it became increasingly clear to me that:

1. The biomechanical and kinesiological implications of such an approach were profound
2. Analysis of *patterns of topography* would yield convincing evidence of an inherent simplicity and efficient organization
3. When altered, topographically fingered scale and arpeggio patterns most consistently reflected the fundamental harmonic *functions* these tonal alterations represented
4. The topographical fingerings of the fundamental forms—scales, arpeggios, double notes, etc.—were *directly* applicable to passages of the piano literature to an astoundingly greater degree than the standard fingerings

5. Patterns for those note/finger groups *seemingly* outside the basic, *core* topographical patterns were discernible; they would specifically function as the connecting *links*
6. From all these, *principles of fingering* that were topographically, physiologically and kinesiologically sound could be distilled and would serve to illumine the fingering process enormously and permit the broadest application
7. Keyboard symmetry as it applies to keyboard solutions is fundamentally reflected in Chopin's pattern

All thoughtful teachers must make decisions about what to teach—and why, when and how. And all dedicated teachers are unceasing in their determined efforts to find better means for developing, encouraging and inspiring the aspiring musicians and artists in their charge. Though I firmly believe that scales and arpeggios, along with other basic patterns such as trills, double thirds and sixths, octaves, etc., are an indispensable part of a student's technical regimen and keyboard study, I know very well how easily tedium can set in. Of course, students can ultimately be directed to various etudes and a wealth of advanced studies; Chopin's, Debussy's and Scriabin's, for example, remain unsurpassed in their challenges and uncanny insight into pianistic needs. They are nonetheless extremely time-consuming and obviously not suitable for the earlier and formative years of study. But even the most talented and devoted of students find that their productive practice time is at a premium. Only the most efficient, well-focused, *relevant* approach to pianistic, musical and artistic development has a chance of being broadly and wholeheartedly accepted.

From such an expanded perspective, I hold that scales and arpeggios are central to musicianship and pianistic training. In the chapters that follow, I not only advocate an approach to their fingering; I also propose concise principles of fingering that are grounded in the topographical symmetry of the keyboard and rooted in both the physiology of the playing mechanism and the kinesiology of its movements in keyboard space. My aim is to offer a rational method for determining optimal fingerings throughout the broad repertoire, to show how the consistent application of just a few fundamental principles may engage both the aspiring and the accomplished pianist in the enterprise. A large swath of excerpts from the extant repertoire are included, to this end.

We are currently enjoying the performances of an amazing number of pianists with outstanding techniques, for whom everything is possible and who would be the envy of most of their colleagues of earlier eras. The standard is extraordinarily high. But why, then, after hundreds of years of experiment and experience, are we still seeing a profession fraught with debilitating performance injury, some of it admitted and some borne in private despair?[23] What is it we are missing? That we are missing something is clear. And surely, what we are missing is what we must look for—what we must find. But like the keyboard itself, perhaps it is that we have been taking another tool, its fingering, for granted.

I hold it foremost that the playing mechanism's natural *functional structure* be wedded to the keyboard's symmetrical topography. This is to be distinguished from, and is not to be confused with, a *functional adaptation* to it. The mechanism's inherent, natural design to functionally accommodate movement and to efficiently transmit and impart force in any three-dimensional space must likewise be properly reflected in movement coordinated within the specific confines and parameters of keyboard space. An exquisitely balanced dynamic of speed, force and control cannot be achieved or maintained without a comprehensive consideration of the keyboard's topography.

There is always a certain attitude toward something familiar, that because we use it or see it everyday we must therefore "know" it; this is also true of any long experience with the keyboard. But such an attitude of readily assumed familiarity also commonly manifests itself as an absence of wonder, an underestimation of potential and, specific to the keyboard, an underappreciation of its symmetrical construction and what it represents.

Consequently, a necessary and thorough reconsideration and reappraisal of *all* that the keyboard might yield regarding fingering issues and related concerns has repeatedly been handicapped by a failure to thoroughly explore its topography. This has been on the minds, in one way or another, of some of the greatest keyboard artists and teachers of the piano for the major part of the history of modern pianism. Many of them frequently subscribed to "unusual" (though successful) fingerings that, for one reason or another, have failed to capture the attention and imagination of the professional mainstream.

We are left with the need to look at the keyboard afresh. We need to see it with the wonder that captivated, stimulated and inspired Chopin. Still, we need to go beyond what Chopin intuitively grasped (he did, of course, what true genius does) and build on the foundation he left us, unfinished as it was. And to do this we must also, at least temporarily, suspend long-held, unquestioned precepts. We must endeavor to encounter the keyboard anew, with "beginner's mind" and "beginner's eye." If we can do this, the keyboard's defining topography and remarkable symmetry will yield and validate its own solutions to the matter of its fingering.

A conceptual "shift" will necessarily follow. It is quite in order and long overdue.

AUTHOR'S NOTE

The matter of editions is rather contentious, and one need only read the extensive writings of several well-known scholars to appreciate the thorny issues involved. I have chosen the texts for the musical examples from among those editions that are both highly respected and widely available. You the reader should note that the fingerings presented herein are not those of any specific editions but are those founded on the topographical principles set forth, and thus they are only incidentally in agreement—in relatively few instances.

Except where indicated otherwise, the text of the musical examples largely comports as follows: *Henle* for Bach, Schubert, Mozart, Beethoven; *Kalmus* for Brahms and Schumann; *Paderewski* for Chopin; *Durand* for Debussy and Ravel; *International* for Rachmaninoff and Scriabin; the Russian editions (reprinted by *Dover*) for Prokofieff and Shostakovich; and *PWM* (Polskie Wydawnictwo Muzyczne, 1975) for Szymanowski.

Measure numbers will be found for all examples to facilitate comparison among the many editions (where there are more than one) in matters of fingering as well as dynamic markings. The repertoire excerpts and the fingerings for the Fundamental Forms will be found to be of immediate value for practical implementation. But it is surely so that a serious study of all that the keyboard's symmetrical topography holds will yield extraordinary fruit over time.

FUNDAMENTAL FORMS
AS FOUNDATION

1

The highest technic, broadly speaking, may be traced back to scales and arpeggios . . . the teacher is largely responsible if the pupil finds scale practice dry or tiresome.
—Joseph Lhevinne

Scales . . . are the essence of beautiful playing . . . the beautifully balanced use of power and distance.
—Abby Whiteside

THE DEVELOPMENT AND CULTIVATION OF A FLUID, musical, artistic scale "line" remains one of the most difficult of pianistic challenges. A line with shape, clarity, perfectly gauged tones and expressive content is a tremendous achievement, deceptive in its simplicity. Indeed, no aspect of pianism is as technically revealing as a scale or arpeggio passage, nor as essential. Scales and arpeggios, after all, not only are the bedrock of some of the most beautiful melodic lines in piano literature but abound as embellishment, dramatic commentary or other passagework of varied configuration. And yet, their role in the technical training and artistic development of pianists remains controversial. The continuing discourse on the importance of the study of these fundamental forms reflects distinct differences in philosophy and pedagogy.

There are opinions on all sides of the argument, and one would have no difficulty citing numerous "authorities" in the concert as well as the pedagogical fields. All concede that the study of scales and arpeggios (the horizontal, melodic extension of chords) is irreplaceable as a foundation for harmonic understanding. But many are convinced of their indispensability to pianistic development and, like Mme. Rosina Lhevinne, have both recommended and required that their students practice *all* scales and arpeggios *on a daily basis* as a necessary part of their technical training. And some, less experienced and less informed, have gone so far as to insist on scales and arpeggios as the exclusive means of technical development.

On the other side of the debate, there are those who consider scales and arpeggios of minimal significance as a technical foundation for pianism, insisting that time is better spent mastering the particular passage and deriving technical benefit exclusively from the challenges presented in the musical composition under study. A few deny benefit of any technical training whatsoever, believing the physical response will properly and correctly follow the mind and ear. Some even disparage the study of scales and arpeggios not out of any particular conviction but out of sheer distaste for what they have experienced as tedium and boredom. Still others hold with the great pianist Moriz Rosenthal, who was reported to have winced at the suggestion, saying that he never practiced scales because they "encouraged unevenness of touch"! Significantly, the illustrious pianist and teacher Walter Robert deemed it necessary to publish an article, "In Defense of Scales" (1962).[1] And the controversy continues.

I have always considered scales and arpeggios to be an essential focus of keyboard training at every level of expertise. Their systematic study provides a unique and unsurpassed opportunity for unlocking the mysteries of the keyboard and perceiving the intelligence behind the organization of the keyboard and its tones. Scales and arpeggios between them encompass all the intervals the pianist will encounter over the entire range of the keyboard. Just as the stepwise progression of scales requires use of the hand in its anatomically more "closed" state, so the larger intervals of the arpeggios, in complementary fashion, require the use of the hand in its physiologically extended, more "open" state. Furthermore, in the early years of piano playing scales and arpeggios can be called on to encourage and develop continuity, fluency and a positive physical and mental stamina as well as keyboard familiarity.

Also important, their study is fundamental to developing a strong sense of tonality, which is essential also to the development of transposing skills and a clear communication of compositional structure. Moreover, the sustained practice of scales and arpeggios nurtures a ready physical and alert aural response to the music at hand and enhances the visual, intellectual and musical comprehension requisite to good sightreading. And always, there is that artistic goal: achievement of a vital, fluid, musical scale line, expressive yet refined.

Central to the rationale for scale and arpeggio study is the issue of fingering. Scale and arpeggio fingering patterns are first consciously correlated to note patterns. By means of repetition, these patterns of *movement* become reflexive. However, such an acquired, ultimately automatic response ought to be neurologically, physiologically and kinesiologically sound. I can understand and sympathize with the arguments of those who object to scale and arpeggio practice, but I am nonetheless convinced that the problem lies not with the scales and arpeggios *per se* but with most of the generally accepted or "standard" fingerings assigned to them. And it is those fingerings—not the study and practice of scales—that need to be challenged.

The standard fingerings have become so universally accepted that it seems almost heretical to challenge them. Indeed, to do so is almost as drastic a step as questioning the value of the scales and arpeggios themselves. In thousands of methods and syllabi, the all-white-key C scale has become enshrined as the ideal model. The operative principle here is to assign the thumb to the tonic (but the fifth finger to the initial tonic, LH ascending and RH descending). Each octave then consists of alternating three- and four-finger/note groups; this allows the minimum number of thumb shifts per octave division and a consistently recurring sequence in consecutive octaves.

Example A

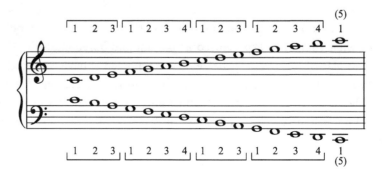

NATURAL FINGERING

The scale fingerings that do not conform to this model—notably those with black-key tonics—are deemed to be aberrations necessitated by the increase in the number of black keys and the resulting decrease in the number of white keys available to the thumb.

Example B

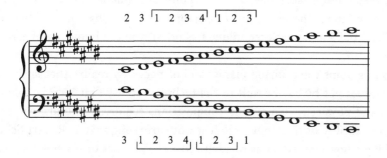

Numerous attempts to revise these "standard" fingerings obviously have not had any significant impact. An understandable reluctance to alter habits of teaching and playing has been reinforced by many anatomical and physiological misconceptions regarding the hand and the attendant playing "mechanisms" (forearm and upper arm/shoulder complex). As one very fine concert pianist remarked, in response to my inquiry as to whether she was aware of a particular treatise (Moszkowki's) proposing alternate scale fingerings, "How can there be any other fingerings for the scales than the ones we use?"

Yet most experienced pianists and teachers generally agree that certain scales and arpeggios are simply more comfortable ("lie better," "fit") or more "natural to the hand" than others. It is probably fair to say that the standard fingerings for the flat-key major scales (with the exception of F for the LH) are generally found to be best suited to the hand and to "lie well" within it. In fact, the above-mentioned "aberrant" black-key tonic scales, major and minor, are among the most comfortable. Similarly, those major and minor arpeggios that have only one white key that is assigned to the thumb are the most comfortable—or put another way, the most *pianistic*. There are clear reasons for this. For now, suffice it to say that the scales and arpeggios that best fit the hand all have the fourth finger assigned to a black key. That the fourth finger on a black key, rather than on a white key, would be most easily followed by the thumb on a white key is readily demonstrable. One need only play the standard fingering for the G scale, RH ascending and then LH descending, beyond the range of an octave to feel the difference. Keep in mind that these patterns are intended to prepare the student for similar technical challenges encountered in the music to be performed.

Again, one of the strongest arguments for the practice of scales and arpeggios is the securing of a familiar, favorable and ready response when encountering these same or similar patterns in learning or sightreading a composition. Yet many editions contain fingerings for scale or scale-derived passages that are quite at odds with the conventional fingerings but nonetheless revealing in their ease of execution. Conversely, many editions do not employ the conventional fingerings in such passages even when these would be superior to those recommended. Absent a thoroughly rational approach, no consistency is possible. What is the point, the student may ask, of devoting years to learning specific fingerings for specific note groups if they cannot be consistently and confidently applied? Years of study and practice would then be preparation for what?

The standard fingerings are not, for the most part, based on principles that can be broadly and consistently applied, either to scales or arpeggios, highly chromatic passages or those that enjoy a variety of related keys or key regions. So it may indeed seem that the benefit of an extensive study of scales and arpeggios is extremely limited, even questionable, past a certain point of pianistic training. And to further complicate matters, the persistent but erroneous belief that the practice of scales will of itself build a pianist's technique has often resulted in overemphasis on such practice.

At some point the aspiring pianist will of necessity realize that such a narrow emphasis does not by itself result in the technical ability that increasingly lengthy, complex and physically demanding compositions require. Naturally, she begins to suspect the futility of this approach. It is not surprising that E. Robert Schmitz, in his striking study, goes so far as to advise that the practice of scales etc. need not be a significant focus of pianistic training since they are but a "small detail."[2]

Nevertheless, the literature of the piano abounds with scales, arpeggios and similar, related passagework. And so the search for the most suitable, most successful fingerings must continue. Once again, I believe that wholesale adoption of the standard fingerings is largely responsible for an underestimation—and paradoxically, an overestimation—of the role of scales and arpeggios in acquiring and maintaining keyboard skill and in achieving artistic, expressive pianism. Fingerings that are less than ideal necessarily demand a greater expenditure of time and effort, often for still less-than-satisfactory results. Thus they lie at the heart of resistance to the teaching as well as the practice of scales and arpeggios.

However, the absence of a consistent, systematic approach to fingering does not mean there is none to be found. For this we turn to Chopin and the keyboard itself—to the influences of topography, temperament and symmetry.

TOPOGRAPHY AND TEMPERAMENT

How did it happen that the full implications of keyboard topography—the common currency of all brands of pianism—elude so many for so long? How was it that Chopin's emphasis on his Fundamental Pattern—revelatory and revolutionary in its time, and thereafter accepted by so many as obvious, useful and thoroughly rational—bore relatively little fruit in matters of fingering fundamentals and pedagogical impact?

One can trace a very impressive "line of succession," so to speak, from Chopin to Mikuli to Michałowski and their students. Among them are Kaczyński, Koczalski, Moszkowski, Godowsky, Landowska, Neuhaus and Rosenthal—and their students in turn.[3] But what has been handed down from them must be said to have had a mainstream impact only at the margins, at best. Still, in one way or another—consciously or unconsciously, documented or not, and in varying degrees—all have continued the "tradition" and kept alive a certain sensitivity and receptivity to the essence of Chopin's thinking in these matters. So what was missing? What was it that would unify and clarify the seemingly disparate bits and pieces of Chopin's pioneering pedagogical legacy—and take it still further?

The ongoing and pervasive influence of all-white-key C major as the foundation for early studies and its firm establishment as the premiere model for scale and arpeggio fingerings certainly obscured the implications of Chopin's revolutionary insights.

For him, the role of the enharmonic major keys (B/C-flat, F-sharp/G-flat, and C-sharp/D-flat) would now be paramount in a more pianistic pedagogy for pianists. But this reversal, in effect, of the Circle of Fifths in the introduction and study of scales understandably posed great obstacles for development of a new methodology and its widespread, even if not universal, acceptance.

Ultimately—and relatively recently as these things go—only Heinrich Neuhaus seriously decried the pedagogical "tyranny of C major"[4] with his accustomed and unrestrained vehemence. He called for establishment of a new regime: one based on Chopin's Fundamental Pattern. In regard to pianism, the Circle of Fifths would indeed then be literally turned on its head. Enharmonic F-sharp major/G-flat major, not C major, would now be the starting point in this circle, a new point of reference. As reflected in the Fundamental (whole tone) Pattern, we will explore its alteration to reveal topographical symmetry and establish consistency in the fingering of the major and minor scales and arpeggios.

Before Chopin's time, F-sharp/G-flat was not a key in abundant use. Beethoven's own excursion, his F-sharp Sonata Opus 78, with its warm, tenderly lyrical first movement, is a comparatively late one. And Schubert's sublime G-flat Impromptu, Opus 90, is still alternatively published in G major, a supposedly "easier" key but also one better suited to those pianists not availing themselves of the benefits of equal temperament at the time.[5] The growing acceptance and adoption of equal temperament as an improvement over earlier systems of tuning is the likely explanation for the genesis of Chopin's new insights. It represents, at the very least, a happy collusion of circumstance. But to quote Jean-Jacques Eigeldinger, "Chopin's reasoning . . . is exclusively pianistic; indeed, the entire reasoning of the *PM* [*Projet de méthode*]—including some theoretical notions—is founded on the structure of the (equal tempered) keyboard."[6]

Stuart Isacoff, in his enlightening and fascinating study *Temperament*, notes that the enharmonic keys in particular were, for the most part, formerly avoided because of the particular limitations of mean and well-tempered tuning. These were eschewed in favor of those keys having fewer sharps and flats. C major, for one, was considered "pure," while F-sharp major, for example—the key at that point in the Circle of Fifths bearing the brunt of the necessary tempered adjustments of the other keys, sharps and flats, preceding it—was commonly considered the key to be most avoided.[7]

But the advent of equal temperament, initially in organ tunings, now liberated the composer to enjoy and employ formerly problematic key and interval relationships. New key schemes, modulations and harmonic relationships could also be investigated; the basis for a chromatic harmony was secured. Compositional liberation and exploration meant ongoing keyboard liberation and exploration. And pianists were consequently free to experience what we now consider the most "pianistic" keys. For at least one of the Romantic Era's greatest geniuses, composer-pianist Chopin, it was "a marriage made in heaven."

Bach's familiar and significant forays into blatant, unabashed chromaticism are well known, the extraordinary *Chromatic Fantasy and Fugue* and the key scheme of the monumental *Well-Tempered Clavier* (though he was not the first to do this) being prime examples. Notwithstanding, ongoing experimentation and continuous controversy as to the superior method of tuning were the order of his day and through most of the Classical Period—and remains so in some quarters![8] But so it was that the compositional style of the respective periods was also considerably, and inevitably, influenced by key choice tied to practical considerations, chiefly instrumentation, as well as individual aesthetics. The technical concerns of the keyboardists naturally followed from this. And what did *not* concern them is as important as what did.

The now-familiar arrangement of the keyboard's black and white keys only gradually evolved. Inherent in it is a symmetry that is not only borne of the artistic and practical advantages of equal temperament but, upon closer examination, is also the key to the pianist's ideal physiological connection to the keyboard. And it was Chopin who, early on, understood this phenomenon best and set about to transform the pianist's approach to the keyboard accordingly.

With the near universal acceptance of equal temperament in his time, the enharmonic keys and the problem of "in tune" thirds needed no longer to be avoided or handled with due diligence. A heightened chromaticism generally (mediant, enharmonic and other common-tone relationships specifically) contributed to a compositional and expressive expansiveness that was both artistic and individual. Exploration and exploitation of those keys now felt to be instinctively comfortable—more pianistic, in our terms—eventually became the order of the day, reflecting and representing the trajectory of the Romantic epoch's visions and ideals.

The enharmonic keys of the Circle of Fifths, formerly uncharted territory, were now particularly ripe for exploration and integration. Chopin's Fundamental Pattern and his iconoclastic methods of pedagogy were his unique and extraordinary response to this new invitation to reconsider former limitations and stake new ground. Rise to the occasion he certainly did.

SYMMETRY AND SOLUTIONS

Unfinished at his death, Chopin's *méthode* would if completed have transformed pedagogy in its aftermath, though we cannot know to what degree. As it stands, only RH fingerings are specified; LH fingerings, long unattended by comparison (the famous D major Piano Concerto of Joseph Haydn contains *not one* LH scale passage in any of its three movements!), can only be inferred. Yet several otherwise quite vague statements, however they may be read, clearly point to *all* scale fingerings consistently determined from the Fundamental Pattern or related to enharmonic majors B and D-flat with their arrangement of the five black keys.

That Chopin was, at the very least, moving in this direction is certain. And given the prominence and scope of his challenging passages for the LH—notwithstanding his preferential key choice—it is not likely that he subscribed to what were, even then, "standard" LH fingerings for the keys in question. It is also interesting to speculate that he may have been simply derelict in his lack of guidance for LH fingerings. But no doubt he remained a "revolutionary" in this matter as well.

In his manuscript, the fourth finger on a black-key "pivot" as the key to the full pivoting action cannot be concluded from the root-position full-diminished sevenths serving as representative of their arpeggio fingerings (also RH, one octave only for C—and rather telling). But their inversions ultimately necessitate the fourth finger pivoting action on a black key (see Chapter 3); as with the enharmonic scales, it is unavoidable. Moreover, the equal tempered octave was calibrated, then as now, to the span of the average hand, with a tritone dividing it in two—a predisposition to such "positioning."

But we also know that Chopin showed no hesitation for employing the thumb after the fifth in passagework. And it is important here to note that an extension of the Fundamental Pattern itself affords no other more practical, more "pianistic" alternative, if the thumb is to remain assigned to a white key (see Chapter 11).

Yet Chopin clearly stated his preference for a black-key pivot, even while admitting the weakness of his fourth finger; that he insisted scale study be inaugurated with those scales having five black keys only further corroborates this contention. His student Karol Mikuli, for example, confirms this in his introduction to Chopin's Mazurkas for Schirmer: "They facilitate the passing under of the thumb and the passing over of the fingers."[9] Clearly it was not solely a matter of a neutralization of finger and key lengths.

Chopin's unreserved admiration for the design of the keyboard, recognition of its symmetry and appreciation of its natural fit to the hand are well documented. And such attention to what we now see indisputably as topographical concerns relating to the physiology of the hand signifies that a revision of the already standard LH fingerings would not likely have eluded Chopin's genius for the keyboard and its music. But we really have no way of firmly authenticating this; the record of even his closest, most devoted students is silent.

It is Charles Eschmann-Dumur's remarkable observation that provides the next rational step in properly wedding the fingers to the keyboard's topography. It is the missing link in the evolution of Chopin's Fundamental Pattern and is, in fact, at the very heart of what establishes it as "fundamental." With the advent of Eschmann-Dumur's discovery, neither it nor its implications can any longer be ignored. This elemental five-finger, whole tone pattern (see Chapter 1) is at the very root of pianism. It follows, therefore, that it should be at the very root of its pedagogy—what Neuhaus, far into the next century, ultimately sensed and unequivocally proclaimed.

Moritz Moszkowski, in the concluding "Remarks" to Part I of his monumental *School of Double Notes, Op. 64* (1901), observes: "Of the Major scales there are always two which correspond by identity of movement, viz. those scales which have *the same number of opposite accidentals* (sharps or flats). Take for example the scale of A flat major (four flats) and E major (four sharps)." He presents these and then decries as "illogical" certain scale fingerings for the LH, such as G and F, vis-à-vis their RH counterparts. And before applying this principle to "establish the identity of movement in the corresponding scales" in thirds and sixths, he informs us that "Mr. Charles Eschmann-Dumur in his *Technical Pianoforte School* was the first, to my knowledge, to indicate these anomalies of fingering. . . ."

Referring only to Eschmann-Dumur's treatise and leaving matters of topographical and intervallic symmetry ("mirroring") without remark, he instructs that the fingering for the LH descending major scales of the same number of sharps or flats must be the "same" as that for the RH ascending. He then draws on certain scale fingerings of Karl Tausig and William Mason to "prove that the fact of *analogies* in major scales is as yet almost unknown, or at least neglected." For him this was what he called the "leading principle."

What is most significant about Moszkowski's own observations is his recognition of what he calls "identity of movement." Whether away from or toward the torso, parallel or contrary, this identity of movement can only apply to the pivoting action itself: where it occurs and how it occurs within the complementary patterns, indeed, how the movement itself is mirrored.

But what he missed, or perhaps did not know—and his double note fingerings (as well as Franklin Taylor's) reflect this—was the origin of this "leading principle" in the symmetrical construction of the keyboard as reflected in Chopin's original Fundamental Pattern. Recalling that the RH pattern spelled in B major (five sharps) exactly mirrors that of the LH spelled in D-flat (five flats), one easily notes that the reverse (RH in D-flat, LH in B) is true as well.

Absent this connection, Moszkowski had thus considered only one piece of the puzzle. For it is Eschmann-Dumur's discovery that complements and reveals Chopin's pattern as the acorn (Neuhaus evokes "Columbus's egg"[10]) that it is: all fingering combinations evolve and flow in some way and to some degree from this basic topographical orientation. This would presuppose a willingness to reappraise the unique role and movement potential of the fourth finger, and even the fifth.

What will be found to be equally remarkable is the revelation of a physiological attunement that is most natural and efficient in all respects. All aspects conspire (in the true sense of the word) toward the most pianistic resolution in matters of fingering.

There is, so to speak, a "hierarchy" of pianistic orientation and adaptation that proceeds from the Fundamental Pattern, from a wealth of black keys to their dearth. These primary patterns, or *core topographies*, are universally operative and also represent a complementary continuum of physiological orientation and accommodation: from highly pianistic to less pianistic. By extension—literally, figuratively and intellectually—they establish the unavoidable context for any solution to technical difficulties at the keyboard.

A topographical journey is a fascinating one, and we really do not have to work hard to find these core patterns operative at every turn. For the topographically aware, they are readily identified and everywhere to be found. From this "core" the process of fingering is ever moving toward one that is rational, consistent, and practical—yet physiologically sound. It is a natural approach enlisting the innate symmetry of the hand and the keyboard, and our innate need to simplify.

As the great Sviatoslav Richter observed in regard to piano playing, "Symmetry! Everything has to be symmetrical."[11] And it all begins with Chopin's Fundamental Pattern.

PRINCIPLES IN PRACTICE

For all his classical training and extraordinary pianism (he arrived in Vienna in 1829, just two years after Beethoven's death), Chopin had no doubt already grasped the defining influence of the keyboard's topography. And it would now be in the forefront in all matters of pianism, and therefore foremost in matters of fingering.

Pedagogically, he most definitely broke the mold in advocating the enharmonic major keys as the pianist's foundation, rather than one that progresses from all-white-key C major. Patterning divorced from topography was correctly perceived as alien to the development of a more inherently "pianistic" approach. And this was not a matter of mere methodology. His compositional key choice bears witness to his insight, his conviction, and his experience. In this, one should look beyond key signatures: closer scrutiny of the topographies of related keys supports this bias even further.

Much has been made about individual differences of the hands as it applies to fingering choice, but certainly training, skill and accustomed usage and response are influencing factors. It is rare that there are genetic anatomical and physiological *deficiencies* rather than *differences*, such as size or fleshiness—although less rarely than is commonly supposed. Ortmann has painstakingly laid them out in a thorough and intriguing manner. But this is an important distinction, and he reminds us at the very beginning of his extensive discussion, "The spatial relationships of the keyboard are fixed."[12]

The keyboard's topography is an irrefutable fact of its design and construction. And like keyboard space, it too is unalterable. Although the pianist may deal with them in sundry ways, the challenges posed as a result remain—no matter the individual hand or peculiar "preferences" or perceived "differences." It is on this that the fingering *principles* presented herein, distinct from any commonly accepted organizational *strategies*, are founded.

The core topographies also represent patterns of organization and are likewise subject to considerations of strategy. But they are not arbitrary in that they are inherent in and integral to the hand's structural orientation to the keyboard. They are therefore *primary* in their influence, whether or not consciously enlisted in the matter of fingering choice. Keyboard topography bears great impact, whether the response to it is positive or negative, whether it is constructively enlisted or recklessly and carelessly ignored.

THREE WORKING PRINCIPLES FOR A BASIC STRATEGY

Throughout our exploration of alternatives to the generally accepted standard fingerings for scales and arpeggios, three main "working principles" may be taken to be axiomatic in the pursuit of a natural, topographically oriented approach.

1. *Long fingers on short keys, short fingers on long keys.* This axiom represents the very essence of a topographical approach. As reflected in Chopin's Fundamental Pattern, it is the fundamental orientation of the pianist's playing mechanism to the keyboard; from it the core patterns and their "pivotal" implications evolve. It represents the foremost natural adjustment of the hand to the biplanar keyboard's topographical demands.

2. *Fourth on black, thumb on white.* The requisite tonal alterations of the Fundamental Pattern that correspond to the diatonic major scales represented by the Circle of Fifths reveal core patterns reflecting operative core principles; these may be translocated as well as transposed. A consistent application of the fourth finger as ideal black-key pivot in diatonic scales and arpeggios follows from this.

For passages in which note groups are extended by means of the thumb-under and hand-over pivoting action, the general statement can be made: the fourth finger is best assigned to a black key when followed or preceded by the thumb, whereas the third is best assigned to a white key. Range of movement is a determining factor in this, since the longer third may serve to better adjust for greater distance (interval) as well as key depth (see Chapter 10).

All-black-key and all-white-key topographies are disadvantaged in not having significant topographical distinctions, mainly key depth and height, that would otherwise positively impact the assignment of fingers according to relevant length (except in matters of substitution). But biokinetically, the fourth finger has the ability nonetheless to function as the stronger, more secure pivot for thumb-under movements. The third will be found to be superior only in faster repetitions within a smaller movement range and where a quick "get-away" (finger retraction) is necessary, as in applying the "French" fingering to the chromatic scale, for example (see Chapter 4, Online Supplement). For extended passages, the fourth will most frequently be found indispensable, as well as unavoidable. Indeed, it should be favored; proper and adequate training reinforces this very important role.

3. *No unnecessary stretches or adjustments*. In regard to range of movement, it is most important that fingerings be considered with the aim of reducing or eliminating any unnecessary stretches or adjustments. The natural position of the hand is the point of departure and the point of return, just as the anatomical position (its "midline") is that for the arm, and the seated position of the performer is that for the upper torso.

This axiom is of great biokinetic significance. The fingers represent individual movement axes and must be properly aligned to optimally transmit vertical force to the keys. Prolonged overextension of hand is to be particularly avoided in favor of a "closed-open" alternation.

Practical application of these working principles in the search for optimal fingerings points toward solutions that are demonstrably superior. They concisely reflect a physiological and topographical consistency in the fingerings for the fundamental forms as they derive from and relate to Chopin's Fundamental Pattern.

THE MAJOR SCALES

The black keys belong essentially to the three longest fingers.
—C.P.E. Bach

One cannot overpraise the genius who presided over the construction of the keyboard, so well adapted to the shape of the hand. Is there anything more ingenious than the higher [black] keys— destined for the long fingers—so admirably serving as points of pivot. Many times, without thinking, minds who know nothing about piano playing have seriously proposed that the keyboard be leveled: this would eliminate all the security that the pivot points give to the hand, [and] consequently make the passage of thumb in those scales involving sharps and flats extremely difficult.
—Frederic Chopin

CHOPIN'S PITHY COMMENT, articulated with his usual economy and grace, reveals just what determines a *pianistic* fingering: long fingers on short keys, short fingers on long keys and a black-key "pivot" as the ideal. The case for a topographical approach to fingering could not be more clearly stated.

Concerned as he was with finding a comfortable, "natural" physiological accommodation to the keyboard, Chopin deemed the five-note pattern E-F♯-G♯-A♯-B most suited to the hand. Although some teachers and pianists[1] have rendered this pattern as the whole-tone sequence E-F♯-G♯-A♯-B♯, Chopin is specific and unequivocal in his instructions, but only for the right hand. The confusion arises, I believe, from the attempt to find a symmetrically equivalent pattern that can be more satisfactorily played by both hands simultaneously. However, the LH "mirror" of E-F♯-G♯-A♯-B is F-G♭-A♭-B♭-C. Both LH and RH then achieve positions of superior alignment, with the thumb a whole step from the second finger and the fifth finger a half-step from the fourth.

Example 1.1

Chopin's assessment of this five-note pattern as most natural had implications for scale study as well. He proposed that teachers should begin with scales that include all five black keys since only these contain the three successive black keys most suited to the long second, third and fourth fingers. He therefore prescribed B major for the right hand and, according to Jan Kleczyński,[2] author of *How to Play Chopin: The Works of Frederic Chopin and Their Proper Interpretation*, D-flat major for the left hand. Significantly, these are the scales that contain the fundamental five-note patterns discussed above.[3]

The B (C-flat) and D-flat (C-sharp) scales have only two white keys and the thumbs, being short fingers, are assigned to them. Both scales reflect what was, by that time, the "ideal" objective of a consistently recurring three- and four-finger/note group per octave and, consequently, a minimum number of thumb shifts per octave; but they are unique in that they each permit only one practical solution. The three adjacent black keys demand the use of the fourth on a black key—if the thumb is deemed best on a white key. Although proposing a number of possible fingerings for each of the other scales, C.P.E. Bach postulated this fingering as the only possibility for these scales.

Example 1.2

In extending these scales beyond one octave, the fifth finger, if used at all, can be employed by the RH only at the highest point of the B-major scale. The four-finger/note group necessarily determines the fingering, resulting in the thumb on a white and the fourth on a black key. Like Eschmann-Dumur, we may also observe that, contrariwise, the four- and three-finger/note groups of the B scale (five sharps) in one hand exactly mirror those of the D-flat scale (five flats) in the other hand in terms of fingering, intervals and succession of white and black keys.

Example 1.3a

(LH)   Db Eb F   Gb Ab Bb C   and   E F♯ G♯ A♯   B C♯ D♯   (RH)

Example 1.3b

(LH)   C♯ D♯ E   F♯ G♯ A♯ B   and   F Gb Ab Bb   C Db Eb   (RH)

Kleczyński also indicates that the four-finger/note group was indeed the prime determinant of Chopin's approach to pianistic fingering. Employing the "English"[4] system of fingering, he writes: "Taking it that each scale has two fundamental positions, viz., that of the thumb, first, second, third, and of the thumb, first, second fingers, [Chopin's] pupils commenced with the scale of B major for the right, and of Db major for the left hand forming the hand in the manner already described at each fundamental position."[5] Further on, Kleczyński is even more specific: "This is the Key to an even execution. . . . Of the scales, taking always for the hands the positions, *first* [emphasis added], thumb, 1st, 2nd, 3rd; and second, thumb, 1st, 2nd."[6]

Example 1.4

Karol Mikuli, probably the most well known of Chopin's students, informs us that F-sharp major (enharmonic G-flat major) was also among the scales first recommended for study. C major, on the other hand, was saved for last. As Chopin put it, "It is useless to start learning scales with C major, the easiest to read and the most difficult for the hand, as it has no pivot." Instead Chopin established the enharmonic major keys as the starting point for further pianism and the foundation for developing what he called the "mechanism."

LONG AND SHORT, BLACK AND WHITE: THE FUNDAMENTALS OF A TOPOGRAPHICAL APPROACH

The marriage of the physiological structure of the hand and the physical characteristics of the keyboard is at the heart of a topographical approach to fingering. The correlation of the varying finger lengths with differences in the length, depth and height of black and white keys equalizes the distance through which leverage is applied in the *vertical* movement of the key, thereby eliminating unnecessary motion to and from black keys.

Larger intervals, of arpeggios for example, simply represent greater *horizontal* distances between fingers and keys, but the same principle of short-long, black-white applies. Of course, resulting differences in the position of the arm relative to the torso and the keyboard do require attention to alignment as well as to other physiological and kinesiological implications of movement in keyboard space.

Nothing is more central to the determination of the most pianistic fingering than the role of the "pivot" finger. In truth, all fingers can and do function as pivots at one time or another. In legato playing, for example, each finger acts as a pivot to the next; proper alignment and the controlled transfer of weight are assured by means of lateral adjustments of the hand to the forearm. There are also the less subtle pivoting actions of hand and thumb ("hand crossings") as well as the oscillating action employed in movements such as "forearm rotation." What concerns us here, however, is the pivoting action of a finger followed by the thumb, ascending in the RH and descending in the LH: the coordinated actions of both pivot finger and thumb manifesting in the fully circular rotations of all joints involved.

Chopin refers to various pivots and pivoting actions; the quote at the beginning of the chapter, for example, refers to "long fingers" *plural* as ideal pivots. His bias, though, does seem to have been toward the third finger as the pivot of choice, probably owing to its central position in the hand and to the fact that its length affords more space and requires less distance for the "passing under" of the thumb. However, as the longest finger the third is most suited to accommodate key *depth* and is therefore ideal as a *white key* pivot. It is otherwise best assigned to a white key preceding a black-key pivot taken by the fourth. The relatively shorter length of the fourth finger is compensated by the height of the black key, and the depth of the white key by the greater length of the third—significant factors in appreciating the fourth finger's role as the ideal black-key pivot. This is readily exemplified by the scales of G major (RH ascending) and E natural minor (LH descending).

Example 1.5

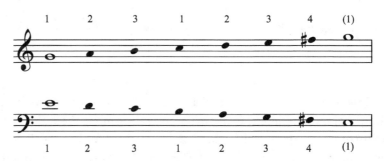

Moreover, the fourth finger, if properly aligned, is at the center of the axis of the forearm and is uniquely designed for its central role in the pivoting action with which we are concerned. Contrary to common perception, then, the fourth is not to be avoided or simply endured; it is—anatomically and physiologically—ideally and best suited as a black-key pivot finger.

Chopin's sense that his own was weak and "out of practice" certainly predisposed him to favor a finger other than the fourth for this essential action. Nonetheless, his advocacy of the pianistic five-finger patterns and his method for inaugurating scale study suggest that he intuited the crucial role of the fourth finger. And although Chopin did consistently employ the third on a black key followed by the fourth on a white key, he did not advocate a RH pattern of E-F♯-G♯-A-B and what would be its LH corollary, F-G-A♭-B♭-C. Nor did he, to our knowledge, refinger those scales having four or fewer black keys. It is, after all, quite possible to conceive these scales with the third finger consistently assigned to a black key, the fourth finger then taking a white.[7]

Example 1.6

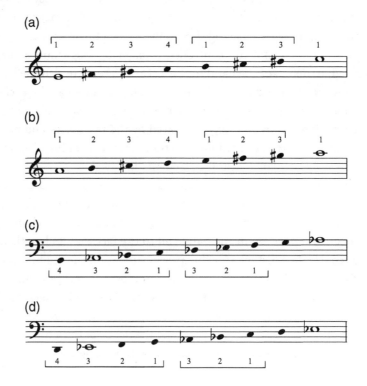

One essential point about Chopin and pianism: it is interesting to note that most of Chopin's major works are written with key signatures of four or more sharps and flats. He was so favorably disposed to these keys that he required his students to begin their work on Clementi's "Préludes et Exercices" with the second volume, in which these key signatures predominate, "and above all to study the first *Etude in A flat*."[8]

Chopin very much appreciated the comfort provided by an abundance of black keys. Knowing his thoughts on the matter, it can be fairly said that his choice of key most likely represents pianistic considerations over those of *ethos*, the unique quality or emotional content of a particular key or mode. Chopin's preference for these keys suggests that on some level, at least, topographical considerations were at play. For it is indeed these scales and arpeggios, particularly those with black-key tonics, that reveal the role of the fourth finger as pivot. As we shall see, this is a fundamental determinant of pianistic fingering and the key to a topographical *system* of fingering for these fundamental forms.

THE FLAT KEYS

It is commonly appreciated that the standard fingerings for the major flat scales are, with the exception of F in the LH, refreshingly systematic. The fourth finger of the RH is always assigned to the B-flat, a black key; the fourth finger of the LH, again with the exception of F, is always assigned to the fourth scale degree, the new flat, which is also a black key. The thumbs fall to white keys.

The F scale fingering for the LH is clearly the aberration, resulting from the insistence on assigning the thumb to a white-key tonic, or key note. The standard F fingering is that of the standard C major fingering transposed.

Example 1.7

5 **4 3 2 1** **3 2 1**

CDEF G ABC

FGAB♭C DEF

In the RH, however, a similar insistence on assigning the thumb to the tonic, although still avoiding its use on a black key, results in an alteration of the standard fingering for the C scale pattern.

Example 1.8a

1 2 3 **1 2 3 4** 5

CDE FGABC

Example 1.8b

1 2 3 4 **1 2 3** 4

FGAB♭ CDEF

The fourth finger is assigned to the B-flat. Thereafter, the fingering and orientation is constant since the fourth finger is always to be found on the B-flat. The F-G-A-B♭

grouping could be considered fundamental to the RH fingerings. In terms of the C major scale, it is then merely the alteration of the four-finger F-G-A-B pattern.

Example 1.9

<u>1 2 3</u> <u>1 2 3 4</u> (1)

<u>C D E</u> <u>F G A B</u> C

F G A B♭ C D E F

B♭ C D E♭ F G A B♭

E♭ F G A♭ B♭ C D E♭

A♭ B♭ C D♭ E♭ F G A♭ (B♭)

D♭ E♭ F G♭ A♭ B♭ C D♭

(F) G♭ A♭ B♭ C♭ D♭ E♭ F G♭

<u>C♭ D♭ E♭ F♭ G♭ A♭ B♭ C♭</u>

C D E F G A B C

As a comparison of C major with C-flat major (enharmonic B) reveals, the C fingering for the RH is simply transposed one half-step lower (F♭-G♭-A♭-B♭-C♭ is, of course, the enharmonic equivalent of E-F♯-G♯-A♯-B). And in the C-flat scale one finds the tonics, and fingering, for all RH major flat scales (F, of course, begins on white-key F, not white-key F♭). The fingering remains constant; the scale degrees are altered according to tonality.

Example 1.10

1 2 3   1 2 3 4 (1)

<u>C D E</u>   <u>F G A B</u> C

C♭ D♭ E♭   <u>F♭ G♭ A♭ B♭</u> C♭

D♭ E♭   <u>F G♭ A♭ B♭</u> C D♭

E♭   <u>F G A♭ B♭</u> C D E♭

<u>F G A B♭</u> C D E F

(F) <u>G♭ A♭ B♭</u> C♭ D♭ E♭ F G♭

(F G) <u>A♭ B♭</u> C D♭ E♭ F G A♭

(F G A) <u>B♭</u> C D E♭ <u>F G A B♭</u>

<u>C D E</u> <u>F G A B</u> C

As for the LH fingerings, the effort to derive the F scale from C is wholly inconsistent. A look at those for the remaining flat key major scales undermines any notion of the standard C scale as model.

By contrast, the operation of the single principle *fourth on black and thumb on white* is easily discerned. How would the LH fingering of the F scale benefit from application of this principle? We need merely to assign the fourth finger to the B-flat to arrive at a topographical accommodation conforming to the other LH flat scales: the fourth finger is on the fourth scale degree, the new flat. Now the LH fingering pattern—3-2-1/4-3-2-1—is the same for all major key flat scales.

Since C major consists of seven white keys, the standard LH fingering for C major, though determined by reflecting the RH fingering sequence contrariwise, is nonetheless arbitrary; again, no defining black keys. Assigning an ascending pattern of 3-2-1/4-3-2-1 to these seven white keys now enables us to consistently apply the *same* fingering pattern proceeding from C major through the enharmonic keys of the Circle of Fifths. The topography, and therefore the fingering, of the enharmonic scales D-flat (C-sharp) through C-flat (B) is the same.

Example 1.11

$$
\begin{array}{llllllll}
3 & 2 & 1 & \underline{4} & \underline{3} & \underline{2} & \underline{1} & (3)
\end{array}
$$

$$
\begin{array}{llllllll}
\mathbf{C} & D & E & F & G & A & B & C
\end{array}
$$

$$
\begin{array}{llllllll}
\mathbf{F} & G & A & B\flat & C & D & E & F
\end{array}
$$

$$
\begin{array}{llllllll}
\mathbf{B\flat} & C & D & E\flat & F & G & A & B\flat
\end{array}
$$

$$
\begin{array}{llllllll}
\mathbf{E\flat} & F & G & A\flat & B\flat & C & D & E\flat
\end{array}
$$

$$
\begin{array}{llllllll}
\mathbf{A\flat} & B\flat & C & D\flat & E\flat & F & G & A\flat
\end{array}
$$

$$
\begin{array}{llllllll}
\mathbf{D\flat} & E\flat & F & \underline{G\flat} & \underline{A\flat} & \underline{B\flat} & \underline{C} & D\flat
\end{array}
$$

$$
\begin{array}{llllllll}
 & & & \underline{G\flat} & \underline{A\flat} & \underline{B\flat} & \underline{C\flat} & D\flat\; E\flat\; F G\flat
\end{array}
$$

(1)

$$
\begin{array}{llllllll}
\mathbf{C\flat} & D\flat & E\flat & F\flat & \underline{G\flat} & \underline{A\flat} & \underline{B\flat} & \underline{C\flat}
\end{array}
$$

The fourth finger is now consistently assigned to the fourth scale degree. The third finger on the tonic at either extreme (through D-flat) is physiologically and kinesiologically ideal and is readily experienced as such.

Proceeding topographically, we have discovered an approach to the major flat scale fingerings that is thoroughly rational and wholly systematic. Moreover, as noted above, these fingerings are demonstrably more pianistic. Indeed, systematic scale study can now begin—perhaps even *should* begin—with the flat keys, a formerly daunting prospect given the confusion generated by the topographical inconsistency of the standard fingerings. Also importantly, as the examples here indicate, we see that it is possible to encourage pianistic comfort by beginning with the scales for the enharmonic keys and working "backward" toward C major, as Chopin recommended, or proceed from C major for theoretical emphasis should teacher or student so desire.

THE SHARP KEYS

All standard major sharp key scale fingerings for the RH are topographically correct. For those having white-key tonics, the fingering pattern follows that of the C scale and the new sharp, a black key, is the raised seventh degree, or leading tone. In fact, the three- and four-finger groups are each exactly the reverse of those for the LH flat keys: 3-2-1/4-3-2-1 becomes 1-2-3/1-2-3-4. For the enharmonic major keys (B, F-sharp and C-sharp) the fingering is that for five black keys, comporting with Chopin's Fundamental Pattern.

Example 1.12

$$
\begin{array}{llll}
\text{1 2 3} & \underline{\text{1 2 3 4}} & \text{(1)} \\
\text{C D E} & \text{F G A } \mathbf{B} & \text{C} \\
\text{G A B} & \text{C D E } \mathbf{F\sharp} & \text{G} \\
\text{D E F\sharp} & \text{G A B} \mathbf{C\sharp} & \text{D} \\
\text{A B C\sharp} & \text{D E F\sharp} \mathbf{G\sharp} & \text{A} \\
\text{E F\sharp G\sharp} & \text{A B C\sharp} \mathbf{D\sharp} & \text{E} \\
\text{B C\sharp D\sharp} & \underline{\text{E F\sharp G\sharp} \mathbf{A\sharp}} & \text{B} \\
& \underline{\text{(E)F\sharp G\sharp A\sharp}} \text{ B C\sharp D\sharp } \mathbf{E\sharp F\sharp} \\
\text{C\sharp D\sharp} & \underline{\text{E\sharp F\sharp G\sharp A\sharp}} \mathbf{B\sharp} \text{ C\sharp}
\end{array}
$$

Here, too, it is the LH that suffers from the insistence on assigning the thumb to a white-key tonic, with the result that the standard fingerings for G, D, and A are not topographically correct.

Example 1.13

$$
\begin{array}{ll}
\underline{\text{(5)}}\text{4 3 2 1 / 3 2 1} \\
\text{G A B C D} & \text{E F\sharp G} \\
\text{D E F\sharp G A} & \text{B C\sharp D} \\
\text{A B C\sharp D E} & \text{F\sharp G\sharp A}
\end{array}
$$

But an application of the leading principle "fourth on black, thumb on white" easily determines the topographical solution for these keys.

Example 1.14

<u>4 3 21 / 3 2 1</u>

(F♯)G A B C D E F♯G

DEF♯ **G A B** C♯ D

(F♯ G♯)A B C♯ D E F♯G♯A

The LH fingerings are now topographically consistent, with the fourth finger assigned to F-sharp throughout.

Analogous to the relationship of C major to C-flat major, in which the RH fingering was simply transposed one half-step lower, our alternative LH fingering for C major needs only to be transposed a half-step higher for C-sharp. Working from the enharmonic keys, we see that our new C major fingering is simply that of C-sharp transposed.

Example 1.15

<u>3 2 1 4 3 2 1</u> (3)

C D E F G A B C

C♯D♯E♯ F♯G♯A♯B♯ C♯

Keeping in mind this alternative grouping for C major and applying our topographical principle to each successive major sharp key in the Circle of Fifths, we now learn that for the LH the fourth finger pivot will always be F-sharp. All the LH scales for these keys can now also be viewed as being derived from the four-note group of our alternative fingering for the C scale or from the alteration of the pianistic five-note pattern E♯-F♯-G♯-A♯-B♯ (enharmonic F-G♭-A♭-B♭-C).

Example 1.16

3 2 1 <u>4 3 2 1</u> (3)

C D E **F G A B** C

(F♯)GA B C D E F♯G

D E **F♯ G A B** C♯D

A B**C♯D** E **F♯G♯A(B)**

E **F♯G♯A B** C♯D♯E

B**C♯D♯**E **F♯G♯A♯B**

F♯G♯A♯B C♯D♯E♯F♯

<u>C♯D♯E♯**F♯G♯A♯B♯**C♯</u>

C D E F G A B C

As with the flat scales, the theoretical value of scale study need not be eclipsed by concern for pianistic comfort; one may proceed from C major through the enharmonic keys, or proceed from the enharmonic keys to C major.

MAJOR SCALE FINGERINGS AND THE CIRCLE OF FIFTHS

Experimentation demonstrates that the leading principle of **fourth on black and thumb on white** allows *only one* topographical solution for each major key, sharp or flat. A formula for the symmetrical system underlying topographical fingerings for all the major keys can be simply put as follows:

	Left Hand	Right Hand
Sharp Keys:	Fourth finger on F♯	123 1234
Flat Keys:	321 4321	Fourth finger on B♭

For LH flat keys to D-flat: *the fourth finger is always on the new flat*, which is the lowered seventh degree of the preceding key and the fourth degree, or subdominant, of the new key. For RH sharp keys to B: *the fourth finger is always on the new sharp*, which is the raised fourth degree of the preceding key and the seventh degree, or leading tone, of the new key.

The fourth finger on B-flat (RH) and the fourth finger on F-sharp (LH) signals the importance of the fourth finger as black-key pivot. In addition to relating the major scales as they mirror each other topographically, these fingerings may be perfectly correlated to the Circle of Fifths since all are derived from the four-note group of the enharmonic major keys (B/C♭-F♯/G♭-C♯/D♭). The LH flat and RH sharp fingering groups are in inverse relation and simply transposed, culminating in enharmonic scale fingerings that are constant because of their five black keys: the RH fourth finger remains on A-sharp/B-flat and LH fourth finger remains on G-flat/F-sharp.

Likewise, the pattern of tonal alterations from key to key is consistent, conforming to the tonal system that the Circle of Fifths represents. Keyboard topography, fingering, physiology and tonal principles are remarkably cooperative.

That this simple formula displays such consistency and symmetry should not be surprising. As noted above, the standard fingerings for the RH major scales *are* topographically correct. By identifying the specific elements that make them so and ensuring that they are consistently reflected in the LH fingerings, we arrive at a rationally determined formulation, one that is as logical, systematic and instructive as the Circle of Fifths itself.

Example 1.17

CIRCLE OF FIFTHS
Major Scales

LH: 4th on new flat (4th degree) to enharmonics

RH: 4th on new sharp (7th degree) to enharmonics

RH: 4th on B-flat

LH: 4th on F sharp

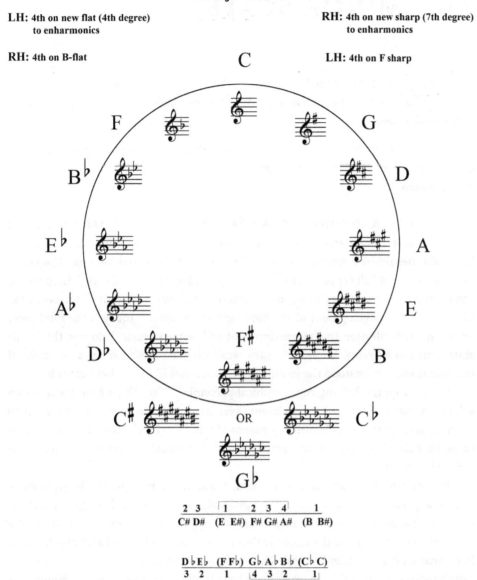

```
2 3   1   2 3 4   1
C# D#  (E E#)  F# G# A#  (B B#)
```

```
D♭ E♭  (F F♭)  G♭ A♭ B♭ (C♭ C)
3  2    1      4  3  2   1
```

For instructional purposes the four-note groups and their enharmonic equivalents can be initially presented within the five-finger whole tone patterns E-F♯-G♯-A♯-B♯ (LH) and F♭-G♭-A♭-B♭-C (RH). The pedagogical sense of this relatively slight alteration of Chopin's pianistic pattern is considered throughout this discourse, but developed significantly in Part IV. For now, suffice it to concur with the great Heinrich Neuhaus, who, despairing of the prevailing pedagogical preoccupation with all-white-key C major, wrote: "In time, by no means immediately, I came to the conclusion that it is with these five notes that one must begin the whole methodology . . . of learning the piano, that they are its cornerstone, its Columbus's egg, the seed of wheat which yields a thousand-fold harvest. This little formula is truly weightier than many heavy tomes."[9]

The reader is directed to Appendix 1 for easy reference to all the single note major scales.

2

THE MAJOR CONNECTION
AND MINOR SCALES

When we recognize that major and minor form one Whole . . . we arrive unconstrainedly at a perception of the Unity of our system of keys. . . . We possess one single key.
—Ferruccio Busoni

Since the fourth finger is the only one occurring once only in each octave, scale fingerings can be deduced from the position of the fourth finger.
—Ernst Bacon

THE PHYSICAL AND TONAL ORGANIZATION OF THE KEYBOARD is, with the advent of equal temperament, truly a source of wonder (*pace* aficionados of "irregular" and other non-ET tuning systems). Taken quite for granted for some time now, most of us do not fully appreciate the genius behind it. After the Greeks' discovery of the overtone series underpinning our Western tonal system and the later evolution of notation, the development of the keyboard as we know it today is the next most important contribution to the development of Western music. I do not think this statement too extreme. We might again recall Chopin's exuberant praise—himself the genius who understood the piano and its mysteries like no other before him.

By applying the leading topographical principle of **fourth on black, thumb on white**, we have uncovered a consistent, systematic, and informative approach to major scale fingering that is well represented by the Circle of Fifths. We have begun to see that the physiological, topographical and theoretical aspects of scale study can indeed be harmonious.

But we also encounter this integrated, harmonious interplay of topographical and tonal principles in searching for the most pianistic minor scale fingerings. These proceed from alterations of the major scale having the same tonic, or key note (the "parallel" minor), or from the major scale a minor third higher and sharing the same key signature (the "relative" minor). The topographical fingerings for the major scales can therefore be immediately brought to bear in eliminating the inconsistencies of the standard fingerings.

To fully appreciate these relationships, let us first review the origins of the three forms of the minor mode: *natural, harmonic* and *melodic*. The form commonly referred to as "melodic" is actually a hybrid, composed of the melodic minor ascending and the natural minor descending.

The Greeks also gave us the *Aeolian* mode, which comes to us as our *natural* form of the minor scale:

Example 2.1

Constructed of whole tones but with half steps between the second-third and fifth-sixth degrees, its tones are also those of its relative major C but begun a minor third below, the submediant (sixth degree) of the relative major. Although the half steps are now found to occur on different scale degrees, they still reinforce the *same* tones as those of the relative major.

In the natural minor, therefore, the half steps—the *tendency tones*—continue to establish and reinforce the strong tonal degrees of the relative major: the half-step between 2-3 that of the third degree, which is the tonic of the relative major a minor third above; and the half-step between 5-6, that of the sixth degree, which is the subdominant of the relative major. Fundamentally this is the essence of mediant relationships, deriving as they do from the relative major-minor. They are tonal relationships of a major or minor third above or below the tonic of a key or root of a particular chord, which may in turn be altered for mode or harmonic function. C and F have this relationship to the tonic of A natural minor (nm).

Example 2.2

Because C and F are the tonic and subdominant of the relative major; the "tonality" of the natural minor itself is therefore vague, or "unstable"—hovering, as it does, around C. However, the raising of the seventh degree enables it to function unmistakably as the leading tone, a tendency tone, to the tonic. A tonal center and a specific tonality is thereby firmly established with the additional reinforcement of the augmented second (sixth-seventh degrees) and its implied resolution. This is the *harmonic* form (hm).

Example 2.3

But this augmented second, by itself an interval formerly considered not "singer-friendly," was, along with the tritone (augmented fourth/diminished fifth, the *Diabolus in Musica*) routinely shunned. We recall that C.P.E. Bach apparently did not deem the harmonic form important or "legitimate" enough to propose fingerings for it.

However, raising the sixth degree by one half-step eliminates the augmented second. All the intervals of the third through seventh scale degrees are now whole tones, with the essential half step leading tone function preserved. Ascending, the first tetrachord is minor; the second is major. This is the *melodic* form (mm).

Example 2.4

The raised sixth and seventh degrees impart an upward momentum toward the tonic; their lowering reverses that direction, toward the dominant—a relaxation of the upward tension, if you will—and the descending scale reverts to its natural minor form. What is commonly called the melodic minor is this dynamic combination of the two forms; it is a *hybrid* form.

Example 2.5

Taken together, these minor forms are highly chromatic; as such they are colorful and versatile but, tonalitywise, relatively unstable. The chromatic possibilities within the parameters of the second tetrachord are illustrated in this example:

Example 2.6

Richard Franko Goldman writes, "Music seems to demonstrate the hypothesis that major and minor are, in fact, not completely separate and distinct in practice."[1] And he then goes on to quote Busoni (*Sketch of a New Esthetic of Music*): "When we recognize that major and minor form one Whole . . . we arrive unconstrainedly at a perception of the Unity of our system of keys. . . . *We possess one single key*."[2]

The single leading principle **fourth on black, thumb on white** can be seen to be a unifying principle and the Circle of Fifths a unifying concept. Few and versatile, topographical fingerings also function as a *physical* link to the keyboard. Stability is maintained in the midst of instability—a central principle that is also fundamental to a healthy piano technique.[3] And we move increasingly toward that "perception of the Unity of our system of keys."

THE MAJOR SCALE CONNECTION

It is with the minor scales that topographical thinking really comes into its own. The enharmonic keys, with their abundance of black keys, again lead the way, and it is with these that we can begin to appreciate the role played by the major scale topographical fingerings. Like the major scales, the standard fingerings for all forms of the minor scales having black-key tonics are topographically correct regardless of the tones altered. All fingerings are that of the parallel major, relative major, or both (RH: G♯/A♭ hm). Only B-flat melodic minor for the LH ascending (hybrid mm) is derived from neither.

The RH standard fingerings for all *harmonic* minor scales having white-key tonics, except C, are topographically correct since their leading tone is a black key and the fourth is assigned to it; the fingerings are those of the parallel major. And for the RH *melodic* minors having white-key tonics, the standard fingerings for all ascending scales are also derived from the parallel majors and are topographically correct—again *except for C.*

Example 2.7

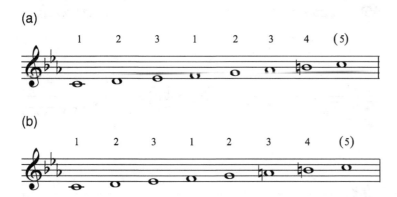

But for the RH descending scales (natural minor form), only C and F are topographically correct since their fingering comports with their respective relative majors, E-flat and A-flat. That of A remains unchanged but is all white keys.

Example 2.8

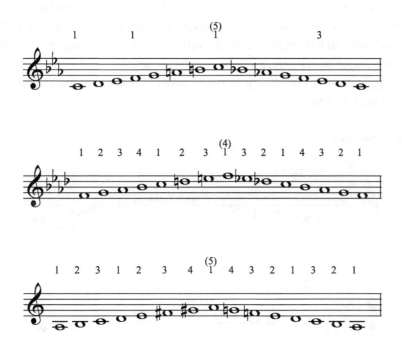

The RH standard fingerings for descending D-E-G-B are topographically incorrect since their lowered seventh is now a white key.

Example 2.9

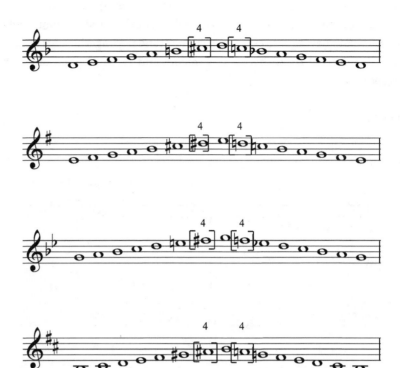

The descending form of the "melodic" minor being the natural minor, it has the notes and topography of the relative major. The descending fingerings are therefore adjusted for the new topographical orientation (even with the standard approach, it is instinctively done for C-sharp and F-sharp in the RH). Possible fingerings that transition from ascending to descending are easily determined (see Appendix 2). For this hybrid form, all RH fingerings are then those of the parallel major ascending and the relative major descending, *again except for ascending C*.

The application of the leading principle readily reveals the pianistic alternative for the minor forms of C.

Example 2.10

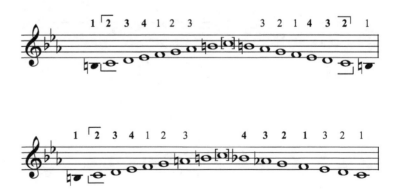

The LH standard fingering for C harmonic and melodic minor is also topographically incorrect.

Example 2.11

(a)

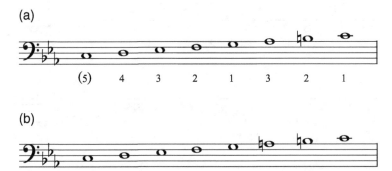

(b)

But correctly adjusted for topography, the fingering is that of its relative major E-flat (melodic minor descending).

Example 2.12

(a)

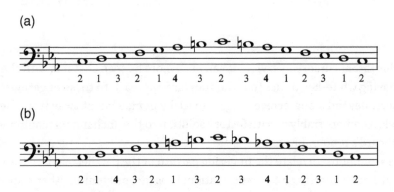

(b)

The standard LH fingering for all forms of the other minor scales having white-key tonics derive from the fingering for their parallel majors and are topographically *incorrect* except for A natural minor descending (all white keys), B (one of the enharmonic scales) and E. Both forms of B and E derive from their topographically correct parallel majors.

Example 2.13

Example 2.13 (*Continued*)

From this rather cursory overview, it can once more be seen that it is with the minor scales having white-key tonics that the standard approach to these fingerings mostly falls short. Beyond a one-octave range, especially in movement away from the torso, they yield a demonstrably unsatisfactory solution to the unchanging requirements of the keyboard's topography.

The attempt to correlate the fingering pattern of the parallel major to the parallel minor, although boasting a *theoretical* rationale, is inconsistent in other respects and results in fingerings that are not topographically oriented. But topographically based minor scale fingerings that comport with those of the relative major are no less—and they are arguably more—relevant theoretically, far more practical in application and infinitely more pianistic.

Indeed, the standard fingerings for the minor forms further conspire to cast C major as the poor model that it is—the enharmonic keys notwithstanding. And from a topographical perspective, it is again the LH that suffers in particular. A solid suspicion that the standard white-key tonic fingerings are a significant factor in the common occurrence of a less agile, less facile, less dependable LH technique vis-à-vis the RH does not require a great leap.

The application of ***fourth on black, thumb on white*** unfailingly provides us with topographical alternatives to the standard fingerings. One could say that this principle is the "irreducible minimum." But how else might we consider fingerings that will orient us topographically, and what might we learn from this? Are there other relationships, and would they confirm and validate what appears to be an inherent and coherent organization? Are they easily remembered?

A comparative analysis of the topographical solutions for the *major* scale fingerings reveals still further consistency and further validation of our leading "pianistic" principle. The outcome is by itself interesting, remarkable, and difficult to ignore. Besides serving us well in our efforts to arrive at fingerings for those minor scales still needing to be topographically adjusted, it offers us a set of *guidelines* readily available for application to any unusual or otherwise challenging passages.

Example 2.14 illustrates the assignment of fingers of either hand to the black keys of the major scales. It represents what turns out to be a methodical sequence of *five* possibilities corresponding to the *number of black keys* in each scale (i.e., as introduced in the Circle of Fifths).

Example 2.14

(1)	G/F	One:	4th finger		
(2)	D/B♭	Two nonconsecutive:	4th	and	3rd
(3)	A/E♭	Two consecutive, one single:	3-4	and	3rd
(4)	E/A♭	Two groups, two consecutive:	3-4	and	2-3
(5)	Enharmonics	Three consecutive black keys:	2-3-4	and	2-3

And as follows (Example 2.15):

Example 2.15

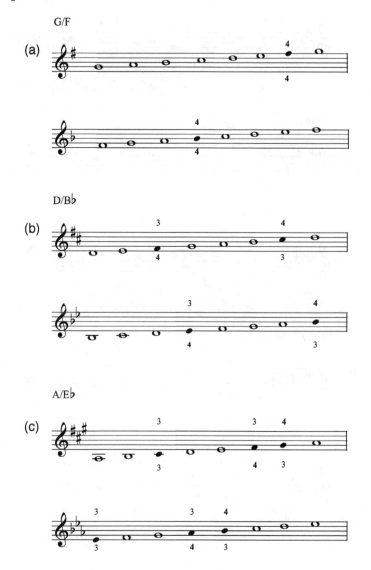

Example 2.15 (Continued)

E/A♭

(d)

B/D♭

(e)

F#/G♭

(f)

C#/C♭

(g)

NATURAL FINGERING

As we have already noted, all major scales having the same number of black keys are identical as to fingering, interval construction and topography. Because the fingerings are based on topography, **all black keys or black key groups coordinate in each** hand—a far more natural, comfortable, and rational synchronization than what is afforded by the standard fingerings. Moreover, the coordinating of the pivoting actions promotes shoulder joint stability.

What I am therefore calling the *major scale connection* is primarily a topographical connection, not a theoretical connection—although it will also prove to correlate in this regard to a surprising degree. For instance, the topographical alternatives for the standard, nontopographical fingerings of C minor (Examples 2.10 and 2.12) can be seen to comply with the guidelines set forth in Example 2.14.

For both hands, the melodic minor ascending is fingered as (1), descending as that of E-flat, its relative major (3). The harmonic minor is fingered as (2), but in the LH the fingering should also be seen as that of its relative major with a raised dominant, this raised dominant now functioning as leading tone.

THE HARMONIC MINOR SCALES

As with the major scales, the standard fingerings for all harmonic minor scales having black-key tonics are topographically correct. All have the fourth assigned to black keys and thumbs to white; all fingerings are those of the parallel major, the relative major or both.

Except for C, the standard fingerings for all RH scales having white-key tonics are topographically correct and derive from the parallel major. For the LH, only B and E are topographically correct. And it is noteworthy that only these scales support two possibilities for each hand, because of their **BWBW** core pattern:

For B harmonic minor RH:

Example 2.16a

Example 2.16b

For E harmonic minor RH:

Example 2.17a

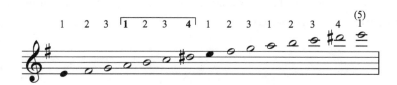

Example 2.17b

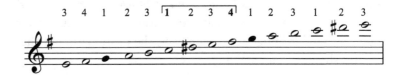

For B harmonic minor LH:

Example 2.18a

Example 2.18b

For E harmonic minor LH:

Example 2.19a

Example 2.19b

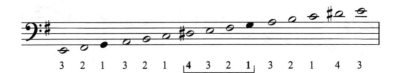

These two scales typify the ease with which the topographical fingerings coordinate and exemplify the topographical advantage in regard to optimal fingering choices. Because there are two possibilities for each hand, there are four combinations for both hands together (HT):

For B harmonic minor:

Example 2.20a

Example 2.20b

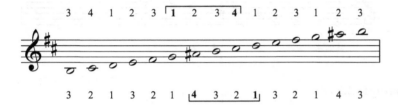

Example 2.20c

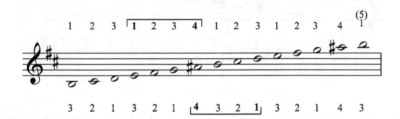

Example 2.20d

For E harmonic minor:

Example 2.21a

Example 2.21b

Example 2.21c

Example 2.21d

Since the fingering for the harmonic minor form of C is the anomaly in both hands, we will adjust it for topography first. For each hand there is only one possibility that satisfies the topographical arrangement of ***fourth on black, thumb on white.*** Looking back to Example 2.14, we see that it conforms to (2) and is *related topographically* to D and B-flat. The coordination of both hands is also the same: the RH third finger synchronizes with the LH fourth finger; the LH fourth finger synchronizes with the RH third. This coordination is something the hand already knows; there are no awkward intervals, and no need for special adjustments.

Example 2.22

Beginning with G, a fifth *above* C, we will explore the remaining LH fingerings according to our leading principle.

NATURAL FINGERING

Example 2.23a

2   1   3   2   1   ⌐4   3   2   1⌐   3   2   1   4   3   2

Example 2.23b

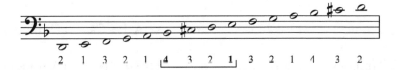

2   1   3   2   1   ⌐4   3   2   1⌐   3   2   1   4   3   2

Example 2.23c

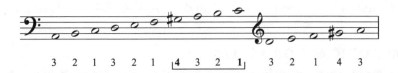

3   2   1   3   2   1   ⌐4   3   2   1⌐   3   2   1   4   3

An issue regarding the LH fingering for F harmonic minor is revealing in that it appears at first to be the only harmonic minor scale that is out of sync with the black-key assignment for the major keys (see Example 2.14). If fingered according to its topographical arrangement (3), the thumb would have to take a black key. Here again, the leading topographical principle is validated and the fourth finger is assigned to the D-flat.

Example 2.24

2   1   3   2   1   ⌐4   3   2   1⌐   3   2   1   4   3   2

And with F hm a fifth *below* C hm, both are in fact topographically related: the fourth finger takes the fourth degree of their respective relative majors. The topographical fingering for F hm is now consistent with its relative major A-flat.

Taken together, the topographically adjusted fingerings for the harmonic minor scales entirely conform to the topography of the major scales in the assignment of fingers to black keys. Like the major scales, they admit of only one solution—again except for B and E, which are unique in having two topographically correct possibilities. And similarly, all patterns are merely intervallic alterations of the now-familiar black-key, white-key topographical patterns.

The *core* patterns (four-note groups) of the harmonic minors do not consistently mirror symmetrically in the way the major scales do. Because of the augmented second, their tetrachords are of different interval constructions; but they do mirror topographically. And nonetheless, certain recurring patterns do mirror each other in regard to interval as well, thanks to the keyboard's remarkable organization. There are identifiable symmetries, all interesting in those terms and all manifesting important root relationships. Example 2.25 is presented with these in mind.

Example 2.25

LH				**RH**	
(D minor)	B♭-C♯-D-E	and	C-D-E♭-F♯	(G minor)
(G minor)	E♭-F♯-G-A	and	G-A-B♭-C♯	(D minor)
(C minor)	A♭-B-C-D	and	D-E-F-G♯	(A minor)
(A minor)	G♯-A-B-C	and	B-C-D-E♭	(C minor)
(F minor)	D♭-E-F-G	and	A-B-C-D♯	(E minor)

THE MELODIC MINOR SCALES

Like the major scale, the melodic minor form is constructed entirely of whole and half steps. Ascending, the melodic minor can also be considered to be the *parallel* major with a lowered third degree and descending the *relative* major begun on the sixth scale degree.

The standard fingerings for those keys having black-key tonics are topographically correct, owing as they do to the very few white keys available to the thumb. In terms of both fingering and topography, only F-sharp mm does not contain the enharmonic major scale group of three consecutive black keys, either ascending (it is, interestingly, E major topographically) or descending (relative major A).

The fingerings for the E-flat and B-flat melodic minor scales are consistent both ascending and descending, whereas the fingerings for the F-sharp and C-sharp for the RH and G-sharp/A-flat for the LH are not. The topographies of these require a change of fingering descending if the thumb is to avoid taking a black key.

Example 2.26a

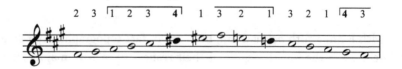

Example 2.26b

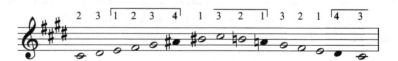

NATURAL FINGERING

Example 2.26c

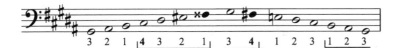

3 2 1 ⌊4 3 2 1⌋ 3 4⌋ 1 2 3 ⌊1 2 3

It is instructive that most pianists make these changes without thinking—another manifestation of a "pianistic sense." And the accepted fingerings for these reflect the fact that, at bottom, topography operates as the *prime* determinant. Just as we begin the black-key tonic scales with a finger other than the thumb or fifth, this is—like the major flat key scales themselves—a further example of the ideal models "hidden" among the commonly accepted fingerings.

SUPPLANTING A FLAWED MODEL

What has contributed to the confusion surrounding the issues regarding a direct application of scale and arpeggio fingerings to passagework is the very form of the standard fingerings for the white-key tonic scales. Except for F and B, they are fingered from tonic to tonic from thumb to fifth, the fingering sequence unchanged ascending or descending. In reality, the demands of extended passagework are rarely met—and inadequately—with this model.

By the student's intermediate years it is a significant handicap. The fingerings found in sonatina collections, for example, are frequently inconsistent with its application; the absence of familiar black-key "markers" is a particular difficulty. Later, we will explore the extent to which this impractical standard "principle" has repeatedly undermined the very large number of sincere attempts to arrive at more successful double note fingerings.

It stands that the most commonly recurring topographical patterns hold the key to a more consistent accommodation. And there remain still the several options for initiating, linking and closing them—just as we have always had to account for transitions from pattern to pattern in the fingering process.

From the topographical perspective, there are only four black and white key combinations (four-note groups, mirrored in both hands) for all twenty-four major and melodic minor scales:

LH	RH
BBBW	WBBB
BBWW	WWBB
BWWW	WWWB
WWWW	WWWW

With the introduction of the 2+ (augmented second) in the harmonic minor form, there is one more:

BWBW	WBWB

These topographical groups represent the four-note groups (thumb on white, fourth on black) for all the minor scales. As with the major scales, one merely subtracts the fourth finger to arrive at the three-note groups, which are also topographically correct.

Beginning with the most pianistic groups—those having the largest number of black keys—they are as follows:

	LH	RH
(1)	B/BBW	WBB/B
(2)	B/WBW	WBW/B
(3)	B/BWW	WWB/B
(4)	B/WWW	WWW/B
(5)	(WWWW	WWWW)

Amazingly, *all* thirty-six major-minor scales are made up of only these five black-key, white-key finger groups when fingered according to the leading topographical principle **fourth on black, thumb on white.**

For our purpose, the Circle of Fifths diagram could well be turned on its head. The Circle of Fifths, now inverted, represents the all-important *pianistic progression* topwise, the *harmonic progression* bottomwise.

Example 2.27

INVERTED CIRCLE OF FIFTHS

Major-Minor Scales

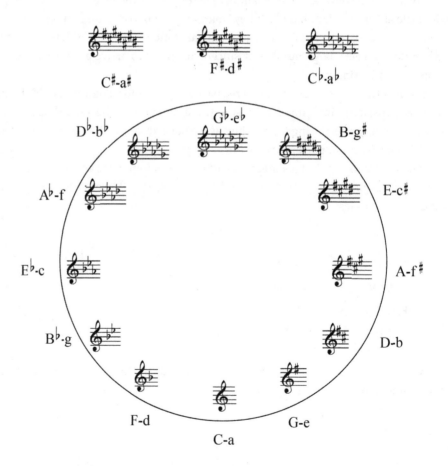

The reader is directed to Appendix 2 for easy reference to the single note scales for all minor forms.

CHORDS, ARPEGGIOS AND EXTENDED HARMONIES

3

Scales should use exactly the same production as arpeggios. There is no difference between them as far as the need of a blended activity goes. But the diatonic progression does not show up that need as do arpeggios.

—Abby Whiteside

After all, in Beethoven or Mozart—or any composer, for that matter—the scales and arpeggio passages are melodic lines.

—Constance Keene

CHORDS AND THEIR INVERSIONS (played as a sequence of simultaneous, or *vertical*, soundings), broken chord figurations, arpeggios and other arpeggiations of closed or open harmonies (nonsimultaneous, or *horizontal*, soundings) all represent what Goldman refers to as a triad's "extension in time." He then goes on to say that "harmony is not only identification and connection of chords; it is a matter of deploying sounds in a time continuum, of giving *motion* to chordal sounds, of manipulating the notes of the triad horizontally (or melodically) as well as vertically."[1]

Although there are many examples, we can consider three well-known compositions by Bach (*Well-Tempered Clavier* Book I, Prelude I) and Chopin (Prelude, Opus 28 No. 1; Etude, Opus 10 No. 1); all are in C major, and each begins a cycle of compositions related to a specific tonal scheme. The highly expressive and lyrical Impromptu in Gb, Opus 90 No. 3 and the alternately delicate and dramatic Impromptu in A flat, Opus 90 No. 4 (D899) of Franz Schubert are contrasting examples of rather lengthy "extensions of time," as well as notable for their harmonic and textural subtlety. And one must include the vast number of Schubert's vocal accompaniments, a genre that he elevated and transformed.

Indeed, the rhythmic activity of the familiar Alberti bass pattern serves the function of sustaining a particular harmony or harmonic progression, which was of practical value at a time when keyboard instruments were limited in that capability. Now, though, we are most likely to consider it a mere stylistic hallmark, idiomatic of so much music from the Classical Period, the earlier keyboard sonatas in particular. And although arpeggios may often be appreciated and considered chiefly as embellishment figures or accompaniment patterns—even if imbued or suffused with a certain *bravura*, dramatic, or other emotional content—they nonetheless fundamentally extend individual harmonies, or the harmonic structure itself, in time.

With the advent of the damper pedal and other technological innovations, harmonies could be sustained and rhythmically extended for even longer duration and over a progressively greater range. Beethoven made much use of this new potential for great dramatic and expressive purpose; his piano sonatas of the so-called middle period reflect both his experimentation and his liberation. And with Chopin, his contemporaries and others after them, harmonies are not only transformed; *sonorities* are created.

For pianists in particular, the concept of arpeggios as harmonies extended in time is an interesting and useful one, as it is reflected in biokinetic corollaries that are significant in their impact on execution. Horizontal movements, now occurring in an expanded keyboard space, must likewise be more expansive. And yet, these very same movements are compressed *in time* as tempo increases. But gravity continues to act on momentum progressing forward in time; horizontal and vertical forces both interact and counteract. There is, too, an energetic expansion commensurate with the emotional content of a composition and the expressive intentions of the performer. Consequently, the need for attention to balance (and counterbalance), appropriate alignment, adequate and *timely* adjustment for key depth and the dynamics of shoulder complex stabilization is significantly heightened. Arm use and finger choice must necessarily bear greater scrutiny.

In playing arpeggios, the pianist must now negotiate larger intervals with the hand most frequently in extended position. Movementwise, there is a greater likelihood of a "blurring of the lines," so to speak. What I am here referring to is that incoordinate result of a lack of distinction between what E. W. Grabill (*The Mechanics of Piano Technic*, 1909) has insightfully termed *distributive* movements—locating movements occurring in the horizontal plane—and *dynamic movements,* or tone-producing movements occurring in the vertical plane. "Clean" playing is very much a product of these well-differentiated and well-timed movements.

With arpeggios the problem is compounded. Either unnecessary stretches must be eliminated or interval distance minimized if the muscles involving the lateral extension of the fingers are not to be misused or overworked. Moreover, there is an increasing tendency to "reach," or lead with the fingers, which must be avoided, rather than fully deploying the mechanism of the upper arm. A highly skillful coordination of the necessary movements within the keyboard planes encountered—black key, white key, vertical, horizontal and transverse (I have termed movements in this oblique plane *adjustive*)—is required. This is the very basis of a healthy, physiologically sound piano technique.

I have earlier joined others in extolling the pianistic, artistic and expressive merits of a well-executed scale line. Likewise, the line of a well-executed arpeggio is of no mean consequence and reflects great care, precision and technical skill. The exposed arpeggio passages of Mozart and Schubert, for example, are by no means exclusively ornamental or mere textural "filler." And because the horizontal shape of a "singing" melodic line is built on extended harmonies as often as it is of stepwise construction, attention ought also to be given to arpeggio technique once the hand is ready.

We have already begun to see how the pianist benefits from a topographical solution to scale fingering. What can we learn about arpeggio fingering from a topographical perspective?

As horizontal (melodic) extensions of vertical harmonies, arpeggio fingerings are derived from these "simultaneously sounding" chords. From the viewpoint of the standard approach, fingerings for those arpeggios having black key tonics are, like the scales, again considered anomalies.

Chords built on tonic C are the models. Following these, the preferred fingerings for all others having white key tonics are those of their root positions, either hand. Although inversions remain an option, their individual fingerings are generally not given the importance they deserve. Pianists all too often invert the root-position arpeggio without a fingering change. For the RH such fingerings evidence a misguided preference for the third finger over the fourth.

NATURAL FINGERING

But from a topographical perspective, the standard fingering for major and minor arpeggios with black key tonics again point the way. Except for all-black-key F-sharp/G-flat major and its relative minor D-sharp/E-flat, the thumb is assigned to a white key and the leading topographical principle is confirmed. Only the fingering for LH B-flat major (and its mirror, RH B minor) is the exception in that the third rather than the fourth is often favored for the black key due to the interval arrangement.

However, the American pianist William Mason (1828–1908) long ago recognized, and apparently tried to dispel, the thorny pitfalls surrounding the dilemma of fingering for the major-minor arpeggios of B-flat and B. Mason—a student of Moscheles, Dreyshock and Liszt as well as a friend of Berlioz, Schumann, Brahms, Wagner and many other notables—authored the quite impressive, and for its time rather comprehensive, *A System of Fundamental Techniques for Piano Playing*, first published in 1878. And in his discussion of fingering for the arpeggiated triads, Mason also alludes to topographical considerations. The 1905 publication of a *New Edition* "greatly enlarged, revised and improved" by his student William S. B. Matthews (1837–1912), himself an influential pedagogue, has this to say (italics mine):

> *Dr. Mason employs the fourth finger invariably* in the second and third positions [first and second inversions] of the right hand, and the first and second positions [root position and first inversion] of the left, *irrespective of the convenience of employing in some forms the third finger thus near to the fifth.*
> Triad arpeggios fall into four kinds of keyboard relations:
> All white keys: C, F, G, D min., E min., A min.; or
> White with black third: D, E, A, C min., F min., G min.; or
> Black with white third: D flat, E flat, A flat, C sharp min., F♯ min.; or
> All black keys: F sharp, D sharp min.; or
> Irregular, B♭, B major, and B minor.[2]

Obviously, we are to assume the minors for A-flat and B-flat. And enharmonic equivalents are not spelled out, often the practice of the time, as these are assumed.

Except for the small hand, it is rare that the fourth finger is not felt or proved to be superior to the third for the major-minor arpeggios of the LH B-flat and RH B, even though the interval for pivot finger and thumb is that of a fourth. Topography and alignment remain the determining factors; inner humeral adjustment (medial rotation) facilitates their execution.

It should also be noted that B-flat and B are the only major-minor *triads* sharing the same black and white key arrangement; they are symmetrically inverted. LH B-flat major exactly mirrors RH B minor, and RH B major exactly mirrors LH B-flat minor: BWW/WWB and BBW/WBB.

Example 3.1a

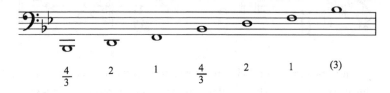

Example 3.1b

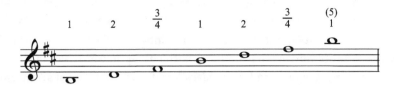

Example 3.2a

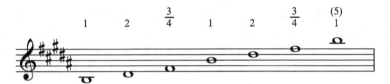

Example 3.2b

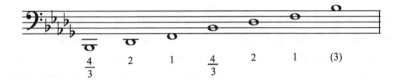

The LH fingerings for both B-flat arpeggios are determined from the second inversion of the four-part chord, those for B major from the root position and B minor from the first inversion.

Example 3.3

Similarly, the RH fingerings for both B arpeggios are found from the root position, those for B-flat major from the first inversion and B-flat minor from the second.

Example 3.4

As might now be expected, LH B minor exactly mirrors that of RH B-flat major and LH B-flat minor mirrors that of RH B major—in topography as well as interval arrangement. The B-flat and B major-minor arpeggios may be "irregular" in one sense, but certainly not in any other.

TRIAD ARPEGGIOS (ARPEGGIATED TRIADS)

The Topography of the Triads

Since to be topographically informed is to be topographically aware, it is useful at this point to take a comparative view of the topographies for *all* root-position triads. Fingerings are easily remembered and consistently applied once *topographical* groups are readily visualized.

	BWB	BBB	WWW	WBW	BWW/WWB	BBW/WBB
Major	C♯/D♭ - E♭ - A♭	F♯/G♭			B♭	
			C-F-G	D-E-A		B
Minor	C♯ - F♯ - G♯/A♭	D♯/E♭				B♭
			D-E-A	C-F-G	B	
Augmented	B♭			E-A-B	C-C♯-E♭-F-G-A♭	D-F♯
Diminished			B	F	C♯-D-E-	C-E♭-G-B♭
					F♯-A♭-A	

The major and minor triads on B-flat and B are topographically related to the augmented-diminished triads built on all other tonics. But, as charted above, one can see that they are yet again anomalies: only the diminished triad for B is WWW in topographical construction, while only that for augmented B♭ is BWB.

For all arpeggios, the significance of such topographical relatedness is to be found in their inversions. In part writing, the use of chord inversions permits a smoother, more melodic bass line and more flexibility in voice leading overall. And so it is with fingerings derived from inversions, particularly when they exhibit topographical similarities and mutual affinities within the wide range of harmonic usage. Root relationships, common tones, tendency tones and enharmonic equivalents are the key. It is in this that they are found to be ultimately—and intimately—related to the passages of a composition.

Major and Minor

Because of their construction, B major and B minor are the only white-key tonic arpeggios having black keys that are topographically correct for the RH in root position. For all others, the preferred fingerings are found in their inversions. The topographical principle is operative in the LH fingerings of all white-key tonic arpeggios whose four-part chords have a black-key third; except for B minor, all root position chords are topographically correct. Looking back for a moment, we can see that Chopin's insistence on first introducing the B and D-flat major scales has its practical counterpart in their arpeggios as well.

Since F-sharp/G-flat and relative minor D-sharp/E-flat are the only all-black-key arpeggios (more about the significance of these keys below) the sequences E♭-e♭-E-e and f♯-f-F-F♯ are instructive and serve as useful models for the major-minor arpeggios.

The four topographies are represented, their fingerings exemplifying topographical application and interaction:

Example 3.5

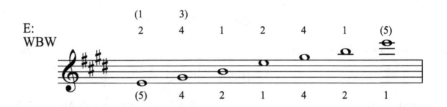

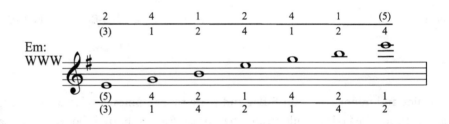

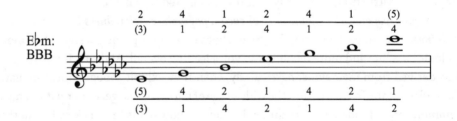

Example 3.6

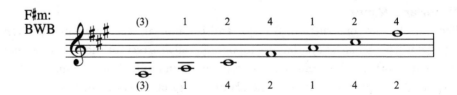

Example 3.6 (Continued)

Fm:
WBW

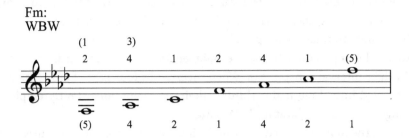

F:
WWW

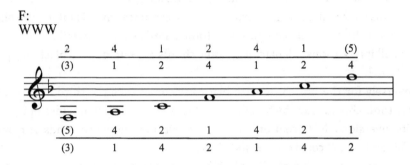

F♯:
BBB

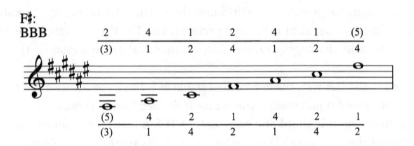

For either hand, the fingering for all-black-key (BBB) and all-white-key (WWW) arpeggios may be that of any of their inversions since there cannot be the defining issue of a black-to-white-key pivot. But those inversions providing a fourth-finger pivot will nonetheless be found to be demonstrably better, even if a little practice (think "physiological reeducation") is necessary at first. The root-position or first inversion of the LH and the first or second inversion of the RH are then to be preferred; viewed contrariwise, these mirror each other.

It is important to consider these all-black, all-white key patterns identical and merely operating in different planes. Such treatment is significant as to orientation, perception of difficulty and comfort. There are, of course, differences in key length and available surface for key contact, but a secure tactile, sensorial response to the black keys is entirely possible—without attempts, usually unconscious, to "create more surface" with the finger itself. But within their respective planes there are no differences in topography. Such a seemingly elementary realization goes a long way to facilitating execution.

Augmented-Diminished

When also considered in their inversions, the topographies for the augmented-diminished triads likewise provide a black-key pivot, allowing consistent fingering throughout. Although their arpeggios are not usually presented in manuals, they are frequently encountered in various combinations, and it is worthwhile to consider them. At the very least, there is the benefit of developing sensitivity to the finer distinctions of thumb-under pivoting.

Because the augmented triads are built entirely of major thirds (M-M) they maintain their interval construction when inverted as four-part chords (the octave may be divided into three major thirds). Their arpeggios consistently employ the fourth-finger pivot throughout for both hands.

Although the root-position diminished triad is constructed of consecutive minor thirds (m-m), the interval between the chord fifth and doubled root (at the octave) is that of an augmented fourth (enharmonic diminished fifth) when written in four parts. It is this larger interval of the tritone that necessitates the RH taking the black-key pivot with the third for all white-key tonic chords except F, while B offers the options of all its positions. All black-key tonic chords accommodate a black-key pivot with the fourth.

Conversely for the LH, those with black-key tonics take the third as pivot; the white-key tonic chords take the fourth. Here too, all white-key B provides options by way of its inversions. Note that only the root-position diminished triads of F and B have WBW and WWW constructs respectively.

This inverse relationship of LH and RH fingerings is in itself interesting, with the exceptions of B and F being particularly noteworthy. It is these two pitches that constitute the tritone (augmented fourth/diminished fifth), the keyboard anomaly in the C major diatonic series of otherwise perfect fifths. But this is further indicative of the innate, and thoroughly remarkable, symmetrical organization of the keyboard.

Looked at another way, the diminished triads of B and F constitute a full-diminished seventh chord if juxtaposed: the octave is divided into four minor thirds (two tritones). Inverting this chord and seen as **G♯ B D F A♭**, we readily understand the significance of this "anomaly": D and enharmonic G♯/A♭ are the *points of symmetry* of the keyboard, a symmetry reflected in both spellings of Chopin's Fundamental Pattern and one that will be explored further. We will see that this remarkable symmetry can be further harnessed to arrive at a comprehensive fingering process that is both rational and natural.

SEVENTH CHORD ARPEGGIOS

Four-part seventh chords are constructed of a vertically or horizontally arranged series of major or minor thirds. With the one voice doubled at the octave, the full chords are then in five parts. In playing them in their vertical arrangement (harmonically), fingering choice cannot be at issue since all five fingers must be put to work—unless the thumb would take two adjacent white keys, i.e. the seconds of an inversion. The topographical fingerings for their arpeggios will therefore be found from either the root position or inversions of these chords and are easily deduced.

Arpeggios of the seventh chords are commonly encountered and recommended for study. Identified by their construction of thirds as well as their distinguishing seventh, they are often named accordingly:

Full diminished seventh	Minor-minor-minor seventh
Half-diminished seventh	Minor-minor-major seventh
Dominant seventh	Major-minor-minor seventh

Major seventh	Major-minor-major seventh
Minor seventh	Minor-major-minor seventh

Example 3.7 is not only interesting harmonically but also revealing as to the fingering. The major seventh chord with lowered third and fifth (enharmonic E♭) may also be considered as a diminished triad, the resolution of the seventh (G♯ to A) delayed. It is "equivocal," to cite Goldman again, in that in its functioning "the sense of a seventh chord as a structural element is lacking."[3]

Example 3.7

Liszt, *Mephisto Waltz*

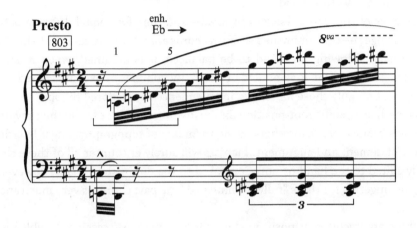

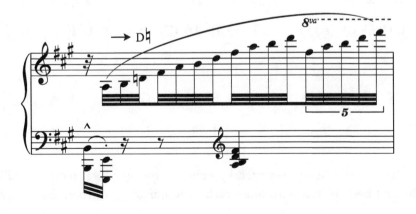

And how appropriate is this internal harmonic conflict, with its opposing tendencies of tones toward upward and downward resolution. The initially unresolved "pull" of inherently opposing forces is an apt metaphor for Faust himself!

THE DIMINISHED SEVENTH ARPEGGIO

The augmented second of the harmonic minor scale early on demonstrates the need to attend to the lateral extensions of the fingers—the "opening" of the hand. (An "open" or "closed" position of the hand is not to be confused with the spacing of chord tones of the same designation.) Augmented seconds may be considered enharmonic minor thirds, but from a harmonically functional standpoint they are different. For the pianist, however, they are aurally and topographically the same. The diminished seventh chord, as it is commonly termed, is constructed entirely of minor thirds—the octave thus divided equally.

Because of this consistency of interval—and therefore equal distance between keys and fingers—the diminished seventh chords are often advocated as being "ideal" for the hand, allowing the hand to be balanced, it is assumed, when in such an extended position. One is reminded of the many volumes of exercises based on this chord, most notably those for "finger independence" by Isadore Philipp.

Nonetheless, some root-position diminished seventh chords and their inversions are more comfortable than others owing to factors of topography, finger length, finger-key placement and alignment. Pianists will surely encounter all of these chords, ideally suited to the hand or not. Compared to the diminished triads, however, the arpeggio fingering for these "fully" diminished four-part chords is very much another matter.

There are twelve root-position chords in chromatic succession. Doubled at the octave, each hand employs all five fingers (LH: 5 4 3 2 1 and RH: 1 2 3 4 5). But since all chords consist exclusively of minor thirds, there are in fact only three chords for each hand, the inversion of each representing four chords. The key to the most pianistic (that is, topographically suited) fingerings for all twelve diminished seventh arpeggios are to be found in these inversions.

Yet again, those chords having black-key tonics lead the way. Giving the thumb to a white key and the fourth to a black key reveals the three topographical possibilities for each hand that, when inverted, represent the topographical fingerings for the arpeggios of all twelve tones. Because each is also an inversion of the other, they may be termed "complimentary."

Example 3.8a

1 2 3 4	1 2 3 4	1 2 3 4
RH: **A** C E♭ G♭ (A)	**E** G B♭ D♭ (E)	**B** D F A♭ (B)

1 2 3 4	1 2 3 4	1 2 3 4
LH: **C** E♭ G♭ B♭♭ (C)	**G** B♭ D♭ F♭ (G)	**F** A♭ C♭ E♭♭ (F)
4 3 2 1	4 3 2 1	4 3 2 1

These three chords are represented by only *two* topographical patterns (BBWW/WWBB and BWWW/WWWB). Since each hand mirrors the other, there are really *only two* complementary black and white key groupings for all twelve diminished seventh arpeggios.

Example 3.8b

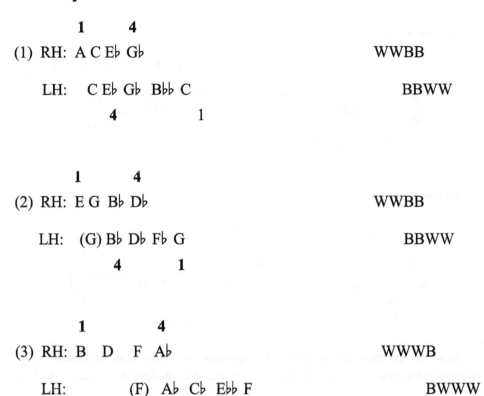

But considered from the viewpoint of keyboard symmetry rather than of root movement, all three complimentary chords bear a direct relationship to the points of symmetry (D and A♭) and Chopin's Fundamental Pattern, as will be shown further on.

The fingering is constant for the individual tones and facilitates chromatic succession. This is readily demonstrated in the arpeggiation of any three consecutive diminished sevenths one-half step apart. (The diminished seventh arpeggios in chromatic order may be found in Appendix 3.)

OTHER SEVENTH CHORD ARPEGGIOS

Topographical fingerings for the arpeggios of the "unequivocal" chords of the seventh may be easily determined. All afford black-key pivots except:

Half-diminished (minor-minor-major)	B
Dominant (major-minor-minor)	G
Major (major-minor-major)	C and F
Minor (minor-major-minor)	D E A

With a white-key pivot unavoidable, the foremost operating principle is *avoidance of unnecessary stretches*. For example, the third inversion (LH) and the first inversion (RH) of the all-white key B half-diminished seventh chord offers a more favorable fingering choice for its arpeggio. If it is compared to the topographical solution for B♭ Dominant seventh (BBWW/WWBB: LH second inversion, RH first), the fingering is easily seen as related. It is consistent, rational and far less strenuous.

Example 3.9a

Example 3.9b

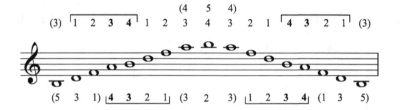

Likewise, the most natural, pianistic fingerings for the other all-white-key arpeggios will be found in the second inversion for the LH and the first inversion for the RH.

Example 3.10

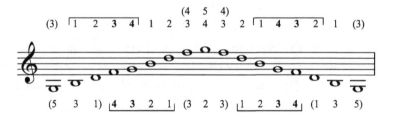

Example 3.11a

Example 3.11b

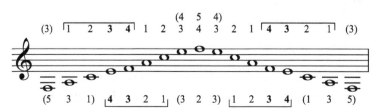

Example 3.12a

Example 3.12b

Example 3.12c

Note that the core patterns for the arpeggios are based on four-note groups derived from a "translocated" extended/open position of the Fundamental Pattern; that is, the three successive black keys assigned to the long fingers are repositioned, or shifted. They are defined not by interval but by topography.

This *translocation* of the Fundamental Pattern is the basis for a topographically correct resolution of *all* arpeggios. As with the scale fingerings, those for the arpeggios have as their core the same five topographical arrangements of black and white keys. These "extended" patterns reflecting the larger intervals of the arpeggios and the wider, more "open" expanse of the hand differ only in *topology*, i.e., the spatial differences or relationships of their distinguishing topographical features and characteristics.

One can easily determine the evolution of the topographical fingerings for the arpeggios as represented by the translocated Fundamental Pattern and its topographical and intervallic alterations. *All* arpeggios derive from this:

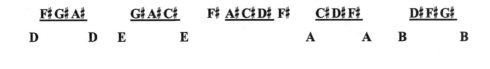

and

G♭ A♭ B♭	A♭ B♭ D♭	B♭ D♭ E♭	D♭ E♭ G♭	E♭ G♭ A♭
D D	F F	G G	B♭♭ B♭♭	C♭ C♭

The core patterns translocated complement those of the whole-tone Fundamental Pattern. The implications for the pedagogy of extended chords and arpeggios are really vast in scope.

EXTENDED HARMONIES, EXTENDED APPLICATIONS

As with the scales, the standard fingerings for major and minor arpeggios having black-key tonics are topographically correct. But for those with white-key tonics, it is the RH that now requires significant adjustment—except for B. Topographically correct fingerings for the arpeggios of augmented/diminished triads and seventh chords will also be found in those inversions positing the pivoting finger on an available black key (thumb on white). For all those involving black and white keys, combinations that are topographically correct and pianistically ideal ultimately comport with inversions that also avoid unnecessary stretching and are thus suited to the most comfortable extensions of the hand.

In the case of arpeggios involving white or black keys only, all inversions are available as fingering options—a sort of "compensating" advantage. Although the third finger has been seen to be most suitable as a white-key pivot (its relative length naturally adjusting for key depth), those inversions involving the fourth finger are nevertheless to be preferred whenever practical, because of the "mechanics" of thumb-hand pivoting and its relationship to the upper arm and shoulder complex stabilization (see Appendix 10).

As in harmonic practice, inversions enable a smoother progression from chord to chord. The maximal vertical space and sufficient key depth necessary for a coordinated and controlled pivoting action are ensured if lateral extension of the fingers (reaching or "stretching" distance) can be minimized or avoided by encompassing the smallest possible intervals. Inversions therefore provide options for more practical and healthful reconfigurations. The hand then functions within a more natural range and with optimal alignment, as consistently as possible.

Application of the leading topographical principle (**fourth on black, thumb on white**) confirms that, like the scales, arpeggio fingerings also conform to the five core patterns. The difference is found only in the lateral distance of the intervals, not in fingering related to topography. Topographically correct fingerings for arpeggios and scales are thoroughly consistent with each other.

The reader is directed to Appendix 3 for easy reference to all the arpeggios.

OTHER SCALE FINGERINGS; CHROMATIC-DIATONIC COMPOUNDS

4

Chromatic scales can be played, if and when necessary, with six different fingerings.
—Heinrich Neuhaus

The process of naming things takes place in the laboratory of the imagination. . . . Identifying the total cast of characters is job number one.
—Russell Sherman

ATTEMPTS TO SOMEHOW SYSTEMATIZE SENSIBLE SOLUTIONS for keyboard fingering have been at the center of an ongoing probe for the most suitable fingerings for centuries. If we grant stylistic differences, advances in instrumental technology, and shifting aesthetics, the fingerings for scales, arpeggios and double notes that are now commonly accepted as "standard" had their own genesis. Even the chromatic scale, one of the most basic and readily comprehended keyboard patterns, is illustrative of that search.

As they have all been handed down to us, they now represent a far simpler organization than that offered by C.P.E. Bach, performance practice notwithstanding. But the search for better fingerings and a better process should never cease—as Debussy wisely intimated ("Let us search for our fingerings"). And composers, knowingly or not, will not let it.

THE CHROMATIC SCALE

Constructed of half-steps only, the chromatic scale can be considered to be fundamental to the pianist's keyboard orientation, both spatially and aurally. Several fingerings have been advocated historically, each held to have certain advantages over the others. It is worthwhile to consider the six fingerings presented here (and in Appendix 4) from a topographical and physiological perspective since all, more or less, are to be found in various editions.

They are best presented and considered beginning on *point of symmetry* D, since black keys and white keys are then maximally synchronized: whether played in parallel or contrary motion, black and white keys coincide.

The **French** pattern is commonly recommended and the one most in use. It is most easily learned and most easily applied. But the **German** or **Mixed** fingering is rarely encountered, if at all. A variant of this "mixed" fingering was recommended and endorsed by the great Theodore **Leschetizky**.[1]

Clara Schumann, in the prefatory notes to her edition of Robert Schumann's *Six Paganini Etudes*, credited Chopin with the so-called **English** fingering. However, Chopin's own méthode advances the French fingering, using only the first three fingers but adding a variant 1-(3-)4.[2] And he "most often played chromatic scales with the last three fingers."[3]

The fifth fingering is attributed to the legendary pianist Sigismund **Thalberg**,[4] whereas the introduction of the sixth has been generally attributed to **Liszt**.[5] Other variants of these chromatic fingerings may be found, and certainly employed, their versatility dependent on the desired placement of accents, tempo/speed and range of the passage. But what we can certainly glean from these fingerings is the fact that only the 1-3 (or 1-2) combination can be considered unique to the chromatic scale. All the others are the basic fingering groups specific to diatonic scale patterns.

A CONSIDERATION OF FINGERING OPTIONS

Less frequent thumb "shifts" are often cited as a compelling reason for advocating certain of the fingerings over others. If this were the chief criterion, Liszt's would certainly be the most favored. Topographically correct, the English fingering, however, is very naturally facile and may be found useful in certain passages. But in this and Thalberg's, the thumb is called on only once more than in Liszt's fingerings. One has only to think of the glissando action itself and the obvious fact that any sustained octave passage requires far more frequent shifts of the thumb, as do other double-note passages such as sixths. But making use of the of the diatonic scale sequence 1-2-3/1-2-3-4 as they do, both the English and Thalberg's fingerings tap into an already learned response. In developing a fingering vocabulary, they might best be considered as *diatonic fingerings applied to a chromatic pattern*.

Of the numerous fingerings for the chromatic scale that have been advocated historically, the French fingering is now generally accepted as the basic fingering, as the one that is most efficient and most universally responsive to the needs at hand.

As for the rest, only a very few are now deemed practical, and their employment is usually limited to special effect.

Overall, the French fingering is conceptually simpler, more consistent, and more facile. It is the recommended fingering for the early years of study, while in the later years it will be found to be the more brilliant, "cleaner" fingering[6] and to afford the greatest versatility in resolving fingering problems. Hereon in this text, a "chromatic fingering" should be taken as the three-finger French pattern for the chromatic scale. And it is this fingering that forms the basis for the variants presented here.

THE SEVEN CHROMATIC FINGERINGS

In his informative, inspiring and provocative treatise *The Art of Piano Playing*, Heinrich Neuhaus writes: "Chromatic scales can be played, if and when necessary, with six different fingerings; I will not give these here as they are so well known."[7] Perhaps he is referring to those six identified above. But with that said, Neuhaus goes on to suggest two more, which he has "derived from dividing the chromatic minor thirds in two parts," separating the outer and inner voices for individual attention. In isolating the inner voice, a second-finger glissando—a "slide" from black to white key—is emphasized and initiates a discussion advocating such application for all fingers.[8] But one need only briefly survey available manuals and other pedagogical materials to reasonably assume that everyone *does not* know them—whichever ones they are that Neuhaus has in mind.

Nonetheless, in addition to the several fingerings for the chromatic scale that we have just considered, there are numerous fingering variants, and far more than six. As with all fingerings, some are better than others. Many are not at all practicable and are challenging merely for their own sake. Obviously, one can think up any number of combinations and apply them to all sorts of patterns. But without consideration of topography, they will undoubtedly be fraught with difficulty. They are rarely necessary, if ever, or physiologically beneficial. And their practical application is severely limited, to say the least.

Collections of technical exercises contrived for our "benefit" these last two hundred years abundantly attest to this. After Isidor Philipp, Alfred Cortot is unrivaled in this, although he eventually narrows the chromatic fingerings down to three "most frequently used" (*Rational Principles of Pianoforte Technique*). As another example, the reader is here referred to No. 14 of Ernst von Dohnányi's *Essential Exercises for Obtaining a Sure Technique*. The chromatic scale is therein fingered entirely as a 1-2-3-4 sequence. Even as an exercise, one must ask why. It is certainly an instance—but only one—of patterning taken to an extreme.

But seven chromatic scale fingerings are recommended here: one basic chromatic scale fingering and six variants. These are the most valuable in practical application and the most beneficial for technical development. Physiologically sound and topographically correct, they are best practiced in a complementary fashion. The French fingering for the chromatic scale is the basic pattern for these indispensable six fingering variants; its simplicity allows the greatest number of short-finger, long-finger sequences. Although they are first encountered and learned as chromatic scale fingerings, they are later *diatonically applied* to great benefit.

These variants will be found to be a superb tool for developing the ulnar (third to fourth/fifth finger) side of the hand. And such a goal is not to be underestimated or overlooked. Apart from the development of strength *and* flexibility in this under-appreciated and most often neglected part of the hand, it is essential for a healthy and successful double note technique. The "end" fingers of the RH are most often called upon to play the notes of the melodic line or an uppermost voice. The "end" fingers of the LH are most often responsible for the clear demarcation of a bass line or lowermost voice (remark that, in the lower range of the keyboard, the piano's strings are progressively thicker and longer, and the key resistance is greater). The mastery of complex contrapuntal passages becomes infinitely easier.

In a relevant remark by Neuhaus: "I think that anyone who has a feeling for the keyboard and *for his hand* [emphasis added] has derived pleasure from playing a complete chromatic scale with only 'half' of his hand (the imaginary dividing line running between the index and the middle finger)."[9] A rather interesting though unusual sentiment—but a revealing anatomical demarcation.

The principle of *short fingers under long fingers and long fingers over short fingers* is unavoidably at work in considerations of suitable fingering for double notes. In these, the potential for a finger-to-finger, note-to-note legato connection is challenged to the extreme, by both the topography of the keyboard and the physical limitations of the hand. Yet by this time most pianists' technique has already been seriously compromised by a lack of attention to the proper and adequate development of the ulnar side of the hand. This is usually underdeveloped or overdeveloped—and often both (flexors, for example, may be underdeveloped while the hypothenar eminence is overdeveloped and extensors overused)—as a consequence. And most important, pronators are generally overdeveloped and overtaxed, another of the chief factors setting the long-term stage for serious disability. The fingerings found in most editions are complicit in compounding these deficiencies, studiously avoiding use of the fourth and fifth and at the same time frequently employing five-finger patterns without intelligent regard for topography.

The seven chromatic patterns that follow are also a unique opportunity for developing the pivoting action of these fingers and for attending to the lateral adjustments that permit their precise alignment with the forearm. For example, the black-key-fourth-to-white-key-thumb sequence may be repeated five times in the course of a chromatic scale octave, compared to one time in the diatonic—and the practice of each sequence in trills of various rhythmic groupings compounds the value. Those fingers assigned to the additional white key are indicated in parentheses in Example 4.1. It must be remarked that 1-(3-)5 is an excellent combination for "contracting" the hand to its palmar center.

Example 4.1

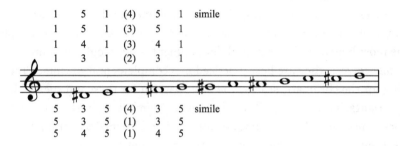

The range of flexion increases for those fingers progressively situated nearest to the ulnar side of the hand; they are thus capable of passing under the longer third and fourth fingers—even the second, although extremely limited in range.

Example 4.2

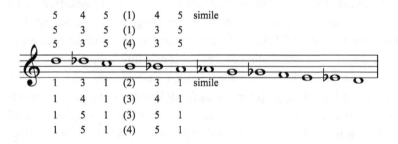

The 5-1 combination plays a key role not only in these fingering variants for the chromatic scale but for all other double note patterns—obviously including octaves—and proper alignment is crucial to its natural use. The mutually opposing action of the fifth to the thumb is, contrary to common perception, of the greatest benefit to pianists. At its most basic, it is an important determinant of hand placement on the keyboard and, therefore, alignment. This oblique, or "diagonal," relationship naturally places the fifth finger solidly in the black-key plane since the hand increasingly elevates as it pivots over the thumb toward the torso.

The anatomical construction of both thumb and fifth is such that their range of movement downward remarkably facilitates vertical adjustments for key depth, a most important consideration in the matter of finger choice.

Although not fundamental in the same sense as those above, the variant shown in Example 4.3 will also be found worthwhile (the "outer" variant espoused by Neuhaus).

Example 4.3

The flexing action of the fingers ("first" joints toward palm of hand) and their optimal muscular-skeletal alignment with the forearm are absolutely essential for these variants to be of any significant benefit. Movements of the longer third over fourth, third over fifth and fourth over fifth—and the shorter fingers under the hand—occur in an oblique plane and require a shoulder joint/shoulder complex that is complementarily and dynamically stabilized throughout their execution. They afford an unsurpassed opportunity for developing a sensitive control of these subtlest movements.

OTHER SCALES, OTHER FINGERINGS
The Whole Tone Scale

This scale of six whole-steps only is counterpart to the chromatic scale of twelve half-steps, or semitones. There are only two possible arrangements of black and white keys, representing the only transpositions possible for the scale: **WWW BBB** and **BB WWW**.

The whole tone scale is particularly instructive. As the basis for Chopin's Fundamental Pattern, it is generally obvious and readily recognized. However, its extension is rarely observed to reveal the **WBBBW** Fundamental Pattern *inverted* (Example 4.4a below: A♯-C-D-E-F♯). This "inverted" Fundamental Pattern—now **BWWWB**—and its own translocation has significant bearing in revealing pianistic fingerings and validating the topographical process.

The available options for any successful execution of this whole-tone pattern in an ongoing sequence, i.e., extended beyond the range of an octave, are also indicative of key fundamentals at work. There are really only two fingering combinations for each that are rational and, in greater and lesser degrees, practicable. For purposes of illustration, it is useful to begin the first on C, the second on G (or B).

Example 4.4a

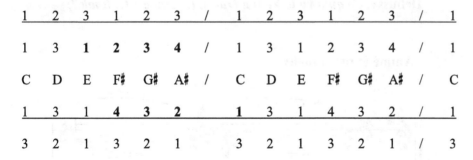

1	2	3	1	2	3	/	1	2	3	1	2	3	/	1
1	3	**1**	**2**	**3**	**4**	/	1	3	1	2	3	4	/	1
C	D	E	F♯	G♯	A♯	/	C	D	E	F♯	G♯	A♯	/	C
1	3	1	**4**	3	2		**1**	3	1	**4**	3	2	/	1
3	2	1	3	2	1		3	2	1	3	2	1	/	3

Example 4.4b

(1)	3	1	2	3	1	/	2	3	1	2	3	1	/	2
	3	1	2	3	4	1	/	3	1	2	3	4	1	/	3
	G	A	B	D♭	E♭	F	/	G	A	B	D♭	E♭	F	/	G
	1	3	1	4	3	2		1	3	1	4	3	2	/	1
	3	2	1	3	2	1		3	2	1	3	2	1	/	3

That the topography of these two whole-tone arrangements is ultimately the determining influence is really quite obvious, and incontrovertible. From a more natural standpoint, the fingerings seen in Examples 4.5a, 4.5b and 4.6 are most efficient and most effective.

Example 4.5a

Example 4.5b

Example 4.6

Debussy, *Ce qu'a vu le Vent d'Ouest, (Prelude VII, Book I)*

Animé et tumultueux

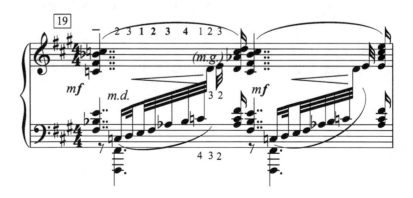

Pentatonic Scales

With the octave divided into five tones, there is, theoretically, any number of pentatonic scales classified and distinguished according to the organization of their individual tones. Composers such as Alberto Ginastera and Heitor Villa-Lobos have based many of their compositions on such individually distinctive pentatonic scale patterns (see Chapter 12, note 13).

But as it is commonly understood, the pentatonic scale is to be found in the black-key arrangement of the piano. A scale exclusively of whole tones and two minor thirds, its fingering when extended beyond its five-note, five-finger pattern is particularly problematical—especially for a span of two octaves or more. There is, however, one regularly recurring pattern that results in the most successful resolution: in regrouping the black keys, D♭ E♭ G♭ A♭ B♭ (BB BBB) becomes E♭ G♭ A♭ B♭ D♭ (B BBB B). The pentatonic cluster can then be seen as an alteration of the Fundamental Pattern (WBBBW becomes BBBBB), with thumb and fifth now fully orienting the hand in the black-key plane.

Chopin's own Etude, his Opus 10 No. 5 ("Black Key"), offers the perfect example. Several fingerings occur in various editions for Example 4.7. But it is Mikuli's that will be found most effective in all respects, one that is grounded in the Fundamental Pattern altered as above (recall that he was Chopin's student). In the example, note how Chopin effects this very resolution with his placement of the rest.

Example 4.7

Chopin, *Etude in G-flat, Op. 10 No. 5 ("Black Key")*

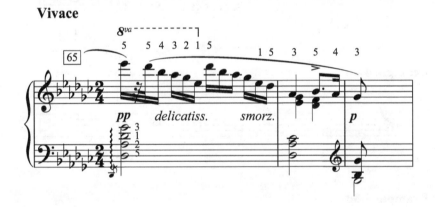

Diatonic Patterns; Chromatic Fingerings

We have seen that several fingerings for the chromatic scale essentially apply finger groups that are fundamental to the accepted organization of the diatonic scales. That is, the octave is divided into two basic groups of three and four fingers so that there is a regularly recurring sequence for each octave of extension. The fingering for C major is taken as a model even though there are no black keys defining its organization or marking its topography.

In fact, as we have seen with the chromatic scale, there are many diatonic finger groupings that can be applied with regularity if the span is not confined to an octave. In the case of C major, it is the steady succession of white keys that permits this, not the orderly succession of half-steps as with the chromatic scale. And such fingerings for C major are often found; Moszkowski's several "special" fingerings for C major double third scales are of particular interest in this regard.

This basic grouping (4+3) should nonetheless be regarded as specific to the diatonic scales; so it is first taught and so it is first applied. As a fingering pattern for chromatic sequences, it could therefore be said to be a *diatonic fingering chromatically applied*. The French fingering, however, is not only peculiar to the chromatic scale but is distinctive in comparison to the others. Although found to some extent in other "traditional" chromatic fingerings, regular and consistent employment of the first and third fingers is not at their core.

In the 1-3/1-2-3/1-2-3-4 chromatic sequence (English fingering) the basic 1-2-3/1-2-3-4 diatonic pattern is chromatically applied. But it is perhaps more than interesting that this fingering corresponds exactly to the alternative topographical solution for the E and B harmonic minor scales (initial octave LH descending and RH ascending). In this case, the initial/initiating 1-3 can be seen as a *chromatic fingering diatonically applied*—however briefly.

Even more interesting, application of 1-3/1-3/1-2-3 is an alternative chromatic solution to the fingering of these diatonic scales, as well as B-flat harmonic minor (1-3/1-3 assigned to facilitate the WBWB core group). Schmitz has called such a solution an *acrobatic* fingering, a term Debussy uses for one that imparts a more energetic, robust physical delivery of force to the keys. But it is really best to see it more broadly as a facilitator in its own right.

Example 4.8a

Example 4.8b

Example 4.8c

Again, the French sequence 1-3 /1-(2-)3 distinguishes itself as an exclusively chromatic fingering pattern, in origin and consistency of application: **WB W(W)B**. For our purposes, the designation "chromatic fingering" will now refer to these composite groups of the French pattern, including its other long-finger, short-finger variants.

In recognizing this chromatic sequence as an entity unto itself, we further discover that there are frequently passages in which the most favorable resolution—likewise influenced by topography—is to be found in applying this fingering pattern to a diatonic note sequence. Such a solution via a *chromatic fingering diatonically applied* is exemplified in Example 4.9, from the Cuban composer Ernesto Lecuona's "Gitanerias" (from his *Suite Andalucia*). Others are extant throughout the repertoire.

Example 4.9

Lecuona, *Gitanerias* from *Andalucia ("Suite Espagnole")*

Presto

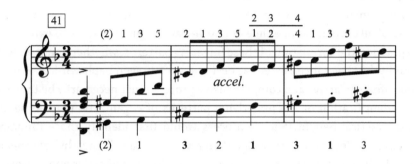

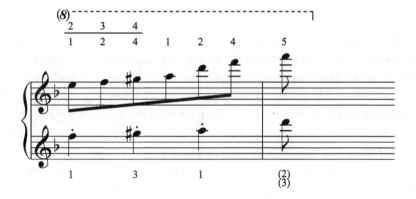

In addressing the solutions available for the extended whole-tone scale, we arrived at sequences of 1-2-3 or 1-3/1-2-3-4 as most practical, the latter exemplifying the uniquely chromatic combination (1-3) diatonically applied. At the same time, the pentatonic fingering did not permit a practicable solution other than a recurring sequence of its five-finger, five-note pattern (1-2-3-4-5).

FUNCTIONAL FINGERING

In expanding our fingering "vocabulary" to include the French chromatic fingering variants and their diatonic application, we have moved significantly closer to a functional lexicon as we embark on further organization and discussion of the essential fundaments of pianistic fingering. Although one may just simply "give a fingering" or "find a fingering," the process is thereby simplified tremendously. And such a logical organization grounded in previous experience with the fundamental forms further secures intellectual and kinesthetic retention.

Recognition of keyboard patterns—their similarities and dissimilarities, interrelationship and interaction—is at the heart of any approach to fingering that seeks to organize in some way the musical patterns of the composition that is to be performed. There are numerous approaches to such patterning, and pianists have historically made use of all of them, at one time or another and to greater or lesser extent.

In practice, the correlation of these fingering patterns, whether or not allied with topography, has been inconsistent at best and spotty, even haphazard, at worst. But ongoing efforts to arrive at a comprehensive process must necessarily be thorough if such an identification of the underlying patterns of organization would be of the broadest practical benefit. Such a process would first identify those fundaments operative at the deepest core; it would then reveal a certain "hierarchy" of other basic patterns, in which some supersede others in function and effective application.

In our present consideration of the keyboard's symmetrical topography and the playing mechanism's physiology correlative to such a potentially advantageous organization of fingers and tones, certain qualifying terms, distinctions, and operative principles have begun to yield a necessary vocabulary relating to the fingering process. A conceptualization that goes beyond recognizing or labeling basic musical patterns and the currently standardized fingerings or their rationale is very much in order and long overdue. We can extend the logic that every note in a composition is in some way functionally related and relevant. To hold therefore that the fingers assigned to the notes of an individual passage are likewise functionally related is not incomprehensible. After all, *function* is what the playing mechanism is about.

Tobias Matthay points to this in words that are, in the present context, quite clear:

> Closely connected with the question of Touch itself is that of FINGERING . . . instead of merely writing down the fingering of a passage, you must always explain *why* it is chosen, and *how* the choice is arrived at. The main principle . . . is, that choice of fingering consists in selecting such finger-*groups* which will easily lie over the piano keys concerned, while at the same time giving due consideration to the necessity of joining such fingering-groups each one to the next or preceding one . . . it is always a finger group which is in question— either a complete group or an *incomplete* [italics added] group. For instance, in teaching the scale fingerings . . . the actual *lie* of these two groups being determined for each particular scale by the position of the black keys, and by the necessity of choosing the easiest position for turning the thumb under, etc. . . . By thus learning where the *whole* finger-group each time lies over the keyboard, we necessarily also learn the place for each individual finger.[10]

Passages abound in such complete and incomplete groups that do not fit easily into recognizable scale, chord, arpeggio, octave or other double note patterns. Moreover, the repertoire has continued to evolve with a compositional complexity and commensurate technical challenge that is, at least initially, daunting. But it does not follow that there is no longer an inherent, fundamental, and comprehensible keyboard organization at work. As ever, the underlying issue is one of perceiving order in chaos—or, put another way, of achieving order from perceived chaos. It is not yet necessary to abandon faith in our rational powers.

The application of what are essentially—and what originated as—diatonic fingerings to chromatic patterns, and chromatic fingering variants to diatonic patterns, plays an essential role in a fingering process that goes beyond the standard patterns largely representative of the Classical style. The pentatonic and whole-tone formulations are uniquely instructive too, as we will see later on. And the role of topographical symmetry will be seen to be neither incidental nor inconsequential. All contribute to a more holistic approach to matters of fingering specifically and technical issues generally. Specific classification facilitates recognition, application, communication and retention.

5

CORE TOPOGRAPHIES AND RATIONAL SOLUTIONS

The wide variation found in the fingering recommended by editors . . . is of more than mere academic interest. It reflects, very distinctly, the individuality of technical *style of the various editors.*
—Otto Ortmann

What is important for the modern performer . . . is to recognize what the earlier types of fingering were intended to achieve and then produce the same effects with more modern fingerings.
—Howard Schott

ALL KEYBOARD PASSAGES ESSENTIALLY deploy the natural position of the hand and its extension, contraction or repositioning. This is the principal rationale for all fingerings. Scale, chord, arpeggio and chromatic fingerings are representative of such adjustments and readjustments of the hand, which then correspond to the intervals of these musical fundaments, individually and in combination.

Thus, five-finger/note patterns have been long held to be the elementary building blocks underlying any rational fingering strategy, as well as the primary method for developing a logical keyboard orientation. For all of these, the basic position is representative of the first five scale degrees, tonic to dominant, allowing for any necessary alterations as to mode or harmony. The major-minor patterns are usually taught in the early years, the raising or lowering of the third finger corresponding to the tonal alteration—a useful theoretical association.

The standard white-key tonic scale fingerings are generally considered as founded on an extension of a five-finger position—LH ascending and RH *descending*—with C major as the model. But except for F in the RH, only the standard LH fingerings for the white-key tonic scales (C to A) exactly reflect these major-minor five-finger patterns. Nonetheless, there are many benefits of accustoming the hand to a five-finger position as both a basic orientation and point of departure. And these patterns do play an important role in any rational fingering strategy. But unless they are further altered, it is not a fundamentally significant one.

The extent to which there is a practical application of accordant fingering principles is what ultimately validates the extensive study of scales and arpeggios as foundation, preparation and "laboratory." Beyond practical application of theoretical instruction, the challenges therein should also fundamentally represent those that will actually be encountered in passagework *to the greatest* extent—a chief failing of the standard approach. Ideally, they ought to be exemplary of a consistent application of fundamental principles and thereby occasion the learning of fundamental movements and responses.

The topographical approach alone satisfies all these expectations to the greatest degree. It is a new look at keyboard organization that is far more logical, eliciting an orientation that is far more natural. And it is one that represents a more comprehensive, more inclusive paradigm—one that transforms the fingering process significantly.

TOWARD A LANGUAGE FOR FINGERING

It is therefore most helpful, even essential, for us to embark on developing a practical vocabulary suitably related to the principles and concepts that are to be employed in such a rational fingering *process*. In this way, any efforts to discuss, communicate and continue to develop them are further enabled and greatly facilitated. Paradoxically, our conceptual framework is expanded at the same time that it is simplified.

Such development of a more comprehensive *language* for this fingering process would enable us to go beyond mere identification or understanding of a passage as to the tonal, modal, thematic, or other relationships it may represent. We would benefit enormously from our ability to discuss and communicate those fingering principles and ordering concepts with greater efficiency, precision and clarity. Schmitz was quite successful in this as he moved us toward a language and terminology for the classification of keyboard movement—much of it also the practical necessity of finding a language where none previously existed. Expert dancers, for example, are unable to imagine any successful training or communication and retention of choreography without a movement vocabulary that has been developed and yet continues to expand. Inextricably tied to movement—to that of the key itself as well as the playing mechanism as a whole—it is important that pianists advance along these lines in matters of fingering as well.

Topography is the essential and obvious link to a natural accommodation of the playing mechanism's physiology to the keyboard. And topographical fingerings reflect exactly the integration of these influences—one fixed and unyielding, the other quite accommodating. A language of fingering coupled with a language of movement could then join forces with the harmonic and structural language of music, all at the service of the further development of a natural pianism. Pedagogy would be more direct and precise—yet appropriately flexible.

AT THE CORE

Elementary five-finger patterns on all twelve tones of the chromatic scale, each of its semitones functioning as a tonic, are indeed basic fundamentals of training. They not only physically engage the entire hand from the earliest years but are useful as a sort of tonal and harmonic "shorthand," if you will. But they are not central to either the standard or the topographical approaches to scale, and certainly not arpeggio, fingerings or their execution (although alterations other than major-minor are entirely supportive of the topographical approach and, at the same time, extremely valuable theoretically).

This can be said of only one five-finger pattern: Chopin's *whole-tone* Fundamental Pattern. *Topographically* altered, it consistently and systematically satisfies the issues of finger length as they relate to key length and key depth. And it is one that at the same time reveals—indeed, *requires*—the ideal solution in the matter of thumb under pivoting.

Fourth on Black, Thumb on White

The *core* patterns that derive from it or are related to it also reflect tonal alterations, and these now take precedence as the *primary* patterns for organization. The natural structure of the hand is compatibly wedded to the keyboard's topography, and physiologically sound fingering follows from this.

From a pianistic viewpoint, the other "elementary" five-finger patterns and their tonal alterations, whether modal or harmonic in origin, must then be considered *secondary* when operative in conjunction with a primary pattern. This distinction will prove apt, for example, when recognizing them in single-note scale fingerings or appreciating their role in determining optimum solutions for extended double third passages. But most important, it is key to a rational solution to the fingering challenges of seemingly elusive passages.

All other patterns, both diatonic and chromatic, will be *functional* while at the same time topographically correct. They play specific roles in the fingering process and the execution of a fingering strategy, and will prove indispensable to a natural approach to fingering.

Considerations of finger/key length, key depth and their neutralization; distant location; interplanar and axial adjustment and orientation; as well as other matters pertaining to the distribution and transmission of vertical force are now reflected in a rational fingering process. And a consistent topographical accommodation is enabled and *ensured* throughout the full range of the keyboard.

THE FIVE CORE TOPOGRAPHIES

There are five primary patterns that derive from the whole-tone Fundamental Pattern or that are reflected in its translocation. Topography is the primary distinctive, distinguishing element. With the requisite alterations for interval, mode or tonality these five-finger topographical patterns constitute the core of *all* (!) diatonic scales and arpeggios. This is in itself a powerful argument for adopting and implementing these fingerings in lieu of the generally accepted "standard" fingerings. That these also represent a consistently familiar, ideal physiological orientation is even more compelling. Clearly, the topographical approach is an extraordinarily efficient one.

In *Practicing Perfection: Memory and Piano Performance*, authors Chaffin, Crawford and Imreh cite rather unsurprising conclusions drawn from their studies of the negative effect that fingering patterns representing previously "unlearned" motor responses have on practice efficiency and performance security. In their comparison of the advantages of "standard" and "nonstandard," it must be understood that the efficacy of the standard fingerings or the "inefficacy" of the nonstandard fingerings is not under study—only the immediate advantage of a learned response over one that must be newly established.

Tempo increases, for example, in which there is less time for mental control or targeted intervention (in which an impulse must first be inhibited before being supplanted), "disrupt" newly established patterns of response that, up to this point, managed to gain an ascendancy. But this is merely to affirm a long-recognized characteristic of any habitual response, whether positive or negative. Learned responses that are relegated to the reflexive, to the automatic, are on the front lines as "first responders," so to speak—an emergency drill, for example. This cannot be read as a judgment or appraisal of the desirability, effectiveness, or efficiency of the response, only a statement of the fundamental nature of any acquired neurological response.

But the following, therefore, may in fact be read—and indeed ought to be read—from the standpoint of our present study, which holds that the standard fingerings not only fail to be comprehensive but are, more frequently than not, found to be altered in application throughout the literature. "Standard" fingerings end up in "nonstandard" applications or simply do not apply:

> The dearth of predictable patterns was a frequent topic of comment. . . . One way to create an organized pattern *where none appears to exist* [italics mine] is to impose one through the selection of fingerings. . . . Of course creating patterns

in this way added to its own burden to memory because the fingerings had to be remembered. . . . Finding familiar patterns greatly reduced the amount of new material that had to be learned. . . . Evidence of [coauthor Imreh's] search for familiar patterns comes from her lamentations about the unpredictability of the music and her use of fingering to impose organization. Evidence of the use of familiar patterns as building blocks comes from the extra work needed to put together bars that contained more of them. Fingering too, provided evidence of the importance of familiar patterns.[1]

The very real implications are in support of any approach to fingering that minimizes the need for learning new motor responses *for already familiar patterns*. And it precisely frames the argument that the learned fingerings for technical patterns and forms must accurately, broadly and universally reflect those actually found in the repertoire. They should be based on more than, and not merely reduced to, what may be a familiar *rhythmic* response of the fingers—or "finger-rhythm sense" as Matthay put it.[2] Although not inconsequential, such a response is not sensorial in the very real and complete sense in which known topographies trigger and reinforce an already familiar response to key contact or tonal associations. Moreover, it is now generally appreciated, fortunately, that the entire body is internally and externally engaged in any rhythmic response to the music or the keyboard.

A comparative study of several fingering solutions for the excerpt in Example 5.1 speaks volumes to all these issues.

Example 5.1

Beethoven, *Sonata, Op. 81a: Das Wiedersehen (Le Retour)*

Vivacissimamente
Im lebhaftesten Zeitmasse

The Craxton (Tovey Edition)[3] and Hansen-Conrad (Henle Edition) fingerings comport with the topographical solution to this otherwise quite problematic passage:

Example 5.2

Beethoven, *Sonata, Op. 81a: Das Wiedersehen (Le Retour)*

Vivacissimamente
Im lebhaftesten Zeitmasse

Topographical Resolution:

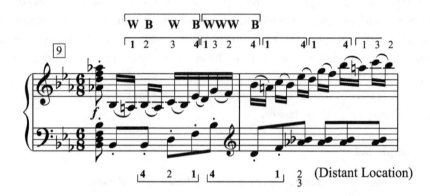

The comparison further points to the advantage gained in approaching an editor's recommended fingering from the standpoint of principles that may be reflected in the broadest possible application. One must be sharply discriminating rather than unreservedly deferential.

Maintaining a rhythm of the fingers—a consistently ongoing, though purely kinetic sense—or the *imposition* of an organizing fingering pattern ("top down" vs. "bottom up," in current jargon) is among the main arguments of those who hold that finger patterns should remain unchanged in spite of topographical change. But ultimately none of these may be divorced from topography. Put another way, attempts to do so are tantamount to a certain kind of physical and intellectual dissociation or "split." The response cannot be the same unless all influencing, impacting factors are the same. "Rhythm of the fingers" is not a compelling argument when considered in the totality of pianism and performance delivery.

Keyboard topography and symmetry are at the core. And only a unifying, integrated response to them—one that engages the hand's own structural symmetry—can result in consistency of approach and maximum effectiveness.

Secondary Patterns

The harmonically or modally derived *secondary* patterns remain essential components of a topographically oriented approach to fingering (they play an important role in the organization and fingering resolution of the diatonic double third scales, for example). Although they represent a basic diatonic pattern that may be altered, they may also be considered triadic since their alteration (second, third and fifth degrees) has much more to do with harmonic changes and relationships than with particular scales or modes. With 5-3-1/1-3-5 as the basic fingering for the root position triads, 4-2/2-4 are then considered assigned to the intervening, nonharmonic (passing) tones. It is in this sense that the five-finger patterns most parallel and reflect the theoretical.

Apart from this, only in the RH do the tonal alterations consistently correlate with the fingering (i.e., first to fifth fingers correspond to the first to fifth scale degrees). But the five-finger pattern M-m (♭3)–d (♭5)–N (♭2) sequenced chromatically is representative of the harmonic implications of these interval alterations and particularly noteworthy in regard to the Neapolitan relationship[4] of the flat second degree.

Example 5.3

FIVE FINGER PATTERN:
MAJOR - MINOR (♭3) - DIMINISHED (♭5) - (NEAPOLITAN) (♭2)

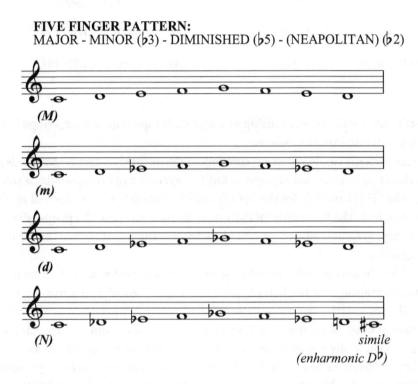

Such five-finger patterns are useful to familiarize and reinforce these particular black-white key combinations, and they are valuable theoretical and aural models. But although triads, four-part chords, their inversions and other extended patterns may be "elemental" from a musical and compositional standpoint, they are nonetheless secondary in terms of fingering influences and considerations. The fact that they converge with topographically correct core patterns more frequently than might first be supposed (e.g., the inversions of four-part chords) does not make this less so.

As I remarked earlier, except for the seven major-minor white-key tonic scales of LH C through A and RH F, the origin of the standard fingerings bears little or no relation whatsoever to the major-minor five-finger patterns. But these patterns remain of significant importance, particularly if the alterations go beyond those commonly employed. With these not only reflecting harmonic relationships but other modal alterations that are so frequently encountered, their role is not only practical but extremely instructive.

For this discussion we will note that the major pattern correlates to the first five tones of the Mixolydian mode and the minor to those of the Aeolian mode. And certain *modal* alterations of the basic five-finger M-m pattern on white-key tonics are, in fact, topographically correct. They exactly represent the finger-note groupings of the topographical fingerings for single note and double note scales.

As fundaments for these fingerings, they are of far more practical—and even pedagogical—value. The (1) major pattern with raised fourth degree (Lydian mode) or (2) with lowered second degree (from upper tetrachord of the so-called Hungarian mode); and (3) the minor (♭3) pattern with lowered second (Phrygian) or (4) with raised fourth (Hungarian mode) are consistently operative throughout the topographical solutions for the fundamental forms.

As an example, such would be the case with the following:

	Left Hand		Right Hand	
(2) G minor:	DE♭ F♯ GA	(1)	G major:	CDE F♯ G
(3) B♭ major:	DE♭ F GA	(4)	G minor:	CDE♭ F♯ G

The reader will recall the relationship of major scale topographical fingerings to that of their parallel and relative minors.

These patterns would represent core topographies for their respective hands and would therefore be classified as *primary*. But for reversed hands they would be *secondary*: for the LH (1) and (4), for the RH (2) and (3). Because they are derived modally rather than from the Fundamental Pattern or its translocation, the pianist does not reap the topographical advantage of a black key for the fourth finger/thumb under pivoting action.

One very important note regarding secondary patterns: forms such as inversions of triads—extensions of the hand beyond the augmented fifth of a five-finger pattern to that of a sixth—are properly considered secondary patterns, as are those of the octave or other large intervals. They do not involve the thumb-under, hand-over pivoting action. Trills and other ornaments should likewise be considered as secondary, whether "fixed" or not—that is, whether their realization is narrowly proscribed or permits more flexible interpretative latitude. But topographical considerations are properly taken in determining their fingering as well.

Functional Patterns

Because the core black-and-white-key combinations are so few yet optimally accommodating physiologically, the topographical fingerings for the scales, arpeggios and other basic technical forms easily and rapidly become an integral part of the pianist's response to the keyboard. However, repertoire passages are as likely to be a complex of various patterns and figurations as they are a continuous sequence of any one or another. And they do not always begin or end on a tonic; tones are altered and key changes occur along with topographies—even if briefly. But any passage, like any phrase, has a beginning, middle and end.

Fingering patterns that function to initiate, link and terminate (end, close, conclude) scales or arpeggios are not a new idea. Pianists have always found it necessary to adopt fingering accommodations for topography and distant location in some way—albeit consciously or inadvertently, efficiently or inefficiently. Recall that all pianists unhesitatingly alter RH fingering groups in transitioning from ascending C-sharp and F-sharp melodic minor to descending natural minor; the ideal topographical accommodation for each is thereby ensured.

It is again worth recalling the rationale for the standard fingerings for the white-key tonic scales and arpeggios. Enshrined with the view that they represent the ideal fingering model is the parallel contention that the black-key tonic scale and arpeggio fingerings are therefore anomalies—this despite their obvious simplicity in organization and logical relationship to each other. At the very least, it is understood that their basic rationale is a very different, albeit related, one: the thumb must remain consistently assigned to a white key. The fingering patterns therefore do not begin with the thumb.

All the black-key tonic major scales in the LH **are** consistent as models and begin with 3-2-1 (F-sharp/G-flat begins with 4-3-2-1 but is consistent with the fingerings for the other enharmonics). However, this is not so for the RH: all black-key tonic scales employ *partial* groups in order to begin on the tonic. It is likewise with *all* black-key tonic minor scales, except for C♯ F♯ and G♯/A♭ in LH. The fifth is not used at all. Presumably, this is what makes them anomalous.

The important lesson to be drawn from this, however, is that once again the standard fingerings for black-key tonic scales and arpeggios serve best as model—not as anomaly. The basic fingering groups are themselves linked by fingers or groups of notes that strategically begin, end, or enable their transition to other fundamental groups. Of course, accomplished pianists have always attempted to do this. Franklin Taylor, who by late-nineteenth-century standards was probably the most rational and comprehensive in setting forth fingering principles and guidelines, did not neglect to call attention to this unavoidable necessity. The following passage is quite instructive in regard to transitional groups, and especially as it implies a preference for consistency of *note* (key) *groups* over finger *pattern*:

> The complete scale has already been described, and all scale passages should, if possible, be fingered with the regular fingering. But this depends very much on the position of the hand at the moment of commencing the scale, and is not always possible. . . . In such a case we have a choice of two methods: either the passage is fingered as if the note on which it begins were the keynote of the scale, or else the [fourth] finger is passed over the thumb every time instead of alternately with the [third] finger, until at length the regular fingering of the scale is reached (which will always be the case sooner or later), after which the remainder of the passage is fingered regularly.[5]

From a topographical perspective, the function of such fingering patterns is to maximally ensure the hand's ideal keyboard orientation within a rational framework. Fingerings grounded in the core topographies, not what were already, even in Taylor's time, accepted as standard or "regular" fingerings (in contrast, we will later appreciate how revolutionary were the discoveries of Eschmann-Dumur, his contemporary), are now to be the norm.

Such an approach to the fingering process necessarily involves more thorough recognition of *all* operative patterns, for what we seek are readily applicable solutions that are both consistent and flexible. Functional patterns play a key role in any successful fingering strategy; they are "how we get from here to there."

The black-key tonic scales are indeed highly instructive. And they are familiar. Their fingerings are not in dispute, whether deemed "anomalous" or not, and offer further insight into topographical accommodation and functional fingerings.

To avoid assigning the thumb to a black key, the standard fingerings for the melodic minor scales on C-sharp and F-sharp abandon their established sequence to effect a fingering change; a linking pattern is required to topographically adjust for the descending natural minor pattern. As noted early on, most pianists manage this transition without even thinking. The function is obvious, the fingering change entirely natural.

The standard fingering logic for the LH B major-minor scales necessitates beginning with the fourth so that the thumb will consistently take a white key. In this case, 4-3-2-1 would function as an initiating pattern and/or closing pattern, and as a linking or transitional pattern if change of direction is involved, as would be the case if the scale first descends before ascending. And similarly for RH F major-minor: the topography also does not allow the thumb to be assigned to a white key without reconfiguring the standard sequence of 1-2-3/1-2-3-4. As with the black-key tonics, the fifth finger is not used in either scale.

Except for these white-key tonic scales of LH B major-minor and RH F major-minor, the standard fingerings as found in manuals are customarily presented without the suggestion of initiating or terminating or closing options. This is true even for the black-key tonics. Presumably this is for the sake of consistency, a well-meaning attempt to avoid confusion in their presentation since they do not conform to the standard white-key tonic sequences beginning and ending with thumb and fifth. But such a practice does the very opposite: in presenting the black-key tonic fingerings for one octave only, recognition of the recurring 4+3 groups is often obscured.

The B-flat major-minor scale fingerings are exemplary. Yet beginning and ending with 3-1/1-3 is a rational and efficient alternative (it is also representative of a chromatic pattern diatonically applied). The basic pattern of four- and three-note groups is perceived with no less clarity—perhaps even more so—and execution is greatly facilitated.

Similarly, 3-1/1-3 will be found to be pervasive as a useful link between patterns of dissimilar topographies or different forms (linking scales and arpeggios, for example). As the gravitational and structural center of hand, the longer third finger on a black or white key is far superior as an initiating or terminating finger to any of the other fingers—particularly when considerations of distant location must take precedence. And the thumb is particularly suited to a white key, owing to its capacity for key depth (due to its range of pronation).

The major scale for enharmonic F-sharp/G-flat provides the best model for initiating and terminating options that are suggested by the consideration of key planes and distant location. Its scale group of three adjacent black keys is fingered 4-3-2/2-3-4 and naturally accommodates the impact of distant location for each hand at, or increasingly approaching, the extreme range of the keyboard. The long fingers are demonstrably preferable as the LH moves away from the arm's midline and crosses the torso to the right, and as the RH similarly moves to the left. But depending on the note groups and topography of a particular passage, 5-4-3/3-4-5 better accommodates the need to adjust for distant location or key depth.

Most useful—and just as interesting from the standpoint of topographical impact—is the option of beginning (initiating) or ending this scale group with 1-2-3/3-2-1. The natural "swing" of the arm, with all this implies as to weight release, acceleration and momentum, is manifest in its curvilinear path of movement away from midtorso and the arm's midline.

The arm's movement through its midline (see Glossary), from one extreme of its range to the other, is perfectly congruent with its journey from elevated black-key plane to white-key plane. Its momentum at this nadir, or lowest point of the "curve," has the potential for culminating in the black-key plane. The "curve" of the arm's movement—its kinematic representation—is totally consistent with the topography; the transition to black key plane is easily effected with 1-2-3/3-2-1 available as a potentially forceful solution.

The arm's movement dynamics as just described elucidate the "correctness" of fingerings such as Liszt's in certain passages of his *Spanish Rhapsody* (excerpted herein). In these it is a *glissando* effect that is intended—with all that the designation implies as to upper arm movement and control. But it is imagery that is rooted in physical experience, such as curve of the arm's path of movement through space—in which topography, interval and range may not be ignored—that ultimately wins the day in aiding in the execution of these passages. Imagining Liszt as a "lion at the keyboard" undaunted by the difficulties of the passage or the "strangeness" of its fingering doesn't really do it. The fingering works for other reasons. The spirit of the passage is something else again.

5-4-3-2-1 is also most useful as a functional pattern. The topographical solutions for LH A major and D, G and C harmonic minor exemplify the benefit of its application as an initiating or closing pattern. Examples 5.4 and 5.5, from Schubert and Schumann, are both in A major:

Example 5.4

Schubert, *Sonata in A, Op. 120*

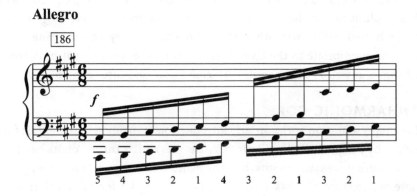

Example 5.5

Schumann, *Variations on the Name "Abegg", Op. 1*

Finale alla Fantasia

Vivace

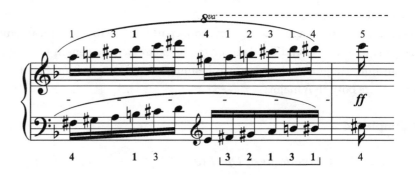

The reader will find numerous examples of these functional patterns and their possible applications in the topographical scale and arpeggio fingerings presented online (indicated within parentheses). A thoughtful study will illumine potential applications appropriate to the specific topographical demands that have been discussed above, as well as the fingering principles that correlate to them.

AN ENHARMONIC CORE

Valid as a representation of the orderly introduction of major key accidentals for root movement by perfect fifth, the Circle of Fifths was earlier turned on its head to represent Chopin's systematic approach to the major scales. As a schematic diagram it is far more practical for pianists who might now see in it a logical devolution of the white-key tonic major scale fingerings from those of the enharmonic keys. Conveniently made possible at the time by the widespread advance of equal temperament tuning, this practical and "theoretical" overlapping of the enharmonic keys reveals a new core for pianists: enharmonic F-sharp/G-flat. This is now the new point of departure, as well as the point of "convergence." This upending or inversion of the Circle of Fifths might also be considered an apt metaphor for the subversion of "Tyrant C"!

From a topographical perspective, this new core is crystallized in the Fundamental Pattern. It is the proxy for all the enharmonic major keys, and their fingerings are relative to it. *They may, in fact, now be seen to emanate from it.* The practical objective in looking at them in this way is to see that they have much to show us as models for finger passages in general—apart from specific scale fingerings. Again, the standard fingerings for C and the other white-key tonic major scales (keep in mind that LH B and RH F are not true to the standard pattern) have little to teach us in regard to principles or strategy having broader application.

By first taking a look at the enharmonic major scale fingerings—those for which the Fundamental Pattern is the centerpiece, or core—we can note that the "partial groups" (as Matthay called them) found therein are prototypes for functional application. The enharmonic minor forms again confirm and further our appreciation of their value for fingering strategy.

FUNCTIONAL APPLICATIONS

At their most basic, these partial groups are best understood as incomplete scale or arpeggio patterns, such as one might encounter in initiating those for C-sharp or F-sharp major and harmonic minor or linking their melodic and natural minor forms. But any single finger or group of fingers that strategically function to ensure the most consistent application of the primary or secondary patterns also should be considered in light of topography. We have already noted certain diatonic-chromatic origins and applications.

In the present context, the key distinction is "functional," since groups of notes may be considered to be partial in many ways, none having to do with function. The three-finger groups of the topographical solutions for the major and minor scales, for example, were earlier shown to derive from the core (primary) patterns themselves. But partial groups may also be considered as deriving from a particular five-finger grouping (the secondary patterns), even a motivic, thematic, or harmonic construct. How they and their fingerings relate to the fundamentally operative groups in an extended passage is the main distinction here.

And functional choices may, and often ought to, reflect more than a strategic assembly of fundamental patterns. As has been touched on, they variously manifest biokinetic support for the movement and energy of the phrase or passage in question. Continuity ("flow") and momentum ("sweep") are facilitated and enhanced by fingering choices that are confluent with the curvilinear movements of the upper arm, that ensure its unifying and stabilizing activity. Here too, adjustments for distant location, black-white key planes, key length and key depth all potentially have an impact on physiological and kinesiological response—and, it should never be forgotten, tonal control and expressive ability.

All of these very specific considerations must therefore influence functional application as well. In this, there is a broad realm of choice. But the parameters established by the primary and secondary patterns immediately focus the pianist on the particular functional issue(s) at hand. The fingering process is undoubtedly less idiosyncratic, far more rational and increasingly "natural."

A FUNCTIONAL PROCESS

Scales, arpeggios, chromatic, double note and other basic patterns organize the notes, keys and finger sequences within the individual tonalities represented. But their organization as they relate to the topography of the keyboard and the physiology of the pianist's playing mechanism goes still further in synthesizing them.

Determining fingerings that best begin a particular passage or phrase, serve as a transition, or link to the fundamentally operative patterns and end or close them are at the heart of a successful and consistent application of the principles advocated in this approach. After first identifying core topographical patterns—there are only five of them!—and then any secondary harmonic or modal patterns, one need only determine how to best assemble them within the passage at hand: to initiate, link and terminate the patterns making up the passage. Initiating, transitional or linking and terminating or closing patterns that are themselves topographically sensitive function to enable us to consistently employ the most effective, rational fingering solutions throughout a passage.

THE DOUBLE NOTE CHALLENGE

2

The principle of the playing of double notes is peculiar to ornamental virtuosity and rests on a tradition of purely harmonic writing. It is particularly manifest in the works of Liszt, Chopin, and the composers who, after them, turned this brilliant artifice of romantic technique to account. . . . The study of double notes should [also] be considered as the best preparation for the practice of polyphonic playing.
—Alfred Cortot

There is value in using a difficult pattern early, but only the kind of pattern which balks until a right balance in activity is established. Octaves and double thirds are examples of this kind of useful activity. They remain difficult and practically unplayable until they are produced in the easiest possible manner. Thus they are extremely valuable in establishing a technique.
—Abby Whiteside

ALTHOUGH MUZIO CLEMENTI is celebrated by many as the first modern keyboard virtuoso, Domenico Scarlatti can arguably claim a definite distinction in that regard. Certainly Scarlatti was the virtuoso counterpart to the more inward Johann Sebastian Bach (along with Handel, all born in 1685) just as Clementi was to Mozart later on. Although Scarlatti wrote chiefly for the harpsichord and Clementi for the piano, both successfully explored and dramatically exploited the keyboard for new technical possibilities, including a variety of extended double note passages.

But it was Clementi who became most famous for double note technique; his double thirds in particular astounded, exasperated and perplexed even Mozart. In the wake of Clementi's own exercises, studies and compositions, succeeding pianists were thereafter roundly challenged: Czerny wrote double note studies, Chopin composed double note etudes, and Liszt (a student of Czerny) adorned and embellished his compositions and transcriptions with whirlwinds and cascades of brilliant double note passages. Double note technique became a hallmark of nineteenth-century Romantic pianism, stock-in-trade for the virtuoso pianist and a necessary staple of serious nineteenth-century pedagogy.

Numerous exercises, etudes as well as fingering formulas and guidelines appeared in response to this formidable challenge, but attempts to systematize double note scale fingerings were less than satisfactory. Though strictures regarding thumb use on the black keys were abandoned with great relief to many, a number of anatomical and physiological misconceptions held sway. A bias toward the fourth and fifth fingers as "weak" was still generally held, with the result that the most widely accepted double third fingerings were those that boasted of employing the fifth finger once only per octave (Liszt, Leschetizky and Franklin Taylor, a student of Moscheles and Clara Schumann). But the use of the fourth was simply unavoidable, *pace* Claudio Arrau.

Apart from an increased awareness of movement occurring within the two horizontal keyboard planes—white key and black key—other topographical considerations played no obvious role in a rational approach to double note scale fingerings. Moreover, here too it was affirmed that any successful solution to the fingering challenges presented should have the advantage of a regularly recurring sequence of finger patterns that would be remain unchanged ascending and descending—no matter the physiological and kinesiological disparities involved.

As we will explore in Chapter 6, the possibility of an imaginative solution to the problem was thus severely compromised even though Eschmann-Dumur's discovery of the topographical and intervallic symmetry of the major scale patterns informed Moszkowski's, and later Taylor's, approach to double third fingering. But as with the now-standard single note scale fingerings, Liszt's influence—and still later Leschetizky's—loomed very large indeed.

"DOUBLE TROUBLE": WHEN MORE IS MORE

Aside from the enormous demands posed by such etudes as those of Chopin, Debussy, Scriabin and Rachmaninoff, the exciting toccatas of Czerny, Schumann and Prokofieff, or the transcendental challenges of Godowsky's transcriptions, double note study itself no longer seems to be a *sine qua non* for pianists or *de rigueur* in their studies. And with such an amazing wealth of literature now at hand, one can easily argue that it is wholly possible to perform even large amounts of virtuoso repertoire without the necessity of a spectacular, or more than adequate, double note technique.

But the benefits of such study in the formative years of technique building go well beyond the ultimate attainment of some degree of "mere" virtuosity. There is an inherent value in double note study that we seem to sense, no matter our disinclination to persevere in it—or frustration when we do. What is at its core that makes this so? What is gained thereby from it? Artist teachers have long upheld it indispensable to the development of a fine, secure technique.

The esteemed artist Claude Frank, when interviewed by Adele Marcus, discussed his current practice regimen. This featured "abstract exercises" in which he is "speaking of exercises which develop and train one aspect of the hand, beginning with a Rachmaninoff exercise in double notes" and later included "scales, thirds, sixths, octaves, et cetera." This prompted Marcus to share:

> I find double-note patterns very beneficial. My first teacher insisted upon double thirds and sixths, chromatic thirds, major and minor, when I was ten or eleven. When I came to Josef Lhevinne at the age of fifteen and a half, he asked me to play a scale. I sat down and tossed off double-third scales in contrary motion.

He looked at me and asked, 'Where did you learn that?' I asked, 'Why? Doesn't everybody do it?'" Remarked Frank: "How wonderful to get that under your belt so early in life."[1]

Apart from obvious difficulty, the commonly accepted fingerings as found in the numerous manuals and exercise collections do little to convince us of such inestimable value. One is again reminded of the great pianist Moriz Rosenthal, who explained that he did not practice single note scales because they "encourage unevenness of touch." And one might say in the case of double note scales that they discourage a good legato.

Although fingering choices for double notes of a fifth to an octave are necessarily limited by the average span of the hand, those for thirds are not. As any good fingering is fundamental to the solution of a technical problem (again Chopin: "Everything depends on fingering"), with double thirds we have the very glaring example of fingerings contributing as much to the problem as to its solution. Indeed, the several "standard" fingerings for them have been an obstacle to successfully countering the challenges of double third study, and to fully appreciating its worth.

And so it is extremely worthwhile—perhaps even necessary—that prevailing double note fingerings be considered from both an historical and a developmental perspective. Engaging the sincere seeker in the *process* of fingering should also include reevaluating every aspect of what is now taken as granted; there are few "givens." Only then can one reliably develop an ability to judiciously appraise a proposed fingering—whether of single or double notes.

Since all the topographically oriented fingerings found herein consistently reflect certain underlying, discernible principles, an understanding of their rational basis leads one to more readily adopt and intelligently apply them in other similar instances. Moreover, these principles both suggest and permit topographical options rather than rigid or fixed application. Were this not so, the mere presentation of another "set" of fingerings would have little more long-term value than that of any other manual.

DOUBLE THIRDS

AN OVERVIEW IN AN EVOLUTIONARY CONTEXT

6

Scales in thirds have the formidable privilege of the most numerous combinations.
—Alfred Cortot

The practice of scales in double thirds provides greater benefits to the fingers and to one's technique in general than plain scales. . . . All the works on the subject which I have studied give a variety (usually bewildering) of alternative fingerings.
—Charles Cooke

DOUBLE NOTE SCALES *OF* THIRDS, for those who prefer this more definitive characterization, remain one of the foremost challenges of pianism; yet relatively few pianists take them seriously enough. They are considered too difficult, too "impractical," or too time consuming—or all of these.

Aside from etudes, it is certainly true that double third passages that are not of trills are rarely of greatly extended length. And for the RH they are most often found chromatically ascending, while diatonic passages are more often encountered descending; for the LH it is the reverse. That is to say, they are most frequently encountered in their more facile deployment. Indeed, even Chopin's famous etude exemplifies this practice in large measure.

Since the Chopin etudes mainly focus on challenging the RH (as do the Debussy and Scriabin etudes), it takes Leopold Godowsky's transcription of the Chopin etudes to squarely challenge the LH in similar fashion.[1] And somewhat like the proverbial elephant in the room, which all pretend not to notice, the now-extensive literature on the technical aspects of piano playing is virtually silent on the subject.

All this speaks more to the difficulty than the value of double third study, a challenge that is compounded by the absence of fingerings that would otherwise clarify and simplify the problem that is, literally, at hand. The various fingerings advocated do little to assuage nagging doubts as to their practical application—even if systematic or consistent in some apparently redeeming way. And even disregarding the compelling issues of voicing and legato connection, the fingerings are fraught with physical challenges that do little to benefit the pianist in the broader development of a healthy, balanced and physiologically sound pianism.

What follows is an overview. A further supplementary analysis will be found in Appendix 5.

One of the commonly accepted fingerings divides the seven double thirds of the diatonic scale into two groups: 3+4 (or 4+3). This is essentially two five-finger groups of three double thirds each, one taking the remaining third by means of a thumb extension from the second finger. However, this use of fingers 1-2 after 3-5 for RH ascending and LH descending—especially on succeeding white keys—is not only uncomfortable and musically problematic but also potentially harmful.

Henri Herz, an enormously admired and emulated pianist in Chopin's and Liszt's day (although not by Chopin himself, as his correspondence attests), advocated this

"1-2 fingering" *except* for certain keys.[2] Herz's approach is most interesting and unique in the relative consistency with which the fifth on a white key is succeeded by the second finger on a *black* key—certainly far more comfortable and effective.

Liszt's solution was to assign a sequence of one five-finger/note group and two successive groups of 1-3/2-4 (3+2+2) for *all* double note scales, fingering unchanged ascending and descending. The fifth finger was thus used only once per octave, the fundamental "five-group" varying from scale to scale. As Liszt's student Tilly Fleischmann put it, "The essential point is to discover the position which will allow the most comfortable transition."[3] This was to be determined *upwards* for each hand; topographical mirroring was obviously of no influence.

Notwithstanding the professed disregard for the thumb favoring a white key, Liszt and most others after him clearly continued to eschew assignment of the thumb to a black key. Most notable was Godowsky, who unequivocally—and unashamedly—stated that he avoided assigning the thumb to a black key *unless absolutely necessary*.[4]

But what is perceived as "necessary" is, of course, the qualifying operative in all of this. "Liberation" of the thumb—that is, acceptance of its usefulness on a black key—is considered the main hallmark of "modern" piano fingering. But as we will see below, the symmetry of the keyboard as reflected in an expanded harmonic language increasingly leaves the pianist with few or no satisfactory options in certain types of passage work. Again, the crux of the matter and its resolution reside in closer consideration of the topographical demands and advantages of the enharmonic keys, and what clues and insights they offer. Topography will indeed have out, and it is best embraced rather than ignored.

Overall insensitivity to topography as a *prime* fingering determinant inevitably results in awkwardness as well as unavoidable, if not insurmountable, difficulties in legato connection. And the resulting tendency toward unwanted, unmusical accents is perhaps even more problematical; a more natural solution is more naturally—more inherently—rhythmical. Although remarkably consistent in rationale, Liszt's fingerings are nevertheless rather complex in organization while still leaving much to be desired as to ease of execution.

Leschetizky's fingerings[5] comport only in part with those of Liszt; he advocates the same finger sequence but often differs in the placement of the five-finger group. His have the advantage of greater simplicity in their organizational consistency, but they likewise do not take topography into serious account. Liszt and Leschetizky's approach to double third chromatic scale fingering also deserves comment in that both are illustrative of an ongoing search for systematic consistency by way of pattern rather than topography. Their fingerings simply employ the double third sequence (3+2+2) throughout a chromatic scale of two octaves, with subsequent repetition thereafter.

This is **Clara Schumann's** approach as well, in which this sequence is also advocated as fingering for chromatic double sixths. Curiously, her solution for the chromatic fourths is not consistent with this sequence; nor is it consistent within itself. Topography is clearly irrelevant to her; at one point she recommends "groups of three successive double notes [3+3+3] for *all* diatonic scales" (by contrast, Moszkowski proposes this option only for C, having no black keys). On "principle," she writes, fingering is to remain unchanged for "scales or passages" ascending and descending—"*with a few exceptions in the case of double notes* [italics added]."[6]

Significantly departing from all the above, **Chopin** and **Karl Klindworth**, a student of Liszt, arrived at chromatic double note fingerings that have survived for their logic and comparative ease. Indeed, the number of fingerings for the chromatic double thirds alone is really quite amazing, as was well noted by Charles Cooke. But eschewing the fifth for the fourth or a glissando thumb for a glissando second, they do not improve over Chopin's or Klindworth's. In fact, it can be said that a greater role for the fifth finger and the glissando action of the thumb—and fifth—are distinguishing characteristics of double note fingering solutions that satisfy the demands of topography while at the same time exploiting its advantages.

In his 1890 *Primer of Pianoforte Playing* (edited by Sir George Grove, first edition 1877), **Franklin Taylor** goes to great length on the subject of fingering—his designation "primer" notwithstanding—and is significantly at odds with his teacher, Clara Schumann, in important respects. For double thirds, he presents charts for the assignment of the fifth finger for each hand, for each mode—identical to those postulated by **Walter MacFarren** (d. 1905), who was for sixty years a professor of piano at London's Royal Academy of Music. In the later *Technique and Expression in Pianoforte Playing* (1897) Taylor himself is no longer wholly in accord with his earlier recommendations for double third scale fingerings. But he does refer to them. (It is interesting that the earlier work uses the English system of fingering, the latter work the Continental system.)

What is significant in the later work is that he now draws particular attention to the importance of black-and-white-key symmetry in major scales having the same number of sharps as flats. But for him, as for others, this means merely noting and applying the same fingering sequence consistently, without further regard to topography and its relation to the structure of the hand. Pattern persists in trumping topography.

C. L. Hanon (*The Virtuoso Pianist*, Schirmer, 1900) provides us with an interesting example of a respectful but not serious "bow" to scales in thirds. After allowing that "thirds occupy a very important place in difficult music," he presents only one basic five-finger pattern, which is then sequenced and thereafter applied to a scale (all in C); a fingering for the chromatic scale in minor thirds; and some double third trill patterns thereafter. The fingerings presented "in the Keys Most Used" employ Taylor's option but omit the enharmonic keys entirely and all minor keys except the harmonic forms of G, D and A. Because of the preponderance of black keys, the enharmonic keys were perhaps still not to be taken seriously by those preferring to live in a white-key world.

Nevertheless, the double third etudes of Chopin, Debussy and Scriabin sport key signatures of five black keys, and each progressively extends the boundaries of the other immensely. But to be fair, it is possible that Hanon simply wished to gear his Studies to what he perceived as the pedagogical needs for a certain level of training. Or perhaps he was humbled in these matters by the monumental efforts of *his* contemporary, Moszkowski.

In his outstanding *Practising the Piano* **Frank Merrick**, in his time a well-known student of Leschetizky, devotes an entire chapter—although not of great length—to the matter of the fingering and practicing of double thirds. His approach is quite eclectic, very imaginative and flexible in that he does not advocate specific fingerings as a foundation for double third scale technique. Instead he proposes "*eleven* different fingerings, applied *regardless of discomfort* to all the diatonic scales in thirds" since "the occasions when orthodox fingerings should be used in an actual piece are rarer than might be supposed [emphases added]"—a rather significant observation and admission.[7] But it is assumed that the reader knows just what these "orthodox" fingerings are, and he goes no further. Topographical *and* physiological considerations are, obviously, of relatively little or no concern.

According to Robert Schick (*The Vengerova System of Piano Playing*, Penn State 1982), **Isabella Vengerova**, Leschetizky's student for two years, approved of Moszkowski's Book II, *School of Scales in Double Notes*, and Book III, *Exercises in Double Notes* (Parts I and II of the School of Double Notes). She also apparently favored fingering these scales in three groups of notes (3+2+2), although preferring two groups (4+3) for some keys, with fingerings the same in either direction. Vengerova also considered Josef Pischna's and Carl Tausig's exercises in double notes highly valuable.

In Pischna's *Sixty Progressive Etudes* **Hugo Riemann** offers fingerings for double thirds "according to Liszt-Tausig." The fingerings presented therein for *most* of the scales correspond exactly to those presented in Chapter 7 as the topographical resolution for RH ascending (first proposed by **J. N. Hummel** in his influential 1828 treatise published in German, French and English) and LH descending.[8] Yet he was, unfortunately, apparently not aware of the principle of major key symmetry. For the LH descending he often uses the same fingering *pattern* without applying it topographically, though he is correctly unconcerned with maintaining the same fingering for each hand in the opposite direction. However, he prefers Liszt's solution for LH ascending and RH descending; **a**nd like him, Riemann does present both forms of the minor. But topographical considerations or concerns clearly do not predominate, as the numerous variants that follow the scales demonstrate.

It is noteworthy that **Isador Philipp's** double third scale fingerings (*Complete School of Technic for the Piano*, Theodore Presser, 1908) for the RH ascending major scales are topographically consistent. These are also noteworthy in that they comport with the single note diatonic scale fingerings: the fourth finger assigned to the B-flat for all the flat keys and the leading tone for the sharp keys (through B). As for the rest, his fingerings are similar to those of Liszt, although only those for the harmonic form are offered for the minor scales.

It is clear that topography and symmetry, as it affords a *consistent* rationale for systematic double note fingerings, obviously eluded Liszt, Philipp, and most other of their colleagues. Even as they were caught up in new experimentation and the then-current disregard for the "old school's" strictures and admonitions regarding black-key thumb use, they remained nonetheless bound by a C major orientation and rigid adherence to certain assumptions regarding patterning. Eschmann-Dumur's unique discovery of the principles of major key symmetry supported by Moszkowski's strong endorsement and transparent application of them had, as yet, little or no impact—most certainly a significant "cognitive lag."

Indeed, Moszkowski acknowledged his debt to Eschmann-Dumur in his *School of Double Notes* after pointing out the asymmetry and "illogical" fingering that most pianists employ for the LH major scales—F and G specifically under discussion. He informs the reader that "Mr. Charles Eschmann-Dumur in his "Technical Pianoforte School" ("*Exercices Techniques pour Piano*") was the first, to my knowledge, to indicate these anomalies of fingering, and this excellent work is hereby recommended to all pianists desiring information on the subject." He then goes on to explore symmetrical application to double third fingerings by comparing certain of them as advanced by Charles (Carl) Tausig and William Mason to "prove that the fact of analogies of fingering in major scales is as yet almost unknown or at least neglected."[9]

Moritz Moszkowski's double third groupings are those of Liszt (3+2+2) *symmetrically applied* RH ascending and LH descending but unchanged in the opposite direction. His *School of Double Notes* is without doubt the most comprehensive and serious attempt to advance double note technique prior to Alberto Jonás's remarkable symposium. It offers a wealth of exercises and challenging etudes in addition to fingerings for the various scales in thirds, fourths and sixths.

Unusual and unique are his "transcendental" double third fingerings, which he proposes as a superior alternative to the "defect" of the "traditional" fingerings, which "always include a succession of two thirds, *the perfect timing of which becomes absolutely impossible*" (emphasis added). Moszkowski therefore set out to devise fingerings that would consistently permit a "true" legato connection: that is, finger to finger, without benefit of glissando, between any two consecutive thirds. Allowing that they were only variously successful, depending on key (read topography!) and tempo, he nonetheless advocated a serious study of them at the advanced level. **Busoni** likewise promoted them in his edition of J. S. Bach's *Well-Tempered Clavier, Book II.*

A close look at certain of these *transcendental* fingerings—those with four or more black keys—from a topographical perspective that is based on Chopin's pattern reveals frequent use of the three long fingers on three consecutive black keys. This comports with the "application" of the *translocated* Fundamental Pattern as demonstrated below in Chapter 7. But for Moszkowski, apparently Eschmann-Dumur's influence served as a conscious one while Chopin's did not; this is perhaps indicative of a greater appreciation of the implications of Chopin's pattern that had yet to develop. On the whole, though, Moszkowski's fingerings cannot be said to represent a symmetrical integration of both men's extraordinary and revolutionary pianistic observations.

It is highly significant that Godowsky's own thinking and experience, on some deep level, is influenced by that very symmetry. He thereby finds certain keys—herein characterized as more "pianistic"—to be more amenable to transcription than others. As Milla Sachania informs us:

> Twenty-one of Godowsky's fifty-three *Studien* transpose the etudes they treat. The left-hand transcriptions tend to be in keys in which the tonic and, preferably, dominant degrees fall on black notes on the keyboard. Eleven, that is half, of the left-hand *Studien* are in different keys from their corresponding originals. Of these, nine shift the music from a white-note to a black-note key. Indeed, *all* the transpositions up a semitone from a white-note to a black-note key concern the transcriptions for left hand alone. Save for [one], which shifts the original from Eb to A, none of the left-hand transcriptions transposes the original to a white note key. It might seem that by relocating etudes to black-note keys, the left-hand *Studien* attempt to challenge the pianist's technique to the limit. Actually, the converse is true, since such transpositions surely *facilitate* performance. This is because. . . .[10]

Sachania then goes on to postulate various possible influences for such facilitation. Having considered the sole transposition from a black-key to a white-key tonic (E-flat to A) to be an anomaly, the author clearly has not given the topographical symmetry of the major keys its due. But Godowsky no doubt recognized this chief influence: E-flat (three flats) mirrors A (three sharps) topographically and intervallically, white-key *tonic* notwithstanding. Whatever the musical or transformational intent of the transcription, topography remained its "friend"—and Godowsky's as well.

It is evident that dissatisfaction with double third fingerings persisted across the board. And the record shows that Godowsky, for one, continued the search for more viable fingerings.

Alfred Cortot's substantially different solution to the fingering of all double notes (*Rational Principles of Piano Technic*, 1928) is to present various combinations and alternatives, all introduced in C major, which are then to be transposed throughout the twelve major and minor (harmonic form only) keys in chromatic sequence. They are to be "employed according to the exigencies of musical execution . . . as their application to the needs of interpretation constantly imposes itself." Topography is not even mentioned; it plays no role in determining a superior choice except, presumably, as it may inadvertently and undeniably be found to produce discomfort. However, the sequences of 4+3 or 3+4 double thirds are advanced as the "the usual fingerings of the scale"; these are simply reversed, pattern unchanged, for the opposite direction.

E. Robert Schmitz (*The Capture of Inspiration*, Carl Fischer, 1935) singularly and admirably set out to intentionally wed the hand's physiology to the keyboard's topography in all matters of fingering, particularly in regard to double notes. He also formulated much that is unique, valuable and fundamental to the biomechanics of playing double notes. The essential and distinctive role of articulating *motor fingers*[11] (what are herein called "pivot" fingers) is of singular importance, as is the impact of keyboard range on finger choice (see the section "Distant Location" in my Chapter 10).

Charles Cooke, in his eminently useful and ever-popular *Playing the Piano for Pleasure* (Simon and Schuster, 1941/1960) advises us that he uses **Tobias Matthay's** system of fingering for the major and harmonic minor double third scales as taught to him by **James Friskin**.[12] Matthay had published his own fingerings in *Double Third Scales, Their Fingering and Practice* and Friskin in *Double Scales Systematically Fingered*.[13] Keyboard topography and symmetry do play a role in Matthay's fingerings to quite some degree (his sensitivity to the black keys of a passage has already been noted).

Charles Cooke (not to be confused with **Dr. James Francis Cooke**, whose 1913 manual *Mastering the Scales and Arpeggios* still wields considerable influence) treats the matter of major and minor chromatic thirds rather extensively, ultimately advancing another attempt to "simplify" by proposing a formula—yet with numerous "exceptions." But later a most important admonition: "You might take note of the fact that—in the ascending right hand and descending left hand—*every inner note of the chromatic major scale in double major thirds is taken by the thumb.*"[14] The italics are his, and the *nota bene* obviously refers to the white keys. I might add, though, that this assignment of the thumb to all the white keys could well be, and should be, applied to the chromatic scale in minor thirds as well.

Although **Ernst Bacon** (*Notes on the Piano*, 1968) does recognize the advantage of what he calls the "symmetrical inversion of the major scale" and its fingering (at the same time extending the principle compositionally), he does not allude to topography per se as a prime influence or determinant. But he does concede differences in double third scale fingerings ascending and descending so that "advantage is taken of the thumb sliding off the black onto an adjacent white key."[15] As with Matthay's enharmonic fingerings, it is this advantage that contributes to the ease of the topographical solution for double note fingerings in the direction of the torso, and as advocated herein.

It is small wonder then that most pianists and teachers approach the study of double thirds with a certain trepidation, much confusion, little commitment and doubtful authority—if they approach it at all. And unlike scales for single notes, it is extremely revealing that there has developed no real consensus whatsoever as to fingerings for double third scales. Absent topography as a more defining, determining influence, it is true that "scales in thirds have the formidable privilege of the most numerous combinations," as Cortot tells us.[16]

From our perspective, an overview such as this serves to highlight the several shortcomings of the surprisingly numerous approaches to double note fingerings that evolved over what now approaches two centuries. Overall, the proposed solutions have managed to address the formidable challenges only in part. And *none consistently build on the fingerings for single note scales*—certainly an attractive and compelling advantage if it can be shown to be possible. Double note scales are, after all, harmonizations of single note scales. As Cortot insightfully admonishes, "The study of double notes should be considered as the best technical preparation for the practice of polyphonic playing."[17] Surely, the fingerings should be up to the task.

But equally important, *intelligent* double third study is indispensable for the development of the entire hand (a benefit nearly all enthusiasts point out) as well as its role in regard to "weight playing"[18]—aside from any other challenges that specific double third passages may pose. And for musical *and* technical reasons, considerations of legato are ever present (always worth remembering: "No legato, no problem!"[19]). A proficiency in double note playing ultimately lends further authority, ease and confidence to one's overall pianism.

Although all the fingerings heretofore proposed and those very few that are generally accepted may boast of a *rationale* arrived at by deliberative process, I do not think that one can claim them to be *rational* in the fullest meaning of the word. Frequently given as they are to inconsistency, even illogic at times—and this apart from the relentless impingement of topographical demands, which are unalterably constant and consistent indeed—Charles Cooke's characterization of them as "usually bewildering" must indeed remain most apt.[20]

THE CHROMATIC SCALE IN DOUBLE NOTES

The fingering variants (Chapter 4) of the single note chromatic scale are at the heart of a systematic approach to the matter of double note fingering. Chromatic double note scales exemplify the application of these indispensable chromatic alternatives.

It must be noted that proponents of the various double third chromatic fingerings are, as with the single-note diatonic minor forms, less than consistent in their agreement as to which of these should be considered among the fundamental forms. Liszt, Leschetizky, Schmitz, Cooke, Philipp and Dohnányi include chromatic major thirds along with the minor thirds, but Hanon, Roskell and the editors of the Royal School of Music manual do not. But the double third diatonic scales consist entirely of both major *and* minor thirds. The inclusion of both chromatic scales in a basic double note regimen would seem to be beyond question.

The chromatic scale in minor thirds, though, can be said to form the basis for all double note scale fingerings. Not only are the third, fourth and fifth fingers fully involved but, as fingered herein, the combination 1-5/2-4 can be seen to be basic to it. The 1-5/2-4 pattern suffices for *eight out of twelve double thirds* and is also important as facilitator for some of the most problematic and potentially awkward diatonic double third scales (Chapter 7). It is ideal as a double third combination, especially if the long fingers take black keys and the short fingers take white keys. Their coordinated actions complement each other for facility and control: for example, flexion of short thumb and fifth and extension of long fingers (fourth moves in consort with the third).

According to Malwine Brée (*The Leschetizky Method*, 1913/1996) Leschetizky considered 1-5/2-4 to be the best combination for double third trills.[21] And Walter Gieseking considers it not only superior as a trill combination but ideal in achieving an "absolute" legato.[22]

For the chromatic minor thirds alone, Jonás has provided fingerings by numerous pianists. In addition to his own, those by Busoni, Klindworth, and Emil von Sauer are only a few.[23] But it is Klindworth who presents fingering that is most natural in both orientation to topography and synchronization of pattern. The topographically based fingerings for chromatic thirds and sixths recommended herein comport with his. In the case of smaller, "growing" hands, fourths and fifths (in which the hand is more extended) are excellent proxies for sixths. Double seconds serve the hand in its more contracted shape. Chromatic double note scales, from seconds to sevenths, are to be found in Appendix 6.

TOWARD A MORE RATIONAL FINGERING FOR DOUBLE NOTES

7

The aspiring student should hasten on to double thirds long before his single notes reach a high standard, for they are muscularly strengthening, they give the mind more occupation per semiquaver [sixteenth note] than the single notes, and their execution automatically keeps all five fingers closer to the keys (a desirable thing in every kind of passage).
—Frank Merrick

A correct fingering is one which permits the longest natural sequel of fingers to be used without a break . . . all varieties of fingering ought to be based upon the principle of a natural sequel.
—Josef Hofmann

THE TERM *RATIONAL* is also used throughout this presentation to distinguish such an approach from one that is best termed *idiosyncratic*. As much as the standard fingerings have become accepted as "gospel," so has the belief that a more systematic, thoroughgoing approach to the matter of fingering is simply not possible. Debussy's admonition (*Cherchons nos doigtés!* Let us search for our fingerings!) is often held as validation for those who prefer to consider fingering solely an individual matter and not justifiably founded on any other basis.

Though there is certainly plenty of room for personal preference, this essentially contradicts the rationale underlying all attempts to organize intervals, keys, fingers and keyboard space into patterns and systematic fingerings throughout keyboard history. After all, we do not teach the scales theoretically and then admonish the student to find the fingering that best suits him or her. Debussy's charge is better taken as a challenge in the face of obvious contradiction and widespread confusion surrounding the issue of fingering at the time—as well as recognition that there is room for individual choice.

The deeper implication, it seems to me, is that there is more thinking and more work yet to be done in this particular arena. And given his revolutionary expansion of the musical language, this would most certainly be true. But as the editor of a publication of Chopin's complete works (Durand: Paris, 1915–16), Debussy surely had his own specific thoughts on the matter.

In fingering too, the matter must be seen as one of striving to order what otherwise might be consigned to chaos. And another most important point should also be made: a rational approach to fingering ought to be one that does service not only to music that *has* been written—that even derives from it or is unique to it—but to music that *will* be written as well. Charles Rosen's appraisal is rather telling in this regard: "The keyboard as it is constituted was perhaps best fitted for music from 1700 to 1880 and has become more and more awkward since then."[1]

A more encompassing approach to fingering must be ever grounded in what is fundamental to the keyboard and the pianist. This can only be achieved if topography *and* physiology are called on to work together for coordinated movement in keyboard space. It is this synchronization and integration that we ideally seek. Fortunately, the symmetry of the keyboard's design is our constant and faithful ally in such a process.

THE CHALLENGE: "USEFUL . . . DIFFICULT . . . UNPLAYABLE"

It is fair to say that double notes generally—one should not forget that they include octaves, though usually considered by themselves as a fundamental form—and double thirds specifically are universally recognized as representing the supreme keyboard challenge.[2] Pedagogical opinions vary as to whether or not they should be introduced early on in the development of a technique or whether they constitute a degree of challenge that should be met only at the more advanced, if not most advanced, stages of study. And some, of course—as we noted earlier—simply despair of the matter.

Diatonic double third scales are especially fraught with frustration on every level (and forget about other diatonic double note scales; excepting octaves they are usually off the radar screen entirely). I am constantly reminded of a very fine pianist-teacher's response to my inquiry as to her opinion about teaching them to students and what thoughts she had about their fingering. Her immediate reply was simply, but firmly, "No one can do them!" Of course a great many pianists can do them—today and certainly in the past, when double notes were part and parcel of any serious training for a virtuoso technique.

The remarkable and very individual pianist-teacher Robert Goldsand, a protégé of Moriz Rosenthal (a student of Mikuli and Liszt), was particularly acclaimed for his astounding double thirds, which merited a large part of the distinction and respect he enjoyed among aspiring pianists.[3] That he required all his students to seriously undertake the study of all double note scales and the most relevant of the extant double note studies and repertoire was, of course, no surprise; it was a hallmark of his teaching. And Josef Lhevinne? His recording of Chopin's double third Etude, Opus 25 No. 6 surely remains the inimitable standard.

That rare talent coupled with assiduous practice can result in such an achievement is without question. But Robert Schmitz[4] and Abby Whiteside[5] are among the very few who have left for us any significant insights as to the mechanics and biokinetic dynamics of double notes. Although expressed in different terms, both understood that verticality of key contact and initiation (what Schmitz called the "verticalization" of finger action) are at the bottom of any solution to the problem of successful and easeful double notes. And both understood that the upper arm was the indispensable key to double note distribution (as all else) throughout the keyboard. They did not see the problem as one of mere patterning or the solution that of relentless determination.

Perhaps readers of a similar bent will welcome a more in-depth overview of other such "indispensables," as a helpful and informative corollary to the genesis of the topographically symmetrical fingerings for the diatonic double thirds that are presented below. To emphasize yet again, all fingerings are tools, and their effective implementation depends on knowledge as well as skill. That said, one always does best with tools of precision—and certainly those that best fit the hand. Topographical solutions best meet the unique challenges of double third diatonic scale fingerings:

1. Movements in all three planes—vertical, horizontal and oblique—must be exquisitely balanced.
2. Double notes are not played exclusively in one key plane but most often in black and white planes simultaneously.
3. Disparities of key depth are magnified when two fingers of varying lengths—and movement potentialities—must now be played simultaneously and with coordinated precision.[6] Fortunately, long fingers may be also be employed when vertical adjustments for key depth are necessary.

4. Articulation (see Appendix 9) must be maximally applied to achieve legato in two voices. Attention to pivot/motor fingers, their correct alignment and coordinated action is essential.

5. A more sharpened sense of alignment and the structural balance of the hand is necessary for an optimally coordinated movement of the key in its vertical plane. Force is to be transmitted as close to the perpendicular as possible. Establishing adequate verticalization for finger action is fundamental.

6. Double notes necessarily limit the extent of lateral and inward or outward adjustments; neutralization of finger/key lengths is especially required.

7. The central, unifying role of the upper arm and its coordinated horizontal movement (circumduction)—inward and outward, and laterally—is paramount.

8. Although the range of lateral extension of the hand and fingers is minimal because of the intervals, the full musculature of the hand is otherwise active in either its contracted or neutral shape (position). Alternation of finger flexion and extension in counteracting finger groups (primarily in the first joints, the basis for articulation), palmar contraction (cross-tension), and application of the principles of modeling for sensorial reinforcement contribute to a healthy development of the hand (see Appendix 9).

9. Placement of the hand requires a familiarity and sensitivity to the varying resistance points of the key for movement at those closer to its fulcrum. Commensurate transfixation of the joints is necessary for adequate leverage and well-coordinated action.

10. The need for shoulder joint/shoulder complex stabilization is intensified. This is particularly so regarding the crossing of long fingers over short fingers in movement away from the torso.

Double Third Fingerings away from the Torso

A rational solution to the problem of optimal fingerings for diatonic double third scales would obviously demand application of the very same principles as those for determining topographically oriented single note fingerings—perhaps the ultimate validation of the topographical approach set forth herein. And we are not to be disappointed: it is really quite remarkable how consistently these apply, and how pianistic the result! The keyboard yet again sheds more of its mystery.

Having established the fundamental four-note core group (fourth on black, thumb on white) for each single-note scale, we find this devolution not difficult: for double thirds it is now a five-finger group, thumb on a white key (RH ascending, LH descending). Let us take the double third scale for A major, identifying this *primary* (P) five-finger group.

Example 7.1

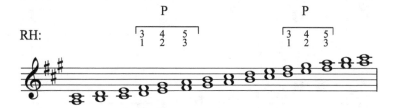

Example 7.1 (Continued)

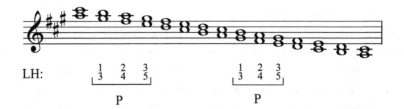

LH:
```
    1  2  3          1  2  3
    3  4  5          3  4  5
    P                P
```

Only one other five-finger group, thumb on a white key, remains within that octave. This is the *secondary* (S) group (in fact, an "expansion" of the three-note group of the single note scale) in which the fourth finger is not assigned to a black key. It is found a perfect fifth above (perfect fourth below) the primary pattern (group) in the RH or a perfect fifth below (perfect fourth above) in the LH, the thumb now displacing the fifth finger.

Example 7.2

RH:
```
    S          P          S          P
    3  4  5                3  4  5
    1  2  3                1  2  3
```

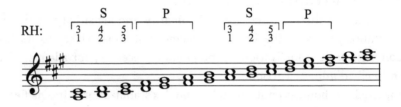

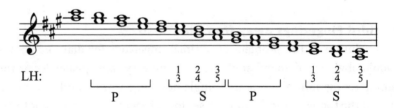

LH:
```
                    1  2  3          1  2  3
                    3  4  5          3  4  5
    P          S         P         S
```

This leaves only one remaining double third "linking" the two groups to be fingered. In assigning 2-4 to this third, the longer fourth succeeds the shorter fifth, bringing the second in its place.[7]

Example 7.3

RH:
```
    S          P      4     S          P      4
                      2                       2
```

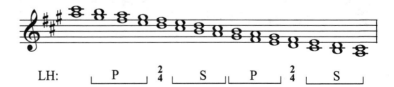

LH:
```
    P      2     S          P      2     S
           4                       4
```

NATURAL FINGERING

The still longer third next succeeds the fourth, establishing this *secondary* five-finger group.

Example 7.4

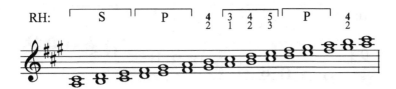

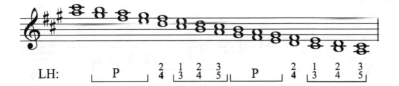

The basic formula for double third scale fingerings moving away from the torso evolves as P + link + S (3+1+3 for the seven double thirds within an octave):

13-24-35 / 24 / 13-24-35

The following are illustrative of the application of this basic formula to (1) keys having a maximum number of black keys, (2) a preponderance of white keys and (3) white keys exclusively. For RH B major and LH D-flat major, the fifth on a white key is followed by the fourth on a black key. The 2-4 link is **BB** with maximum advantage:

Example 7.5a

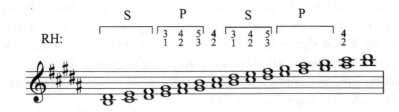

Example 7.5b

For keys having one to three black keys, the 2-4 link is **BW**:

Example 7.6a

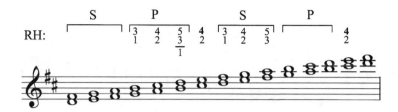

Example 7.6b

In the foregoing it should be noted that the fourth is always on a black key (of the primary group) prior to its displacement by the second finger of the link; the longer fourth succeeds the shorter fifth. For all-white key C and A natural minor, the 2-4 link is **WW**.

As noted, the combination 1-5/2-4 must be considered the basic double third pattern. It alone has the potential to maximally ensure a successful legato connection from finger to finger and key to key over an expanded range, but tempos more than moderately fast are not amenable to this otherwise satisfactory execution. For all-white-key double thirds in particular, topography provides no "markers"; nor does it afford concomitant physiological relief.

An excellent solution for predominantly white-key topographies lies in judicious alternation of a five-finger group with successive sequences of 1-5/2-4 strategically applied. There is in all this, in fact, an important axiom at work. And it is one that will repeatedly be found beneficial in naturally adjusting fingerings that might initially seem awkward: *the first, third and fifth fingers may often be profitably interchanged when assigned to a white key* (note Example 7.6).

Reflecting this most natural option, the basic formula for fingering double thirds in movement away from the torso would now be represented as

$$\text{13-24-3(1)5 / 24 / 13-24-3(1)5}$$

Toward the Torso

Again, double note scales are essentially harmonized single note scales, two voices in each hand. And these individual voices are to be treated as such in that a continuous legato is to be achieved as much as is physically possible. A necessary or unavoidable break in legato ought best to occur in the less prominent voice—in the "harmonizing" or textural voice—and consistently in the same voice. It is most desirous that the legato line be maintained in the outer voice for RH ascending and LH descending, the inner voice in the opposite direction. This is the chief musical, and therefore technical, aim of successful double third fingerings. Though less subtle, more extroverted bravura passages may abound in them, double thirds (and sixths) ultimately demand considerations of voicing, texture, "color" and warmth; the compositions of Chopin, Liszt, Schumann and Brahms immediately come to mind. To arrive at effective double note fingerings, this should always be taken into account.

Although it is possible to finger a succession of double thirds without ever assigning the thumb to a black key, the potential for high velocity and maximal legato connection is often greatly compromised. In movement toward the torso, for example, the 35-24-13-12 pattern allows us to take advantage of the thumb's ease in moving from B to W. This *glissando* action is innately compatible with the gravitational pull exerted on the arm, the shift of the thumb being naturally concurrent with the direction of pronation. From W to W, the long familiar extension of the thumb that opens the hand from a fifth to a sixth, as from root-position chords to those of the first (RH) or second (LH) inversions, is employed. But the standard use of this fingering for each hand in the opposite direction as well (RH ascending, LH descending) puts the player at an unnecessary disadvantage in that proper and adequate upper arm (humeral) stabilization now requires far more conscious attention.

Earlier we noted that the standard RH fingering for both the F-sharp and C-sharp melodic minor scale (hybrid form: melodic minor ascending, natural minor descending) is instinctively adjusted when descending to accommodate topography. In spite of this universal precedent, it has not been commonly held that a scale fingering *could*, or even *should*, differ ascending and descending. As we have seen, few have dared to recommend otherwise. But entertaining this possibility, we move closer to a consistent, *unified*, topographically oriented, and physiologically sound solution to the problem of diatonic double third scale fingering.

This topographical formula (3+1+3) for movement away from the torso obviously does not work satisfactorily in movement toward the torso.[8] But by similarly dividing the double third scale into two five-note groups yet employing the 2-1 extension (the pattern of four thirds is now 35-24-13-12) we find that a consistent and superior pianistic solution results. Since the pivoting action of hand over thumb is the key physiological determinant, it is demonstrably most desirable that this occur with the thumb on a white key. This corresponds with the hand's natural tendency to elevate (1 to 5, W to B is very natural) when crossing over the thumb. Positioned first in the black key plane, the fifth finger is in its diagonal (laterally oblique), opposing relation to the thumb (see Appendix 10) and, in its alignment with the forearm, ideally placed to engage the key for vertical action.

Again the enharmonic major scales of five black keys serve as models, having only two white keys available to the thumb. For every scale in each hand, therefore, the 35-24-13-12 pattern can be assigned to only *one* group of notes if the thumb is again to be positioned on a white key as a pivot for the next note group. The long third finger, whose action favors extension in the direction of the torso (LH ascending, RH descending), conveniently makes most efficient, coordinated contact with the black keys that follow.

Example 7.7

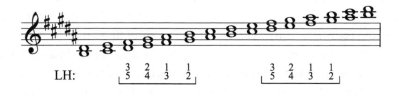

LH:
$$\begin{matrix}3 & 2 & 1 & 1\\5 & 4 & 3 & 2\end{matrix}\qquad\begin{matrix}3 & 2 & 1 & 1\\5 & 4 & 3 & 2\end{matrix}$$

RH:
$$\begin{matrix}5 & 4 & 3 & 2\\3 & 2 & 1 & 1\end{matrix}\qquad\begin{matrix}5 & 4 & 3 & 2\\3 & 2 & 1 & 1\end{matrix}$$

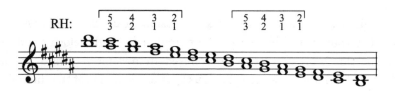

Example 7.8

LH:
$$\begin{matrix}3 & 2 & 1 & 1\\5 & 4 & 3 & 2\end{matrix}$$

RH:
$$\begin{matrix}5 & 4 & 3 & 2\\3 & 2 & 1 & 1\end{matrix}$$

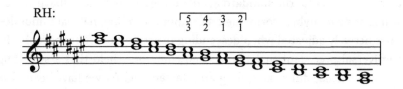

Example 7.9

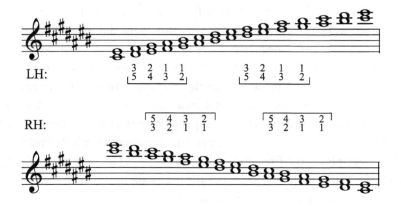

LH:
$$\begin{matrix}3 & 2 & 1 & 1\\5 & 4 & 3 & 2\end{matrix}\qquad\begin{matrix}3 & 2 & 1 & 1\\5 & 4 & 3 & 2\end{matrix}$$

RH:
$$\begin{matrix}5 & 4 & 3 & 2\\3 & 2 & 1 & 1\end{matrix}\qquad\begin{matrix}5 & 4 & 3 & 2\\3 & 2 & 1 & 1\end{matrix}$$

The fourth finger of the topographical core group is displaced by the third finger (again Chopin's cryptic "down one finger"?): the four double thirds of the RH ascending and LH descending 13-24-35 / 24 pattern becomes 35-24-13-12, now an extended primary group.

Example 7.10

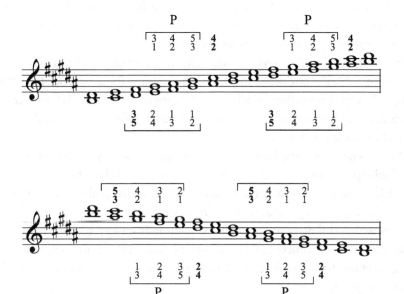

As we might expect, this displacement of the fourth with the third finger of the core pattern consistently establishes the RH descending and LH ascending topographical fingerings for double third scales throughout the Circle of Fifths. This extension of the core topographical group provides the basic pattern for diatonic double third scales in the direction of the torso; the secondary groups remain constant. As with the topographically oriented scale fingerings for single notes, the double third fingerings exemplify simplicity, unity and consistency.

This single formula, away from the torso (3+1+3) and back (4+3), is the basis for all topographically oriented diatonic double third fingerings:

13-24-35 / 24 / 13-24-35 and 35-24-13-12 / 35-24-13

With it—and from it—fingerings that meet all the desired criteria for good double third technique may be determined simply and rationally. *And they are built on, and employ, the topographically correct fingerings for the single note diatonic scales!*

FINGERING OPTIONS: OTHER TOPOGRAPHICAL ADJUSTMENTS TO THE BASIC FORMULA

As with the single note scales, and for similar reasons, it is in movement away from the torso that difficulties are most pronounced if topography is not taken seriously. And yet there are fingering options that are particularly useful in movement away from the torso, that naturally orient the hand to the keyboard and effectively enlist a coordinated response. We have just touched upon one of these "axioms" in addressing the correlation of thumb, third and fifth—which might well be considered the "architectural pillars" of the hand. We should explore this further.

White-Key Options for the Third Finger

One of the challenges inherent in *all* approaches to double third fingering is successive use of the third finger: it must engage the key vertically, immediately traverse the fifth finger obliquely and then contact and vertically engage its new key. Along with the horizontal movement of the upper arm and lateral adjustment of the hand to the forearm, movement in all planes must be finely tuned. Especially at a fast tempo, this is demanding of mental and physical coordination to quite an extreme. It is not for nothing that even a great artist such as Walter Gieseking had no hesitation in divulging a "trade secret": he suggests omitting the third finger at faster tempos—presumably the one repeating before the crossing (he is not specific).[9] Dohnányi distinguishes such execution as "blind thirds" versus "full thirds." He further remarks, "It is practically impossible to perceive any audible difference . . . while the gain in ease and clarity is remarkable."[10]

But yet again, topographical considerations lead the way toward an optimal solution of this specific problem: the third finger is employed three times in quick succession within the range of a perfect fourth, or more for melodic minor thirds, for example. This is not as great a challenge from white key to black as it is from white to white, in which the distance traversed is greater from key bottom to key bottom. Within the proposed conceptual framework further ease is nonetheless still possible through certain slight, yet thoroughly consistent, advantageous alterations of fingering for topography.

Employing the **thumb or the fifth in place of the longer third** leads us to an infinitely more comfortable, facile and effective fingering. This works beautifully because it comports with the unique functional anatomy of the thumb, fifth and third as it relates to the architecture of the hand and their movements at the intersection of its transverse axis (thumb and fifth finger) and length axis (third finger). And as with all topographically oriented fingerings, proper alignment for the coordinated movement of the key in its vertical plane is more effectively achieved and assured.

This is a particularly attractive option for scales having a preponderance of white keys.

Example 7.11

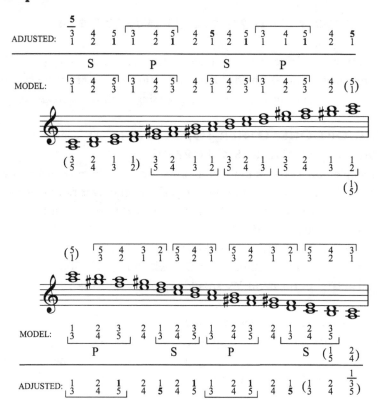

NATURAL FINGERING

Example 7.12a

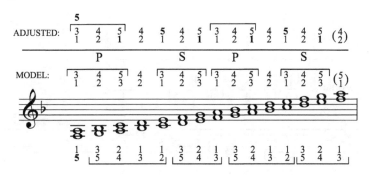

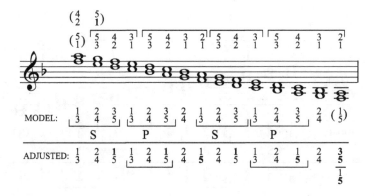

Example 7.12b

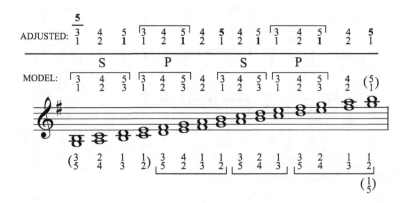

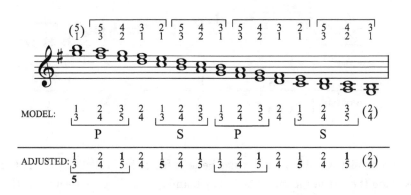

Example 7.13a

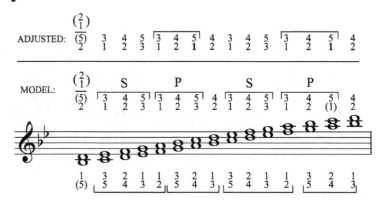

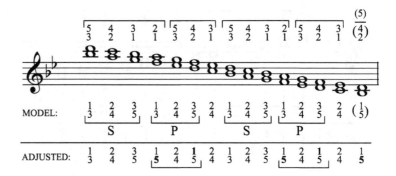

Example 7.13b

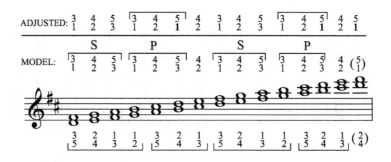

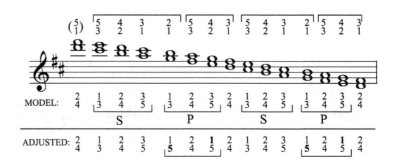

The pianist will derive particular benefit from the availability of this option in executing the harmonic minor scales of B and E, recalling that each has the unique advantage of two topographically correct fingerings for the single note scales, and noting the similarities to both of them.

Example 7.14

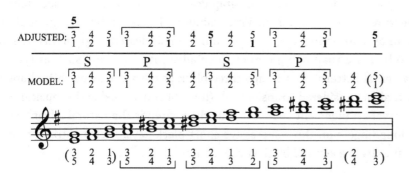

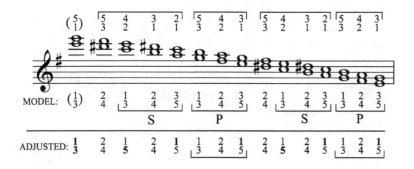

Example 7.15

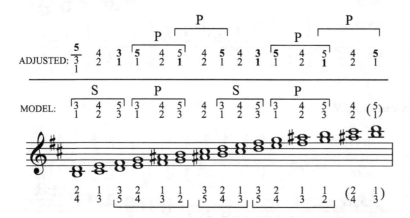

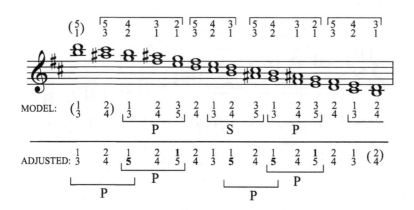

From the Enharmonic Model: Three Adjacent Black Keys

An interesting and very useful topographical option is available in determining the double third fingering for any major or minor scale having three adjacent black keys (i.e., four or more accidentals, RH ascending and LH descending). In this case there is seen to be more than one group of three adjacent black keys such as typifies the Fundamental Pattern. That is, any three-black-key group may be shifted upward or downward, or considered "translocated" (it is not transposed in the musical sense, as the interval arrangement changes). This then extends the natural advantage of the three long fingers on three successive short black keys: their neutralization of the two planes (white key and black key) of action.

Example 7.16

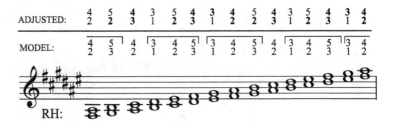

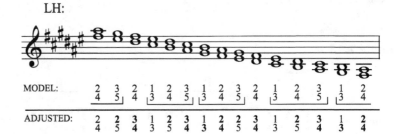

Example 7.17

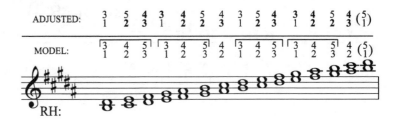

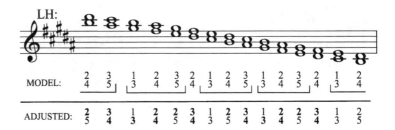

Example 7.18

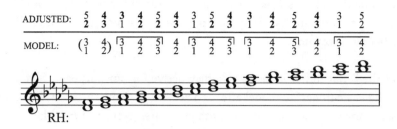

Yet again, the enharmonic major keys lead the way in revealing models for more natural, topographically based solutions. C.P.E. Bach first identified the three long fingers on the three (short) black keys as the most distinguishing feature of—and the key to—a natural orientation to the keyboard, and Chopin builds on this. The pedagogical implications of such a translocation of the Fundamental Pattern are really quite extraordinary and are considered later in Chapter 14.[11]

For now, it is useful to see how this option is also applicable to a scale such as F harmonic minor, parallel to F major but relative to A-flat (four flats). The fingering adjustment, or *refinement*, for this scale is particularly interesting since it also takes advantage of the white-key substitution of fifth and thumb for third. And note the "cooperative" advantage of the fourth finger *glissando* in the LH.

Example 7.19

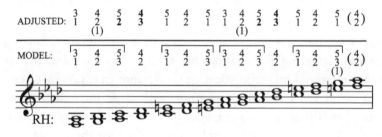

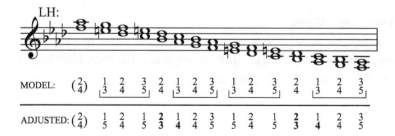

Similar fingering adjustments can yield more pianistic fingerings for a very large number of double note passages, particularly of shorter range. The Chopin Mazurkas, for example, abound in less extended passages in which modal and directional changes benefit accordingly.

A look at the B-flat minor scales is also instructive for our purposes; further refinement of the basic fingering model affords a still more pianistic result. The harmonic minor scale, for example, has the advantage of *three* groups of *two* black keys. This includes one major third (from the Fundamental Pattern) and two minor thirds, which can also be fingered as belonging to two groups of three adjacent black keys. The fingering in Example 7.20 represents a significant improvement, while comporting with topographical principles and practice.

Example 7.20

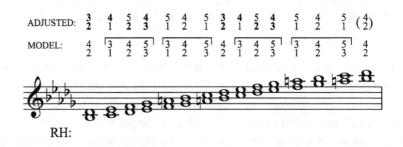

RH:

LH:

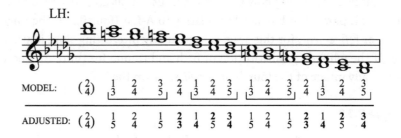

What is further revealing is that such a rational alteration now unavoidably employs those fingering combinations for major and minor thirds that are basic to the double note scales for chromatic major and minor thirds. We see here, then, the extent to which the chromatic fingerings, with their unavoidable topographical "imperative," are fundamentally operative in double third technique. And now, with the use of 2-3 and 3-4, the topographical fingerings for the double third diatonic scales make use of all fingering combinations except 5-4!

The Chromatic Option
Again, a diatonic pattern frequently benefits from applying a chromatic fingering. The single note scale for B harmonic minor is but one example; the alternatives in Example 7.21 may be found appealing.

Example 7.21

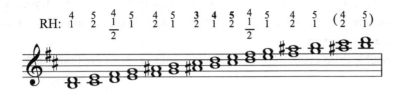

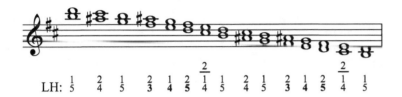

A SYMMETRICAL PROCEDURE

Unique to this approach is the practical consistency of diatonic double third scale fingerings that are "built on" the very same fingerings for the single note scales. These in turn have topographically and pianistically evolved from symmetrical implications of Chopin's Fundamental Pattern, its translocation and its alteration. Such an ongoing recurrence of the core topographical groups is obviously a distinct advantage: a sensorial reinforcement of the hand's most natural orientation to the keyboard is always at work, always contributing to security and comfort.

As with the single note scale fingerings, it is extremely worthwhile to proceed first from the enharmonic major keys in either direction (flats or sharps) and through the Circle of Fifths to C major. And it is not necessary to proceed from tonic to tonic in introducing the double third fingerings for each scale; at this more advanced stage of study, recognition of tonality and the requisite alterations would be, reasonably, a given. Such an introduction best commences from core pattern to core pattern in movement away from the torso (RH flats ascending and LH sharps descending). It not only is less complex but highlights their topographical unity.

Any of the above fingering options is most successfully presented as an alteration or adjustment of the basic topographical formula. In exploring options for any of the diatonic double third scales, it is therefore strongly recommended that the basic formula be first employed for all scales (major keys first here as well) so that any and all adjustments remain conceptually grounded in their fundamental rationale. Again, core pattern to core pattern rather than tonic to tonic is without doubt the superior approach in introducing or learning the fingerings for any of the diatonic double third scales.

If they are initially learned by such consistent and methodical application of the formula, awareness of the keyboard's topographical symmetry is significantly strengthened. Moreover, there will be a dramatic impression of both the technical and strategic advantages to be gained in such "fine tuning" without a loss of conceptual clarity as to what it all rests on. Patient tolerance for the process itself is of enormous value, and the consistency and unity inherent in this approach will be all the more apparent and more fully appreciated. Heightened topographical sensitivity will proceed ever more naturally and spontaneously—a chief goal of all topographical fingerings for the fundamental forms.

The double third scales for the major and all minor forms are found in Appendix 7.

DOUBLE SIXTHS AND OTHER DOUBLE NOTES

8

To play scales in thirds or sixths (diatonic and chromatic scales, in major and minor thirds and sixths, taking into account the Godowsky exercises . . .) is, of course, an excellent thing . . . what would be the sense of the centuries-old and still-not-outworn division of the whole of our piano technique into elementary aspects, if these aspects did not exist in actual piano literature?

—Heinrich Neuhaus

It is absolutely unnecessary to practice the very difficult scales in double sixths in all keys. The chromatic scale in major and minor sixths is sufficient.

—Ernst von Dohnányi

RIGHTLY INCLUDING OCTAVES in his rather cursory, though insightful and helpful, discourse on double notes generally, Neuhaus makes a very important point. It is most beneficial that such difficult passages—any difficult passages, for that matter—should be isolated from the literature for concentrated attention to advance technical development, all without in any way devaluing the compositional context from which they are excised. Certainly, he goes on to say in specific regard to octaves, such an approach is as valuable as, if not more valuable than, "dozens of boring octave etudes." And he continues: "As for the other more usual double notes—thirds, fourths, sixths, sevenths, ninths—I need only say that so much has been written about them and so much composed for their sake that I am reluctant even to start a conversation on the subject."[1]

It is undoubtedly true that "so much has been composed for their sake," but one would nevertheless be hard pressed to otherwise find the issues surrounding the double note challenge addressed in any great length or depth. Only Alberto Jonás, Franklin Taylor, and Frank Merrick have devoted a significant swath of space to any meaningful discussion of double third or other double note fingerings. And only E. Robert Schmitz and Abby Whiteside have seriously attempted to get to the heart of the matter, technically speaking.

Indeed, even more than thumb action and the mechanics of pivoting, the record is remarkably deafening in its silence—especially in the matter of double sixths. One cannot escape the suspicion that such studied avoidance is more likely founded in the complications and contradictions experienced when implementing the generally accepted fingerings for the chromatic and diatonic forms. Dohnányi's extremely "simplified"—even simplistic—advice can be seen then as further attesting to the elusiveness of this highly challenging problem, rather than proposing an effective solution, and in so doing relegating it to the relatively inconsequential.[2]

So what does one do, for example, about double sixths in consecutive intervals of more than a half-step? What does one do about embellishing or cadenzalike passages in which they predominate or form an integral part of the whole (as in Chopin's "Berceuse")? Neuhaus's ensuing admonition follows from this: "If a pianist is interested in the problem of double notes, not only as a performer but as a teacher, he is bound to know the best examples of this type and learn them." But what is it that he or she is to learn *from* them—and how to go about it?

On the surface it would appear that both Neuhaus and Dohnányi are—as are so many others, and in a most important sense—on the same page. But one should note Neuhaus's qualification: his recommendation of supplementary study of Godowsky's exercises in which glissando fingering plays a decided role[3] (as well as a later, most enthusiastic, endorsement of such fingering, including Brahms's exercises for it[4]). The unavoidable implication is that the commonly accepted fingerings for diatonic double sixths do relatively little to unlock or develop a technical mastery that is overwhelmingly "transferable" in practical, artistic application.

On yet another level, many simply dismiss double sixth proficiency as being of little import, despite the demands of a wealth of passagework in the repertoire. Still, it is small wonder they remain unconvinced given the proposed "standard" fingerings that are still in vogue—if taken at all seriously. Once again the pianist is confronted with fingerings for fundamental forms that hardly relate to practical application; they are contrived for the "form" only: unchanged ascending and descending, from tonic to tonic.

Taking in only those extended passages of a purely virtuosic sort in which the demands of more sensitive tonal balance and refined attention to texture are less stringent, if at all existent, we can easily deem them of relatively little consequence. Yet again: "no legato, no problem." And indeed, one recent fingering manual[5] eliminates sixths entirely, without even a suggestion of guidelines for their fingering.

To take such a position is certainly to miss the enormous gain inherent in all double note training—especially if it is based on a more natural use of the playing mechanism and facilitated by fingerings that are more topographically attuned. Full cognizance of the myriad ways in which double sixths appear in the literature would no doubt lead to a welcome change of attitude.

It must again be affirmed that what is needed are fundamental, "operational" principles that reliably serve as the starting point for a fingering application that accounts for the keyboard's topography as well as its topology (given the matter of spatial distance that these pattern forms and passages necessarily encompass). The core patterns derived from Chopin's Fundamental Pattern, and likewise the shared topography of the enharmonic major scales, once more reveal the fundamental basis for natural solutions to the thorny matter of double note fingering. Approached along these lines, there are not—and need not be—significant discrepancies in their fingering from that for the other fundamental forms. This inherent topographical and physiological consistency in the all-important matter of fingering makes for accelerated development of an assured, natural technique for double notes.

Highlighting some of the particular issues encountered in double sixth study is at the same time helpful in appreciating its distinctive value. We may then be further persuaded to seek a rational solution to the problem of biomechanically sound fingerings for these seemingly obvious, yet rather elusive, patterns.

In contrast to double thirds, most past attempts to settle on double sixth fingerings for the chromatic and diatonic scales tended to be very general and rather uniform. This is not the least owing to the fact that successive double sixths are necessarily limited as to choice of finger groups because of their interval span. But what is most unique about them is that, among all the fundamental forms excepting octaves, the fourth and fifth fingers may not be only sparingly enlisted—not a happy situation for "thumb (radially) oriented" pianists, and no doubt a factor in their popular disavowal.

Here too, a brief overview of some other influential thinking on the matter is constructive in further setting an informed context for developing a more natural approach to double note fingering and technique.

MORE DOUBLE TROUBLE

The topographical fingerings for the diatonic double sixth scales presented herein are consistent with those for double thirds. It is worth observing that other double sixth solutions, for the most part, likewise draw on a certain correlation to double third fingering.

Those prescribed by Clara Schumann, Moszkowski, Leschetizky, William Mason, Philipp, Charles Cooke and most others, for example, similarly group the diatonic double sixths according to their consecutive groupings of double thirds within the octave (3+2+2), in which the fifth finger is called on only once per octave. But in double sixth scales (2+2+3)[6] or other extended sequences of sixths, the fifth finger cannot, of course, be so limited in its use. The differences of black-and-white-key allocation are to be seen mainly in assignment of the three group. Among these it is notable that the fingering for the enharmonic scales is generally consistent, and the placement of these groups would indicate a topographical sensitivity to some degree—certainly unavoidable in the case of the enharmonic major scales. Most offer fingerings for the chromatic major as well as the minor sixths.

It is quite noteworthy, though, that, as he did in the matter of diatonic double thirds, Liszt departs from the pack and differs markedly: his solution rests in regular diatonic sequencing of the basic 1-4/2-5 pattern only, and for all keys. The chromatic major fingerings likewise exclusively employ this fingering sequence, but adjusted to avoid the thumb on a black key and aided by a glissando thumb on the successive white keys. The chromatic minor fingerings can also be found enlisting the more common sequence (2+ 2+ 3).[7] Remark again that, on close scrutiny, Liszt's fingering applications do generally exhibit a topographical sensitivity—however consciously— as does his compositional key choice. But it is rather significant that it is eschewed in the matter of double sixths.

Hans von Bülow, Liszt's exceptionally talented student and later son-in-law (he eventually married Cosima), evinced early on, however, a rather fierce resolve to be unaffected by topography even while admitting its unrelenting, irrefutable influence. In his 1868 Preface to a collection of Cramer's studies, he wrote:

> As the chief mechanical difficulty in pianoforte playing, we now lay stress upon
> the unevenness resulting from the local relations of black and white keys, of the
> field forming the scene of action for the performer's fingers. Our aim, therefore,
> is chiefly directed to rendering the fingers independent of that unevenness,
> and, by means of *protracted gymnastic exercise* [emphasis added], to enable them
> to move about on the black keys in a manner as light, free, secure, and distinct
> as when on the white keys, and without stumbling in any combination
> whatsoever of white and black . . . without respect either to the relations of
> black and white keys, or to those of longer and shorter fingers.[8]

What is most significant, of course, is von Bülow's very clear-headed identification of the root cause of that "chief mechanical difficulty in pianoforte playing." But more than 140 years later, one can only infer the enduring effects of advancing such a determined position—*topographical warfare*, one might say—on encountering some of the fingerings advocated for consecutive diatonic double sixths. Even for this most elusive of all double note forms, pattern purposefully persists in trumping topography.[9]

In 1938 Walter Gieseking, among the most consummate artists of any generation, similarly advocated Liszt's double sixth sequencing even while admitting that the "tension of fingers with regard to *legato* sixths 1-4/2-5 is very great. Hence it follows that fatigue takes place quickly." He is silent as to any specific topographical assignment of the fingers, but he allows that a glissando (gliding) thumb permits great relief, the outer voice in any event bearing the burden of legato.[10] Given Gieseking's unsurpassed (recorded) performance of Debussy's Etude IV from Book 1, one can surely assume his practical and artistic application of glissando fingering in that groundbreaking double sixth study.

But just a few years earlier, in 1935, E. Robert Schmitz (Debussy's assistant and close colleague) had published his own double sixth fingerings that sought—as did all his fingerings—to wed the hand to the keyboard's topography and to maximally engage it in a more natural, physiologically attuned manner. Its prehensile capabilities were to be enlisted even in such interval extensions as double sixths—octaves as well.[11] Most significant, however, was his correct understanding that the *upper arm* was the key to negotiating these larger intervals within the hand as they were distributed horizontally in keyboard space.

In noting the dramatically different yet "complementary" artistic and textural aspects of Debussy's above-mentioned double sixth etude (*pour les Sixtes*) vis-à-vis Chopin's, Schmitz does not avoid attempting to guide the pianist toward a more satisfactory, more natural resolution of the extraordinary challenges therein. He begins:

> From a general technical viewpoint, one may say that the performance of double-sixths is often conducive to stiffness and fatigue, *unless the arm technique is adequate in distributing the fingers* [emphasis added]. The attempt to ensure absolute legato simultaneously at both voices of the same hand, by the fingers, is superfluous on the modern piano, and, moreover, tends to create strain.[12]

The increased hand span required in executing double sixths markedly limits the optimal range of movement for lateral adjustments. This means that adjustments for proper alignment must be more exquisitely fine-tuned while at the same time the biophysical demands are intensified.[13] Even more than with double thirds, execution of double sixths and the fingerings chosen to that purpose reflect the technical limitations and musical aspirations of the executant. But fingerings also influence a technical response. Tone quality is always the revealing indicator.

From a developmental standpoint technically, a comprehensive approach to double sixth technique necessarily enlists the upper arm as primary motor and control. And the full participation of the hand and forearm's ulnar side is consequently accompanied by a proportionate deemphasis of radial orientation. Sensitivity to issues of structural (skeletal) alignment and balance becomes further integrated in the pianist's total keyboard response as a consequence; indeed, it is heightened.

Sixths are the aural and theoretical (harmonic) inversion of thirds, and the topographical double sixth fingerings presented herein support and validate the manual—and textural—aspect of this relationship. The benefits are converse as well, and healthy technical balance is therefore to be achieved in concurrent study of both series of double note forms (for the smaller hand, double fourths and fifths are appropriate at first). The primary emphasis on a prehensile finger flexion as the predominant action for double thirds becomes one of lateral extension for double sixths—one might say a *functional inversion* as well as that of interval. This does not mean, however, that prehensile action of finger articulation is of little importance. Quite the contrary, it remains essential.

As with all extended patterns in particular, proper upper arm use is ignored at one's peril. But the intelligent pianist who regularly engages in complementary practice of both thirds and sixths can thereby reap rewards that are extraordinary. Authority and assurance that are biophysically grounded can be counted among them.

The attendant musical and expressive rewards of serious and thoughtful double sixth practice are likewise immense as well as unique. The fingers of the hand's ulnar side become increasingly skilled in their delivery of tones that fall to the RH's melody line and the LH's bass line. At the same time, the thumbs become all the more deft in handling inner voices that frequently necessitate their consecutive (glissando) use, or highlighting harmonized melodic lines in the piano's middle range that require frequent exchange and rhythmic interplay between the hands (late-Romantic "multi-dimensional" styles). The artistically paramount textural and *fioratura* aspects of Chopin's style, distinctly characterizing his "Berceuse" and encountered variously throughout the Nocturnes and other works (one should always consider the *bel canto* style and remember his contemporaries Bellini and Donizetti specifically in this regard), are indeed testament. And there are the inevitable challenges of balance and voicing—even texture—in fugues of all styles (recall Cortot's insightful comments), the numerous concert etudes composed to that purpose, as well as the enormous catalogue of transcriptions of one sort or another.

TOWARD A NATURAL APPROACH

Some of the particular challenges of scales and other sequences for double notes larger than the interval of a third have, so far, only been broadly touched on. But because they literally "extend" the boundaries of double note technique, closer consideration of the specific issues surrounding double sixths (fourths and fifths also) compared to double thirds will prove to be extremely worthwhile. More detail is in order when presenting the rationale for comprehensive fingerings of double sixths. Certain topographical factors may not be readily apparent, and there are fewer combinations of fingering available overall, even to the average hand.

Pivoting is also at issue in double sixth scales, but "thumb under" less so: only in those combinations in which the thumb can effectively manage a legato connection after the second finger. This very much depends on hand size, flexibility (especially knuckle bridge), skilled adjustments for alignment and upper arm coordination. Assignment of long fingers over short is central for movement away from the torso but is mostly "hand over" thumb or short fingers under long for toward-the-torso action. The natural swing of the arm and the recapturing of its rebound must not be lost in either direction; appropriate curves must not be "reversed."[14] Motor finger action (see Glossary) predominates as it articulates the outer voice and coordinates with the glissando (arm "pull") action of successive thumbs or fifths.

In an important sense, the hand is not working in "two divisions" away from the torso since the thumb, when engaged, is always playing in conjunction with the "end" (third, fourth and fifth) fingers. Only in movement toward the torso is the thumb the pivot finger for a hand crossing, as is characteristic of other scales and arpeggios. In double sixth scales, therefore, the fourth finger for a black key as the preferred pivot for a thumb-under action is not a prime consideration. Instead, key depth adjustment and black-white key plane translation are now among the chief influences affecting finger choice and movement. Elimination of unnecessary extensions, neutralization of key depth and application of relative finger lengths for their movements over and under are the means for ensuring optimal verticalization, all correlative to a unifying legato connection controlled by the upper arm.

The third, fourth and fifth fingers—representing the ulnar side of the hand—are the most active motor fingers. Double sixths are therefore especially advantageous in developing the essential articulating capabilities of these fingers. This *articulation with weight* is natural to them given their range of flexion, strength (their tendonous interconnection is a naturally stabilizing facilitator—*not* an inborn handicap) and coordination with the upper arm via the ulna of the forearm.

Overall, the chromatic double third fingerings can, in a most important sense, be seen to set the foundation for a natural fingering for all double note patterns. For seconds the hand is more contracted; for thirds it is a healthy complement of flexion and extension; for double note patterns of larger intervals—fourths to octaves—extension is the predominant activity. But for all, the strategic and topographical assignment of 3-4-5/5-4-3 is integral, the keyboard's symmetry and topography the determining factors in their consistency.

For double sixths, however, the further matter of avoiding unnecessary stretches entails still more frequent shifts of thumb or fifth (depending on hand size, fingering choice and technical proficiency), particularly for passages in the fastest tempi. A properly developed upper arm technique is here of the greatest importance since the technical requirements for sixths are dynamically much more akin to those for octaves than might be perceived at first. Pedagogically, emphasis on double sixth study can be a sensible complement to octaves for smaller hands at earlier stages of advancement; similarly, fourths and fifths help develop a foundation for double sixths at a still earlier stage. Proper alignment and commensurate shoulder joint/shoulder complex stabilization are key elements of a successful technical execution—as always.

The most basic fingering combination for double sixths may be found in their chromatic *minor* fingering: 1-4/2-5. Its topographical application is central to a natural fingering strategy for diatonic scales and other passages of double sixths. Perhaps this is at the bottom of Dohnányi's remark. But keep in mind that this is also the basic combination for chromatic major thirds, and that the minor sixth is the inversion of the major third. And note too the combination's relationship to four-part chords, their inversions and the arpeggio fingerings that follow from them. Again, only their topologies—that is, the spatial distances between the individual black-and-white key components of their topographical patterns—differ.

Such differences of interval appreciably affect the hand's natural accommodation to topography, notably as it is affected by the distinguishing 2+ interval of the harmonic minor scale. A slur pattern of two major sixths that are a step apart—beginning on C for example, all white keys—encompasses the interval of a major seventh; so does the same pattern beginning on C-sharp. But continuing the sequence chromatically, it soon becomes obvious that some topographical combinations bear this sequencing of 1-4/2-5 better than others; a like sequence of minor sixths—although now encompassing a span of only a major sixth—does not fare much better. In all of them, any discomfort or awkwardness arising from placement of the hand is found to be due mainly to a problem of second finger alignment, affecting its capabilities regarding key depth adjustment and vertical action. Indeed, appropriate assignment of the second finger is a prime determinant of a natural, topographical solution to double sixth fingering. In general, the second finger will be best served by a black key when that option is available.

As in the solution for double thirds, we take advantage of two successive groups using 3-4-5/5-4-3. If we assign them to maximize any topographical benefits, each hand symmetrically mirrors the other in movement away from the torso. Likewise, only one sixth remains: that linking the two groups. Employing 1-4 (the link was 2-4 for double thirds) advantages the longer fingers in crossing over the relatively shorter fingers for an ensuing finger legato. Recall that 1-4 is inherently stable. But enlisting the glissando option (employing either 1 or 5, depending on voice and direction) simplifies the linking considerably. Remember that a glissando fingering is fundamentally an upper arm action.

Example 8.1a

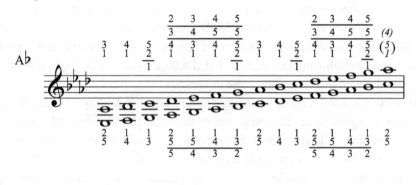

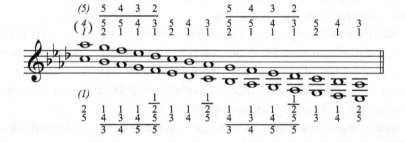

Example 8.1b

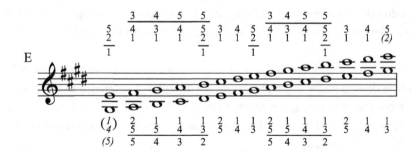

Example 8.1b (Continued)

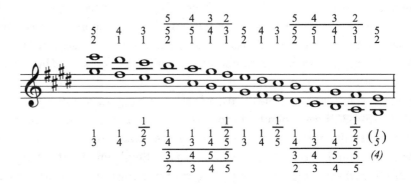

Such facilitation by way of glissando fingering is yet another benefit realized by a developed sensitivity to such topographical arrangements: black to white is most natural but white to white or black to black is perfectly amenable. White to black is more easily accomplished if the interval is that of a half-step; the natural elevation of a hand crossing or an engagement of the longer second—as pivot/motor finger—relative to the shorter fifth also assists in this. These serve to great advantage, particularly for smaller, less agile hands, while sometimes suggesting—or inspiring, if you will—other equally suitable glissando fingering options. But the chief operating principle for all double notes remains: that the legato connection be maximally preserved at all times, in at least one voice or another.

Maintaining the integrity of a single, unifying melodic line or voice is no less important in regard to double sixths than with other double notes. However, more frequent though subtle shifts of hand position are usually necessary, and this inevitably requires that the weight shift from ulnar to radial side of the hand (and vice versa) be managed accordingly. Tempo is undoubtedly an important influencing factor in enlisting glissando (always under the control of the upper arm) or applying other topographically correct options.

Alternate use of legato and staccato between voices remains a most effective way to ascertain effective finger choice, serving also as a basic practice technique for developing control of the necessary weight shift and counteractions that all double notes require. This will prove especially useful in regard to the second finger since 2-1 facilitates the fifth finger glissando option.

In movement away from the torso, care should be taken not to insist on a thumb-under second finger legato connection at the expense of ulnar orientation or appropriate alignment for the outer voice: a rather subtle coordination of arm shift and finger succession better serves instead. But here too, judicious employment of the glissando option permits optimal alignment, perhaps its most significant advantage, while at the same time facilitating and ensuring a legato connection.

For the enharmonic major keys and their harmonic minors (excepting B-flat hm) Schmitz's double sixth fingerings employ the 2-3-4-5 sequence in movement both away from the torso and, for most, toward it (5-4-3-2). This, of course, comports entirely with application of the Fundamental Pattern (and its alteration) but is really quite limited in practice.

The second finger of the group may take a black key following the fifth on a white key, the better sequence for second and fifth, but only if the interval is confined to the half step. And certainly the extension (stretch) of 1-2 can be quite awkward, even uncomfortable, except in the case of very flexible hands or those having a larger-than-average span. Nonetheless, 2-3-4-5 can often be an excellent combination that in many ways simplifies fingering strategy for those hands able to manage it—especially in shorter passages within the more proximate range of the arm's midline. Most pianists, however, will likely find the hand-over pivoting on a black-key thumb less attractive than the glissando option, in which thumb as pivot remains assigned to a white key.

The fingerings for the following enharmonic major scales exemplify a topographical assignment that is consistent with the model for diatonic double third solutions. They also validate the Fundamental Pattern as their core and typify available glissando options.

Example 8.2a

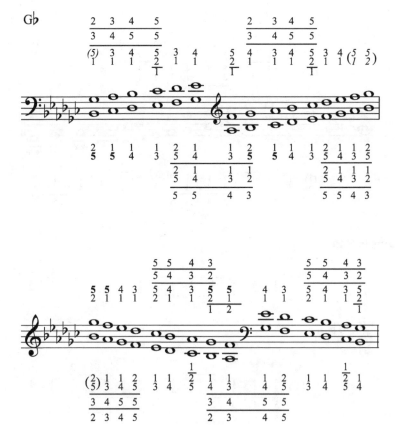

In the G-flat major scale it can be seen that the alternative application of 2-3-4-5, that of the Fundamental Pattern, is most attractive in this key, in that the longer second has the advantage of crossing over the shorter fifth for a half-step only. This is so for the RH ascending and the LH descending.

But this is not the case for the D-flat major scale; nor is it for that of C-flat. For the former only the RH has this advantage. The converse is true for the latter: only the LH shares this advantage.

Example 8.2b

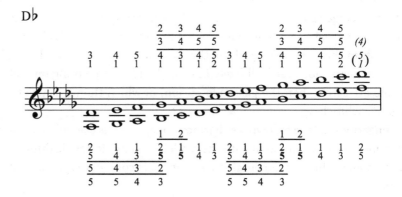

Db

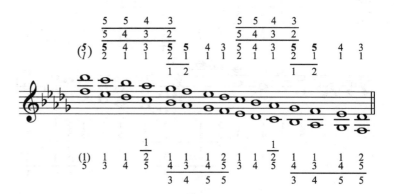

Example 8.2c

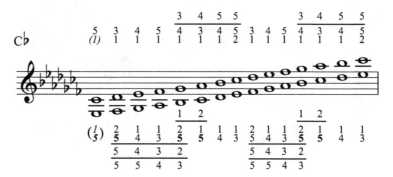

Cb

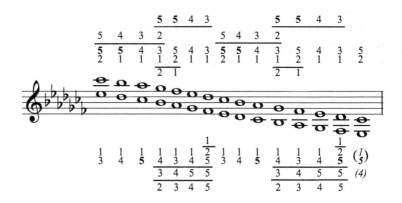

NATURAL FINGERING

In these keys, the glissando options for 1 or 5 are likewise most facilitated by the half-step distance, whether from black to white or white to black.

It should be noted that the fingerings for all diatonic scales—single or double note—are best served by the topographical arrangement of the major scale for G-flat/F-sharp as ideal model. Recall that this is the scale for the enharmonic major key that replaces C as the new beginning point for an Inverted Circle of Fifths (Example 2.27). One might indeed call it the "Pianists' Circle of Fifths" reflecting the unique advantages gained from equal temperament and the keyboard's corresponding symmetry.

Recall too the importance of symmetrical D-flat and B (C-flat) in Chopin's exposition of his approach to fingering and the role of the Fundamental Pattern: he recommended that LH scale study begin with D-flat and that of the RH with B. But only G-flat/F-sharp *begins* with the three long fingers on the three short keys, the unique and distinguishing characteristic of the Fundamental Pattern—the very essence of the core topographical arrangement that C.P.E. Bach likewise saw as the key to a natural fingering.[15] Indeed, Mikuli tells us that "the scales with many black keys (B, F-sharp, and D-flat) were first studied. . . ."[16]

Further discussion of the third finger is also warranted. With diatonic double thirds we recognized that an inherent problem in their consecutive diatonic execution is the ready need for the third finger to be placed and available to activate the next key—its verticalization[17]—immediately after releasing, and retracting from, its key a fourth above or below.

But we also found that substitution of the thumb or fifth for the third frequently eliminated this difficulty, especially from white key to white key where the distance traversed is greatest. This is not an option available for double sixths, however. Any issues of quick succession are greatly exacerbated by the necessity of an alignment appropriate for efficient use of the second finger, and the third must now negotiate the intervening interval from a more extended, outstretched position of the hand. The distance traversed is necessarily greater, even as the components of the executed movement are compressed by time at faster tempi.

It is necessary, therefore, that the third finger be strategically assigned so that glissando application of the thumb may be skillfully employed (remark yet again that the glissando action is primarily that of the upper arm) as an alternative to the second finger for many topographical combinations. Although important for double thirds, glissando fingering has the potential for an even greater role for double sixths. But the thumb's release, retraction and subsequent "repositioning" must be quick and well-timed if its more frequent use is to be of particular advantage.

Chopin's chromatic etude in A minor is especially illustrative of this. Because its harmonies are usually found as (first and second inversion) chords "of the sixth," the basic span of the hand most employed throughout the etude is that of a sixth.

Example 8.3

Chopin, *Etude in A Minor, Op.10 No.2*

Allegro

Opus 10, No. 2 is therefore an excellent study not only for the more obvious development of the "end" fingers in their chromatic assignment but also for the necessary and appropriate action of the thumb in more natural solutions for double sixths in general. A RH staccato (opposing) action of the thumb, coordinated with those other fingers taking the notes of the supporting harmonies, at the same time shifts the weight to the hand's ulnar side—to the end fingers. Remember that the thumb's retraction (and reposition) is along its diagonal, *transverse* axis of ulnar opposition (Appendix 10); the release for repositioning constitutes the thumb's basic playing action, which is at its base. The naturally efficient result is that any uncomfortable stretches (lateral extensions) are greatly minimized, if not entirely eliminated; weight is available to rightly emphasize the outer chromatic lines; and a balanced ulnar orientation can be more easily maintained throughout in collaboration with the requisite dynamic stabilization of the upper arm.

A PIANISTIC APPLICATION

Given a genius coupled with an extraordinary penchant for rational pedagogy, it is probably not at all presumptuous to infer a conscious, logical progression in Chopin's emphasis on double notes in the E major Etude, Opus 10, No. 3 immediately following—the preponderance of sixths in particular. Similarly interesting and instructive, Opus 10 No. 2 and Opus 25 No. 8 also bear fruitful comparison. But even the briefest survey is to essentially suggest a greater role of double sixths underlying the repertoire than is generally granted.

Seemingly not at all related—on the surface of it—are the legato octaves of the B major Lento section of Opus 25 No. 10, in which the end fingers are charged with the melodic line. Excepting further extension of the hand to an octave, topography relates them to the fingerings for the sixths. Owing to Chopin's uncanny pedagogical—and topographical—insight, pianists who would seriously undertake simultaneous and sequential study of the three Etudes, Opus 25 nos. 8–10, could not fail to appreciate and benefit from his crafty and wise technical progression.

There is no doubt that the search for successful double sixth fingerings poses challenges out of the ordinary. One need only compare the attempted and recommended "solutions" of the various editions to appreciate the degree of perplexity that apparently confronted the editors. Even so, one should not too readily discount or dismiss such challenges, but rather work for their resolution. The recurring consistency of the keyboard's topographical symmetry yet again holds the key to enormously simplifying the "problem" of double sixth fingering—and with it, double sixth technique.

Like double thirds, any fingering for double sixths and a consequent "proper" double sixth technique should reflect the inherent character and texture of the intervals themselves. Thirds and sixths are characterized by their propensity for warmth, richness and color. They are not simply harmonizations or "doublings," and their textures are in contrast to the stronger, more strident sounds of the "open" intervals: perfect fourths, fifths and octaves. Such textural characteristics distinguish the works of Brahms in particular, qualities sadly absent in most performances of his *oeuvre* in the current artistic climate. But this propensity is there to be captured wherever thirds and sixths abound.

Chopin's Nocturne in D-flat, Op. 27 No. 2, is an ideal example of the pitfalls of unpianistic fingering even in the search for a more musical, more pianistic execution. The fingering solutions in Examples 8.4 through 8.6 for the ethereal double sixth passage that closes this nocturne speak volumes to these issues. They are pointedly revealing in the degree of their dissonance with the apt poignancy of Cortot's accompanying exhortation: "This whole ending should seem to evaporate in a dream atmosphere."

Example 8.4

Chopin, *Nocturne in D-flat, Op.27 No. 2*

Lento sostenuto

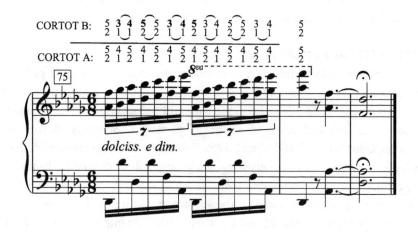

Example 8.5

Chopin, *Nocturne in Db, Op.27 No. 2*

Lento sostenuto

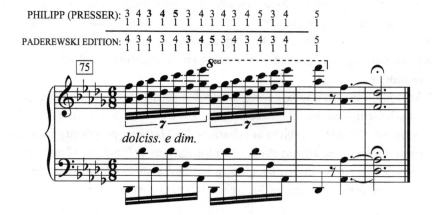

Example 8.6

Chopin, *Nocturne in Db, Op.27 No. 2*

Lento sostenuto

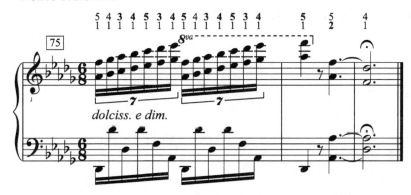

It is to be observed that Cortot's solution B (Example 8.4) similarly reflects the glissando application for the D-flat major scale in Example 8.2b. The important difference, however, is his advocacy of glissando for both 2 and 5. But the topographical solution is demonstrably easier: the legato connection for the glissando 5 is best controlled with the aid of 1-2 in the lower voice.

Example 8.6 exemplifies the pianistic advantage of the topographical solution for the D-flat scale. The glissando option (8.2b above), though useful, is not as conducive to a successful legato in the ascending melodic line given the tempo. But both topographical options have the utmost potential to satisfy the artistic and expressive demands of this Nocturne's sublime closing measures since it is in skilled enlistment of the upper arm mechanism that the sense of "line" ultimately resides. The vertical must not function at the expense of the horizontal. All movement—whereby expression is conveyed—must therefore be in exquisite balance. The fingerings chosen must reflect and ensure this capability.

As is the case for all double notes, the issues regarding finger choice for double sixths essentially revolve around those that will prove most effective in regard to legato connection, elimination or reduction of awkward and impeding stretches (extensions) and optimal alignment. Although sixths are more challenging than other double note patterns, the larger interval distances (their topologies) conveniently enable facilitating options.

Glissando action for fingers other than the thumb and fifth may also be enlisted—a unique, if properly limited and judiciously employed, advantage also afforded by the keyboard's topography and the hand's natural orientation to it. The double sixth etudes of Chopin, Debussy and Scriabin are among those compositions that most firmly attest to an appreciation of these affinities in their composers' choice of key.

The fingering solutions for double note diatonic sequences of fourths and fifths will be found to comport with those for double sixths. Passages of what are called mixed double notes—double notes of chromatic/diatonic "mixed" intervals—are likewise amenable to the very same principles of application. And as Moszkowski tells us: "The works of Hummel, Chopin, Liszt, Brahms, Saint-Saens and many others are teeming with the most complicated combinations of Double Notes. Their extreme difficulty of execution must oblige pianists, even the most skillful, to make them an object of assiduous study."

Yet again, considerations of topography invite the most natural and pianistic resolution in matters of fingering, through a process that is both rational and consistent. The reader is directed to Appendix 8 for all the diatonic double sixth scales, including those for all minor forms.

TOPOGRAPHY, STRATEGY AND SYMMETRY

3

To a large extent the shape of an instrument determines its fingering. It would appear to be most arbitrary in the case of keyboard instruments, for the arrangement of the keys is such that any one of them may be depressed by any finger. For this and other reasons the study of fingering is a treacherous path along which many have erred.
—C.P.E. Bach

As art is infinite within the limits of its means, so its teaching should be governed by the same limits in order to give it boundless potential. . . . So we are not dealing with ingenious theories, but with whatever goes straight to the point and smoothes the technical side of the art.
—Frederic Chopin

THE KEYBOARD BY ITSELF represents a physical organization of tones. And keyboard history in turn is replete with attempts to group its keys—and therefore those tones—into "fingerings" for a conceptual organization and practical application of harmonic and melodic patterns. The ultimate goal is facilitation of expressive and artistic execution of the music at hand.

The capabilities of instruments available to composers of a given period, prevailing notions of performance practice and contemporary limitations of applicable knowledge from the biophysical realm undoubtedly affected and influenced the fingerings adopted and prescribed. But as noted earlier, instrumental innovations and composers' imaginations have always led the way. For the most part, therefore, technical proficiency has lagged behind invention and complexity. One need only be reminded of the vast amount of repertoire, formerly dismissed as "unplayable"—even by the greatest artists of the given era—that is now the common currency of concerts, competitions and conservatories.

Consequently, matters of fingering have mostly developed as a kind of patchwork. This is not to say that many have not attempted to systematize or codify it in some way, nor that much does not follow from any particular rationale. The scale and arpeggio fingerings in common use for so long are obvious examples of this, as are certain long-held precepts and "rules." But contradictions and exceptions to them far outweigh the basic "principles" espoused. As Fielden pointed out, now quite some time ago, development of a science of fingering has indeed remained far behind the curve, so to speak. And nothing has changed since then. The tail has been wagging the dog for some time now.

Generally speaking, we no longer consider that there is any conflict between the *science* of piano playing and the *art* of piano playing. But the study of fingering has been, by default, mostly relegated to the realm of "art" and, amazingly, the search for technical solutions continues without questioning what are now archaic rationales for some basic approaches to fingering. Any conscious effort to seek solutions to technical difficulties must in large measure involve the issue of appropriate and efficient fingering. And it is impossible to do justice to this search without full consideration of the influence of keyboard topography in all its manifestations. Ultimately, this will be found to be unavoidable.

The varying lengths, mutual affinities and natural "individualities" of the fingers in relation to the keyboard's topography, even if that is glibly taken to be only a matter of its surface "geography," demands this consideration. Without topographical awareness and sensitivity, the pianist's movements toward key engagement may be likened to a dancer's attempt to dance, to move coordinately or to coordinate movements, on a constantly shifting floor. The physiological and kinesthetic variables would be daunting, if not overwhelming—not to mention unpredictable and psychologically distressing.

THE CHALLENGE

The variables of the keyboard's topography—its ground, its floor—are known and should be fully factored into the equation. What is needed for this are solid, *natural principles* for a pianistic fingering, each of them having a biomechanical, physiological and kinesiological basis that is relevant to the keyboard's topography and that derives from its demands and influences. These principles would be far more yielding in insight and benefit than "rules," and far more useful and universal than mere "guidelines." They would also be liberating.

Pianism and a pianistic fingering—each as both science *and* art—are neither separate from nor at odds with each other. There is a definite relation of "clean" playing to the degree of clarity and precision of movement necessary for establishing and preserving the vertical plane for key action/retraction (*dynamic movements*).

Likewise, coordinated movements relative to the horizontal/lateral plane and those intersecting all planes obliquely (*distributive* and *adjustive movements* respectively) are involved in locating the key or key groups and bringing the fingers into contact with them. They must also align the skeletal structure of the playing mechanism to best effect tone production in the key's vertical plane. All are essential components of fluency and musical "line" as well. Indeed, appropriate consideration of proportionate movement in these horizontal/lateral and vertical planes parallels the very nature of melody and harmony in their own inter*action*.

There is also the underlying relation of "secure" playing to *dynamically active* joint stabilization, primarily of the shoulder joint/shoulder complex, as well as the physical "grounding" of the entire body. This is to be distinguished from any set muscular or skeletal *fixation*, with its implications of rigidity or varying degrees of inflexibility (here the maxim "strength through flexibility" is yet again validated). Psychological security is proportionate to physical security. And tone "control" presupposes a certain fundamental physical control that ultimately permits it.

The importance of "energy management," its *availability* as well as its deployment, is always at issue. Even in this, the importance of a balanced relationship of vertical to horizontal is manifest. Grounded energy moves vertically along the body's spinal axis; muscular tensions, originating and manifested horizontally to that axis, are impediments to a free, unobstructed flow of that energy. Arthur Rubinstein's practice of oftentimes "standing" in the course of performance was usually viewed as a mannerism or act of showmanship. But in getting more fully into his feet and "going vertical" certain tensions were released and more energy was made available to him. The benefits of this are immediately, and dramatically, demonstrable.

As an art form, music is *one-dimensional* (painting is two-dimensional; sculpture and theater dance are three) in that it occurs and is experienced only in time; it is linear. "Time" is the *sine qua non* and "timing" is the essential component of all coordinated movement. It is fundamental to the successful balance, synchronization and integration of all of the above. An *integrated* rational, musical and emotional response, deeply expressive and highly communicative, is further enabled and facilitated by an approach to fingering that is in keeping with that end. Without this integration, true spontaneity at the highest levels of artistic performance is otherwise not possible. Emotion (affect) is the *movement* of our feelings. The ultimate question is whether or not a particular performance or performing style will be of affect or mere effect, its poor cerebral substitute.[1]

The present work is both a plea and an argument for an inclusive, integrated approach to the resolution of fingering challenges. It is not meant to be a compendium of fingerings; given the vast amount of keyboard literature now spanning more than 250 years, such a task would be impossible. It also does not attempt to survey all recorded efforts to address this complex and seemingly illusive subject throughout that long history. Rather, its chief aim is to promote alternatives to certain prevalent attitudes and practices, and to set the study of fingering on a more rational yet more comprehensive course.

Many of the excerpts found herein are put forth to demonstrate the astounding degree to which basic topographical combinations recur in the extant literature. Others serve as examples for practical application of those natural fingering principles that, when implemented, will also go far to ensure a healthful and easeful development of pianistic keyboard skills. Nonetheless, the "topographical" approach does not preclude certain fundamentals and underlying principles for "strategic" organization, many of long standing and proven efficacy, even though it will depart significantly from many others. For the sake of thoroughness and logical presentation such a context must also be considered.

FUNDAMENTAL STRATEGIES

9

Fingering is the strategy of the hands.
—Wanda Landowska

The rules of fingering have arisen from practical experience . . . some of these [rules] contradict each other in part. . . .
—József Gát

TO EXTEND THE GREAT LANDOWSKA'S THOUGHT,[1] we can assert that fingering is both strategy and tool—it is "means whereby." As such, it is an integral part of the pianist's process of learning, and retaining, a composition.

"Fingering" is an intellectual and practical tool for comprehension, synthesis, and memorization as well as a physical means to achieve desired technical, musical, interpretative and expressive ends. Persistent and consistent repetition is essential for its reinforcement and subsequent relegation to a response that is both reflexive ("automatic") and sensorial. Indeed, "repetition is the mother of retention."

As with all tools, effective employment of fingering options depends on an appropriate choice of tool and its skillful manipulation for the job "at hand." In a most literal sense, it must fit the hand so that the requisite force may be multiplied in the most mechanically efficient manner available.

STRATEGIES FOR THE HAND

It is probably no exaggeration to state that the *legato* action, with its "binding," "joining," or overlapping connection of successive tones, is the chief biomechanical and aesthetic aim underlying all basic approaches to fingering for the modern piano. Topographical considerations aside, experienced and knowledgeable pianists and teachers will generally concede that several principles in regard to the positioning of the hand and the grouping of notes to "lie within it" or "under it" are operative in their approaches to fingering.

The Basic Five-Finger Position

The "basic" position of the hand, neither contracted nor extended, is the stepwise five-finger, five-key position, thumb and fifth on the white keys; individual fingers are assigned to single, successive keys within the interval of a fifth.

This neutral position may be extended, contracted, or transferred/shifted ("translocated") in its entirety or in part.

Extending the Five-Finger Position

At a very elementary level, an *extension* of the five-finger position may be accomplished by an opening of the hand (second through fifth fingers) from the thumb, or the thumb from the hand.

Cadence patterns of triads and their inversions and the basic studies of Hanon books I and II exemplify this action, the five fingers thereby encompassing the interval of a sixth. With skill, the thumb may also be used for the legato binding of consecutive, usually stepwise tones—the so-called thumb legato. Although accomplished organists are well familiar with this technique, it is underemployed and little appreciated by pianists (Francis Taylor is the rare pianist who has written of it; proper training of this valuable action is a sorely neglected facet of pianists' thumb technique). *Glissando* fingerings, the sliding of a finger from key to key, easiest from black to white, may similarly extend, or contract, the position of the hand.

Extending the Hand's Movement Range

But a chief means of extending the hand's range of movement is the "passing under" of the thumb or the "passing over" of the hand, as in scales.

The other fingers of the hand may also extend from the thumb or apart from each other in this. Chords of four or more parts are examples, as are their arpeggiation (as *arpeggios*), which also involves the pivoting action of hand and thumb, but with the hand now in "open" position. Unnecessary stretches are to be avoided—although fingerings for widely spaced extended chord passages often do not comport with this very important basic principle.

Contracted or "Closed" Position

The hand also may assume a contracted position, in which the fingers play in a more "closed" position. Chromatic alterations necessitate such *contraction*, in which the hand must now spatially adjust itself to the requisite half-steps. Typical are chromatic scales of all fingerings, in which the successive fingers used are each spaced a half-step apart despite their natural position in the hand.

Changes of finger for repeated notes and finger substitutions must also enlist such contraction in varying degrees, all involving more or less subtle changes of hand position. Finger substitutions are a common means of shifting the position of the hand.

Translocating

Note groups/patterns beyond the natural span of the hand and not negotiable by means of any of the preceding actions are transferred or shifted by means of the forearm or upper arm.

A series of triads would be an example of this *translocation* at an elementary level. Octave passages, large chords (these also involve extension) and single or grouped notes alternately located at the extremes of the keyboard's range and throughout its several registers are also representative. In such instances, a desired legato effect may be achieved by means of the speed of the arm shift, primarily under the control of the upper arm—with or without the help of the pedal. Where legato cannot actually be physically effected, the *quality* of the arm's movement in space can be translated into an "illusion" or sense of a legato connection, which aids, paradoxically, in both the sounding and the "matching" of tones. This is truly a "felt sense" and is not dependent on visual impression.

Dynamic shoulder joint/shoulder complex stabilization is a prime component in this, as is skillful control of the curvilinear components of upper arm movement.

Distribution and Redistribution

Passages as notated may be *redistributed* between the hands for ease, clarity and tonal control. Regarding the question as to whether or not a particular composer's fingering should be held to be inviolable, it is important that any redistribution enhance and reinforce the passage compositionally (e.g., in the matter of voicing, color, or texture). And it should be in accord with the composer's intent, as best it can be determined, and not simply a matter of "managing the notes." Redistribution must therefore be handled judiciously and with great skill, with care and attention to the sound that results. It should result in a new and different coordination that is superior to what was formerly possible for more efficient and effective tonal control.

For those who object on "purist" grounds, it is worth reminding that such redistribution occurs in any fugue of more than two voices and in other such "multidimensional" compositions in which the tones of a middle register melodic line must be divided between both hands. As for the score itself, any redistribution or absence of it is best considered only as reflecting the composer's own preference for execution.

What must be respected above all are the *implications* of a composer's notation and harmonic deployment; clarity, fluency and the integrity of individual voices are the chief concerns. Difference in tone quality due to awkward or cumbersome execution is not a reasonable rationale for rejecting a more facile execution that may be achieved by means of intelligent and musical redistribution. An orchestral transcription, for example, would not likely be purposely set out to reflect harshness in sonority or an awkwardness inhibiting a fluid, spontaneous rhythmic pulse—unless it was implied by a uniquely stylized character of the passage in question.

Ultimately, the "strategy of the hand" is assignment of groups of fingers to groups of notes (keys) for distribution by the arm variously throughout the range of the keyboard. A topographical approach to natural fingering includes all of the above as basic to the hand's positioning and grouping of the keys; they are reflected in all alterations and permutations of core patterns. As strategy, they remain in accord with both the practice and aims of any commonsense approach to fingering. An approach that allows for a full measure of the keyboard's topography is undoubtedly far more comprehensive, more "overarching." It is one that includes all that is valuable and time-tested but goes well beyond.

STRATEGIES FOR THE FINGERS

It is in the areas of specific finger assignment and use that the standard and topographical approaches depart significantly from each other. Both include the commonsense recommendation that the learned scale, chord and arpeggio fingerings are to be applied to passagework wherever possible. The earlier chapters have considered their differences in great detail.

But certain inferences, practices and "rules" have evolved from standard scale/arpeggio fingerings that are faulty from more than a strategic point of view. For example, the insistence that the initial note of a scalewise passage should be assigned to the fifth finger for the LH ascending or the RH descending too often determines that the scale fingerings as taught and learned will not be applicable and sensorial recognition disadvantaged. This is typically found in the numerous editions of etudes, sonatinas and sonatas of the Classical Period. To the degree that there are topographical advantages—notably in the standard RH fingerings for the major scales—they are now elusive and often appear to be no longer available to the player.

All-white-key C major, with its symmetrical (contrariwise) fingering pattern, has long been considered the basic, ideal model for the single note diatonic scale. But topographically it is the anomaly, along with its relative natural minor A. And as discussed earlier, those scales having black-key tonics give lie to all such arbitrary requirements having no legitimate biomechanical basis.[2] Again, the scales for the enharmonic keys, major and minor, are not the anomalies. Rather, they point us to topographically symmetrical solutions, and Chopin correctly intuited their significance.

As to other preferred uses of the fingers—some having a sound, practical basis, but many others misconceived—it is worthwhile to survey several other commonly held "strategic principles" and their applications.

Short Fingers Under, Long Fingers Over

Short fingers, not only the thumb, may "pass under" longer fingers; conversely, longer fingers may "cross over" shorter fingers. This depends greatly on topography, especially regarding issues of key depth. The 2-5 combination should be avoided in any such crossings—an admonishment also voiced quite early on by Franklin Taylor: "The contraction between the fore-finger and little finger . . . is probably the worse that can be made, and should always be avoided."[3] This has especially great bearing on choice of fingering for double third scales; the topographical fingerings do not employ this combination.

Strong Fingers, Weak Fingers

There are so-called strong and weak fingers, referring to a certain imputed relative strength among the fingers. Generally, the thumb and the third finger are the designated strong fingers while the second, fourth and fifth are considered to be weak.

Neuhaus, however, considered the third, fourth and fifth fingers to be weak[4] while József Gát deemed all fingers to be equally strong if adequately developed and properly used.[5] Gyorgy Sandor[6] does not consider them equal in strength but relates the matter of strength to one of "independence." He considers proper alignment to be a determining factor, as does George Kochevitsky.[7]

Certainly, the underdeveloped musculature of any finger will be "weak" relative to that of a more developed—or even overdeveloped—finger. But biophysically speaking, all fingers have what might be called "weight bearing" capabilities and functions. Whichever the finger choice, all will indeed depend on proper alignment, as well as consideration of their respective movement axes and appropriate action. Here too, form follows function.

Strong Fingers, Strong Beats; Weak Fingers, Weak Beats

Notes occurring on strong beats are assigned "strong" fingers; those on weak beats are assigned "weak" fingers. In addition to the so-called strong beats of each measure (e.g., the first and third in common time and the first in 3/4 time), the first notes of appoggiaturas and slurred note groups are all best taken by stronger weight-bearing fingers. This is complemented by assignment of weak fingers to the note of resolution or succeeding notes. But there are many passages that, in their entirety, may be considered—and harmonically are—extended appoggiaturas or multinote slur groups.

The musical issues here are those of articulation, "long" notes, strong ("down") beats, weak ("up") beats, the initial notes of appoggiaturas and slurs, and notes or note groups of preparation and resolution. All have an important vertical significance, emphasis and dimension. Unlike other instrumentalists, the pianist must initially "give more" to a long note for it to last. And because the relative lengths of long notes play an important role in the structure and shaping of a phrase, there is a certain inherent "hierarchy" of note values. Considerations of topography enable the pianist to enhance and expand its musical, interpretive and expressive substance.

Long and short fingers, key depth, point of key contact, key resistance and direction and speed of force application all have an impact on a musically inferred and required sense of "strong" or "weak." Dissonance-consonance (resolution) and tension-release are represented and realized here in harmonic, structural *and* physiological terms. But at its simplest, musically speaking, this sense is really one of "more" or "less." It is entirely relative in terms of tone production and may be effected in a number of ways.

Avoiding Weak Fingers

Weak fingers are to be avoided. The recommended avoidance of the so-called (incorrectly) weak fourth and fifth fingers is reflective of a gross misunderstanding of the unique physiological structure and biomechanical function of these fingers. It also reflects a bias favoring a "striking" of the key from a position of elevation; from that standpoint the fourth and fifth fingers are quite rightly seen to be at a disadvantage in this regard. Remarkably, several well-established artists, in a number of interviews and articles, have recommended avoiding the fourth finger whenever possible.

However, in octave passages of black and white keys, a chromatic scale for example, it is generally held that the fourth is to be assigned to a black key when following a white key played with the fifth. This is to assist in achieving *legato* (with best results in movement toward the torso). But a very developed sense of alignment and forward adjustment is essential in counteracting what should be only a very temporary misalignment of the fourth finger. Otherwise the essential role of the upper arm is greatly handicapped. The action and release of the thumb must be extremely well timed, with the upper arm always in the lead. For melodic passages in which the lower voice (RH) and upper voice (LH) need not be sustained, this fingering works well, as it also does on adjacent black keys. And for hands that can manage it, use of the third—even the second—can aid in achieving the desired legato connection in this case.

Chopin's "Octave" Etude, Opus 25 No. 10, is an outstanding example of this. The held notes of the chromatic outer sections, in B minor, readily reveal the limitations of injudicious use of the fourth finger on the black keys. At the same time, the lyrical middle section in B major—now with the *advantage* of five black keys!—offers us an ideal opportunity to develop an octave legato.

It is generally viewed that the fifth, because of its relative shortness and "weakness," best functions on a white key—and at the edge of the key, where there is a greater advantage in leverage (one of Schmitz's main contentions as well). But its considerable range of downward movement is almost universally underappreciated— if recognized at all. Movement from the base of its metacarpal, at the wrist, appreciably increases its range of flexion, which is already greater than the other fingers.

This is likewise true of the thumb. And in regard to the pianist's playing mechanism the fifth finger's own complementary role to that of the thumb and its unique significance in the hand's functioning structure is unjustifiably underestimated, if not neglected entirely. The size and prominence of the thumb's muscle mass—its muscle "mound," as we say—is often cited as physiological evidence of its uniquely important role in the functioning of the hand. And yet, the technical terminology for the thumb's mound as it correlates with the lesser mass of the fifth finger nonetheless says even more: thenar eminence is paired with *hypo*thenar eminence. Both, although ostensibly shorter than the other fingers in length, are capable of greater *downward* vertical range and are therefore compatible with any need for key depth adjustment.

Range of movement for both must be considered from their metacarpal base at the wrist.

Most unfortunately, available editions manifest this limited understanding and underappreciation of the fifth finger's potential. In fact, the fifth finger is studiously avoided, by and large. We have seen, for example, that the fingerings for double third scales commonly in use typify such avoidance of the fifth finger (Liszt, Leschetizky, Dohnányi, Cooke et al.): only one five-finger, five-note group per octave is employed. Consequently, the full benefit gained from use of the entire hand is greatly minimized, both in execution and in potential development. Although the 53-42-31-21/53-42-31 (4+3) sequence in current favor takes fuller advantage of the hand's grasp, it has the disadvantage of requiring the extremely awkward and destabilizing crossing of the second finger over the fifth in movement away from the torso. In contrast to both of these approaches, the topographical fingerings advanced herein *maximize* the use of the entire hand and its ability to secure a grasp of—a "grip" on—the keys. Optimum coordination and requisite factors for stabilization are "built into" the fingering choices.

Thumb Shifts

The position of the thumb determines the position of the hand. Shifts of the thumb are therefore to be kept to a minimum in passagework, in keeping with its customary deployment in scales and arpeggios. This follows in extended chord passages as well, despite the lateral distance between the fingers. But an obvious necessity for frequency of thumb shifts in chromatic scales, octaves and other double notes pervades the literature of the post-Classical period. And a biophysically sound use of the playing mechanism (see Appendix 10) supports such frequently recurring thumb use. In fact, with its ability to assist in pronation, the thumb plays a crucial role in implementing the arm's natural swing away from the torso.[8]

Thumb on a Black Key

The thumb may be *freely* assigned to a black key. As specifically advocated, this is to permit consistent adherence to a specific fingering of a motif or other compositional pattern, one that is to be preferred regardless of a particular key and its topographical implications—or comfort.

Even were such an approach ostensibly defended on purely interpretive grounds, it could not possibly be appropriate given topographical changes that are significantly dissimilar when transposed. Differences in key length, width, resistance and—especially—depth would affect physical response appreciably. The entire "mix" would change.

Nonetheless, *any* fingering may be positively affected by the degree to which the player is skilled in such techniques as the "vibratory" movements espoused by Thomas Fielden (advocated and advanced by composer Paul Creston in his *Virtuoso Technique for the Pianist*) or those of weight release and distribution. Famously championed by Isabella Vengerova—but also József Gát, Gyorgy Sandor, the "Russian" school, and many others, these specific techniques are but two examples. However, they are in fact very related and serve as options that better address topographical considerations, particularly in respect to strong-weak beats (accents) as well as repeated notes and sequenced figures.

These *strategies*, with noted exceptions, remain basic to all rational approaches to fingering, whether or not topography is a primary consideration. It is safe to say, for example, that pianists find themselves in agreement about fingering for scales having four or more black keys as well as the fingering alternatives for arpeggios that their inversions offer. All reflect, in one way or another, commonly held fingering "strategies" of long standing.

Commentary aside, there is probably little new here. But for our purposes, strategies—which are nonetheless arbitrary, even if logical—should be distinguished from deeper, more grounding "principles" that might in fact fundamentally govern a particular strategy.

10 FUNDAMENTAL PRINCIPLES FOR A NATURAL FINGERING

The shapes of our hand and the keyboard teach us how to use our fingers. . . . I shall build upon Nature, for a natural fingering devoid of unnecessary strain and extension is clearly the best.
—Carl Philipp Emanuel Bach

The word principle in itself refers to the beginning of something. The word fundamental as used here refers to a foundation. Fundamental principles must then offer concrete initial foundations on which it is possible to construct solidly and develop extensively.
—E. Robert Schmitz

A NATURAL FINGERING *process* is one that follows from the keyboard's fixed physical characteristics as "first cause." The underlying *principles of the keyboard* reside in its topography and topology—the surface features and the distances they represent. The playing mechanism's functional structure and natural ability to negotiate space are wedded to them. It is from these fundamental, "topographical" principles that a topographical strategy may proceed.

All govern a fingering approach that integrates the topographical, physiological and kinesiological. One may of necessity supersede another at times, while others interrelate and interact—may even intersect, literally—to varying degrees. But they are never in conflict; all reflect the body's natural ability to negotiate keyboard space—in fact, any space. At its simplest, topography is all about keyboard space. And technique is all about *movement* within that keyboard space: movement to and from the key, and movement of the key.

Emotion too is about movement. It is the movement of our feelings, our inner visceral reaction to sensory *impressions*; its *expression* in physical space is biokinetic. The piano becomes an extension of our means of expression, giving voice to its physical manifestation within the confines of the keyboard.

As such the piano is a tool ("instrument") and must be properly grasped—literally. The keyboard is the point of contact, the place where the rubber meets the road, where body and instrument meet and—ideally—become one. It is at this juncture that the most natural response permits true spontaneity and expressive immediacy. If it is ever to happen at all, it is here where one should not be able to distinguish "the player from the play."

The principles advanced in this chapter reflect fundamental considerations of topography, physiology and mechanics as they have an impact on fingering choice; movement, energy and application of force are always at issue. Conversely, fingering choice cannot fail to have significant biokinetic implications of its own.

What are these fundamental principles? How are they linked to the keyboard's topography? How do they affect pianism, by application or default? How should they govern finger choice?

At their core, these principles reflect topographical attributes that remain constant. But the several units of the playing mechanism must ever adapt to them within their own limits of movement potential as well as within the limits of keyboard space. And these spatial parameters are largely determined by certain fixed physical limitations of the keyboard. In seating himself at the instrument, the performer establishes a "movement center," the position from which he thereafter adapts and orients himself and his movements to the various ranges of the keyboard—all within these parameters.

But the spatial restrictions encountered are, curiously enough, where the pianist needs them least. Laterally, the extensive range of the keyboard itself prescribes movement, but poses no formidable obstacle within its bounds. Horizontally forward, however, the pianist's movements are limited by the fallboard.[1] And vertically downward the keybed itself limits the scope of movement.

So it is that horizontal movement backward and vertical movement upward are limited only by the pianist's own physiological structure and position. Yet herein lies the most basic barrier—a seductive one at that—to an approach that is biomechanically and kinesiologically most efficient and most natural. The keyboard's spatial limitations encourage excessive movement upward and backward, while discouraging or obscuring the full range of curvilinear movement that is nonetheless possible, even within the relatively diminished parameters described by fallboard and keybed.

The body must nevertheless constantly orient and adapt itself to the keyboard within these established and limited parameters. But in this, a most fundamental article of faith—long held by many if not most—meets its first challenge: were the arm "relaxed" it would fall from the keyboard and tend toward the body, eventually coming to rest in anatomical position at the side of the torso. The upper and lower playing units of the arm cannot maintain any position on or orientation to the keyboard absent muscular control. To the extent that a passive "free fall" can be effected—and this extent is nonetheless considerable—it can take place only within movement parameters initially established and thereafter dynamically maintained by the pianist's neuro-skeletal-muscular system.

This adaptability, if it is to be maximally efficient and flexible, must be rooted in thorough comprehension of the keyboard's topographical attributes and the playing mechanism's options in response to them. The aim must be to establish and maintain such an optimal orientation *throughout the entire range* of the keyboard, even while the performer's lower torso must necessarily remain appropriately centered and grounded—though ever poised for movement.

In one way or another and to one degree or another, these responses constitute *adjustments* of the playing mechanism to planes of movement as they mutually intersect: vertically, horizontally, laterally and obliquely. All movement at the keyboard occurs within these planes, and fingering choice ultimately reflects *and* influences movement choice. Generally speaking, involuntary movements are not indicative of exceptional technique.

Conscious, deliberative consideration and implementation of the following fundamental principles support fingering solutions that most effectively integrate the keyboard's topographical demands with coordinated movement at the keyboard. But seen another way, the keyboard as we have it is designed to fit the hand—as all well-designed tools are.

KEY PLANE

The keyboard is biplanar, requiring *horizontal* adjustments throughout its range. Interplanar movements occur principally within its two planes: a lower one of white keys and a higher one of black, each bounded in front by the fallboard and on either side from bass to treble, the keyboard's *lateral* range.

Biplanar transitions may be effected by in-out, forward-backward movements of the entire playing mechanism that are controlled by the *upper arm*—as in the case of octaves, a series of chords, or any wide interval beyond the hand's natural reach or grasp. Where the basic finger-to-finger legato connection can be maintained, finger articulation (see Appendix 9) can also be enlisted to enable a more coordinated transition and adjustment from plane to plane. These *motor fingers* elevate and displace forward the arm's mass, its weight subsequently released as a force factor in key activation and tone production.

It should never be considered that the thumb simply "plays" or is assigned a black key. Transposition of the thumb to a black key determines that the entire hand *and arm* are now located in the black-key plane. All movement is then oriented and occurs within this black-key plane. Conversely, it should be remarked that assignment of long fingers to black keys—even the fifth—constitutes movement in the white-key plane *if the thumb is so oriented*.

KEY LENGTH

Key length is the principal factor in complementary assignment of *fingers* to the keyboard. This represents an alternative for *horizontal adjustment* of the arm; interplanar adjustments forward and backward ("in" and "out") are thereby kept to a minimum.

The maxim ("working principle") **short fingers on long keys, long fingers on short keys** reflects the inherent compatibility of the hand to naturally adjust for differences in key *length*. But this must also include length adjustments for the (variable) distance from key fulcrum to any subsequent point of key contact—not exclusively that at key end.

Schmitz's approach to in-out adjustments (he was apparently the first to thoroughly consider and analyze these movements) is not only biplanar but also based on the fact that each key, a lever, is played most easily at its very end. This point being the greatest distance from the key's fulcrum, the least degree of resistance is encountered since its leverage is maximized. Others have noted this advantage as well. But this has served as a faulty rationale for insisting that the fifth finger, declared "weak," play on the edge of each white key whenever possible.[2]

Although it is true that resistance at the key's edge is at a minimum, it must also be considered that the playing mechanism functions as a *series* of levers. With the key-and-hammer action itself a series of levers, levers are therefore acting on levers. The angle and length through which force is applied are therefore important factors in overcoming the resistance encountered at the varying points of key engagement. If fingers are assigned topographically *and aligned correctly*, force is multiplied by finger length to optimal mechanical advantage.

But so it is that swinging the key into motion at its endmost point of contact can often result, paradoxically, in *less* sensitivity to key resistance and diminished tonal control. This is precisely due to each finger's individual length, strength and other innate abilities—not to mention such variables as the arm's pull of weight. The in-out and lateral adjustments required for a (less) coordinated response at each key end would therefore necessitate an increase in the amount of movement and energy/force commensurate with the increased range of distance traversed. Tempo (time) is obviously a significant factor.

However, the differences in key resistance at the various points of contact are effectively neutralized or counterbalanced by a *functionally correct* position of the hand (see Appendix 10). This natural placement of the hand maintains the *relative* position of the fingers as in anatomical position and best serves as the point of departure for any necessary lateral adjustments for alignment and leverage. These situate the playing mechanism for the most sensitive and effective response to the resistance of the key—with movement that is minimal and subtle, yet maximally effective.

KEY DEPTH

Key depth is the *downward vertical* corollary for assignment of long and short fingers.

The distance to key surface for initial contact and its subsequent depression to key bottom may also be naturally adjusted by the relative lengths and physiological capabilities of the fingers. At its most basic, finger length relative to key depth is the chief determinant in successful execution of an appoggiatura, whatever the technical approach.

The relative lengths of fingers may be thus assigned to compensate for, or to adjust for relative differences in, *depth*. In this, it is not only finger length that proves advantageous but relative range of vertical movement as well. In order of effectiveness, the thumb, third and fifth fingers best adjust for differences in the level of key *depression* to be negotiated. Recall the advantage gained in their reciprocal substitution when "fine-tuning" fingering for double thirds.

But also note that adjustments for key depth—or for *maintaining* key depth as the upper arm transports the lower arm throughout the keyboard's wide range—may be effected in several ways. Chief among these is elevation or depression of the wrist-forearm, or the entire shoulder complex itself. However, fingering choice is the first "line of defense."

The topographical fingerings for scales, arpeggios and double notes exemplify consistent application of this natural adjustment. It is fundamental to the core topographical patterns and one of the most significant factors in their effectiveness. Its value is especially evident in locations at increasing distance from the arm's anatomical midline (see also "Distant Location" below). *And it is of prime importance in determining the most suitable fingering combinations for trills and other ornaments.*

For example, playing (away from the torso) a white key with the third finger and then a black key with the fourth finger naturally compensates for differences in key depth. The long third finger on the depressed white key complements the relative shortness of the fourth finger and its preparatory contact with the height of the not-yet-depressed black key. The fact that the fourth finger by itself has a lesser range of elevation (extension) is not of any significant account. The upper arm, with humerus inward, naturally elevates as the lateral adjustment of the hand at the wrist brings the fourth finger into alignment with the forearm (more precisely, its ulna) for vertical action. This is similarly the case with the shorter fifth following the relatively longer fourth.

However, this same WB sequence played by the second and third fingers may at first seem to be contradictory. But in fact, the principle holds true: the third, with its greater length and capacity for elevation, can still negotiate the height of the black key relative to the depressed white key, even though engaged by the shorter second finger aided by the range of pronation. In reverse (toward the torso), the *already depressed* black key neutralizes the relative shortness of the second about to play the succeeding white key.

This is similarly the case, away from the torso, when the fourth finger is assigned to a white key following the third on a black key: the fourth finger's larger range for flexion—and therefore key depression—adequately compensates for difference in depth. Recall that, as discussed earlier, the spatial requirements for thumb-under pivoting involving white keys only are yet another matter (see Appendix 10).

Resolution of all topographical issues surrounding key depth is significantly aided by appreciation of the *movement range* for each finger, as well as considerations of length. This is likewise with *any* fingering combinations employing the thumb. In collaboration with pronation and inner humeral rotation, its range of movement downward surpasses that for any of the other fingers.

The topographical fingerings for scales and arpeggios also confirm this principle in movement toward the torso, even though it is the hand that is pivoting on the thumb. In this case, the hand elevates in "crossing over" the thumb, as it does also in its lateral extension from the thumb, unless deliberately restricted. The distance through which any finger must contact and engage a key to its bottom[3] is increased as a consequence. The ensuing vertical distance for key contact and depression is decreased by a subsequent black key, but increased if it is a white key.

This bears greatly on which fingers best succeed the thumb in movement toward the torso: generally speaking, W to W is best taken by the longer third finger, W to B by the fourth—*unless* the horizontal distance traversed (interval size) is better served by the longer third. What is always at issue is relative finger length and range of movement as it facilitates vertical key depression; oblique movement in the service of key depression is remarkably inefficient biokinetically.[4]

The key depth principle derives from the topographical *inversion* of the Fundamental Pattern: BWWWB. It comports with diatonic alterations of the Fundamental Pattern and can be seen to have a sound basis in the hand's natural ability to adjust to the topographical demands of the keyboard in an optimally efficient fashion. It is a prime example of the wedding of physiology and topography. The pianist will find this specific application of great advantage in working out fingering challenges encountered in the repertoire.

KEY HEIGHT

Key height is the *upward vertical* corollary for assignment of long and short fingers. This principle interrelates and interacts with considerations of key depth but chiefly concerns the matter of the horizontal black-white key *planes* to the extent that they are a factor in preserving or creating space to accommodate the requisite curvilinear movement of the fingers.

Recalling the keybed's restriction for vertical movement downward, adequate vertical space *upward* is therefore necessary for the most effective, coordinated action of **short fingers under long and long fingers over short**. This principle also reflects the need to ensure and facilitate the full complement of the mechanism's rotational components for *oblique* adjusting movements within these planes.

Considering the *height* of the key relative to finger length affords the possibility of adequate space for "thumb under" pivoting in movement away from the torso, and for the movement "under" of other short fingers relative to long. The pivoting action of a black-key fourth finger—or even fifth (!)—followed by a white thumb is particularly demonstrative of the advantage afforded by this topographical application.

The longer third naturally provides more space from white key to white key. But in extended patterns such as arpeggios of the diminished triad, the finger length necessary to encompass the larger interval also best augments pivoting space. The principles interact; the topographical considerations intersect.

For the RH ascending or LH descending, the fourth finger on a white key followed by the longer third on a black—or even the third followed by the shorter second—is also demonstrative. Here, key depth and key height correlate with the relative finger lengths.

Key height relative to finger length is an extremely important factor in any pivoting action. As agents in alignment for weight transfer and legato control, *all* fingers in effect serve as pivot fingers. In their articulation[5] of the key and their role in the displacement of weight forward and upward for subsequent release, this principle effectively applied aids in minimizing or eliminating superfluous arm movements and unnecessary stretches.

DISTANT LOCATION

Application of this principle reflects judicious consideration and integration of all the above natural adjustments of the fingers to the keyboard's topography, but as they are specifically encountered in arm movement *crossing the torso and then extending beyond it*.

Approaching these "distant locations"—the upper treble reaches of the keyboard for the left hand, and the lower reaches for the right hand—the *laterally oblique* orientation of the arm relative to the keyboard and torso is the primary determinant for finger choice.

As the upper arm locates the keys and positions the lower arm at such distances increasingly further from its anatomical midline, the need arises for adjustments to establish or maintain key depth due to the corresponding elevation. At these distant locations, the relatively longer fingers are therefore to be favored over the thumb for proper alignment and uniform contact with key bottom. In accommodating distance (reach) that is now laterally oblique relative to the keyboard, they will correlate with any need for the arm's adjustment for key depth via shoulder complex depression. Moreover, use of the thumb in these distant locations is aided in this way, should pattern or strategy dictate: the long fingers guide the upper arm in its optimal orientation for alignment and stabilization.

Maintaining an inward rotation of the humerus (an important dynamic of shoulder joint/shoulder complex stabilization), avoiding so-called ulnar deviation (a "twisting" of the hand toward the thumb) and properly aligning the lower mechanisms within the upper arm's curvilinear (elliptical) movement path optimally enables application of this indispensable principle. It is worthwhile to note how frequently children will instinctively favor using a long finger rather than the thumb at these distant locations.

PRINCIPLES AND PROCESS

Correlation of finger length is the primary natural adjustment to key plane, length, depth and height. But in calculating any keyboard adjustment, the arm's range of movement is correctly gauged from its own anatomical midline, not its distance from the torso. Consideration of relative finger lengths will therefore be indispensable in departing from the arm's midline and in crossing the torso to the extreme ranges (distant location).

Correlative to considerations of key depth and key height in assigning long and short fingers—at the very core of the topographical fingerings for the fundamental forms—it is necessary to establish optimal vertical space for the thumb-under pivoting action. This permits the rotational component of this complex movement ensemble to function with maximum efficiency and effectiveness in its curvilinear path[6]—one that is not an arc, but an ellipse.

Depression of the shoulder girdle/shoulder complex variously aided by torso flexion and rotation at the hip axis most effectively assists in maintaining uniform key depth throughout the keyboard's range (see Appendix 10). In all of this, proper and adequate stabilization relevant to the dynamic functioning of the entire playing mechanism is a chief consideration in fingering choice and plays a primary role in its execution. Shoulder complex stabilization is in turn significantly affected—positively or negatively—by choice and execution.

TOPOGRAPHY, SYMMETRY AND LINES OF ACTION

11

The thumb was passed . . . the hand still retaining its horizontal position. . . . I know from experience that by this method an equal and steady style of performance is attainable even when it is necessary to pass the thumb after the [fourth] or [fifth] finger, as in the Scherzo in B♭.
—Jan Kleczyński

The keyboard as it is constituted was perhaps best fitted for music from 1700 to 1880 and has become more and more awkward since then.
—Charles Rosen

CHOPIN'S RECOGNITION of the important role of the enharmonic scales, the implications of his Fundamental Pattern, and his insights into topography and pianism as further reflected in his compositional key choice remain nothing short of revolutionary. Even considered on its own, Chopin's Fundamental Pattern is not only the exemplar of the symmetrical mirroring of all the major scales but also representational of the hand's most natural orientation to the biplanar keyboard. No other keyboard pattern can lay claim to this distinction. It is "fundamental" by any measure, and not for nothing has Neuhaus elevated it to preeminence.

The patterns that result from its alteration are found to embody all the topographical combinations the pianist encounters, and they give rise to the fundamental principles operative in the hand's engagement with the keyboard. The three adjacent black keys are viewed not as anomalies but the basic points of departure for the hand's topographical adaptation. Indeed, with the third finger assigned to A-flat/G-sharp and the outer intervals extended to octave D, the architectural or structural "pillars" of the hand—representing as they do its transverse and length axes (see Appendix 10)—now encompass the keyboard's points of symmetry. Though the pattern is now D-G♭-A♭-B♭-D/D-F♯-G♯-A♯-D its topographical construction remains the same.

It has been demonstrated that the five core patterns reflecting topographical and tonal alterations may be seen as fingering "proxies" for all major and minor forms of the scales, including double thirds (*primary* pattern). And translocated—one cannot say transposed here—four-part chords are found in them; horizontally extended, these configurations similarly serve as proxies for all arpeggios. Even chromatic fingering patterns are implicitly represented in the Fundamental Pattern, exclusively providing as it does for the half-step topographies of WWB on the thumb side and BWW on fifth finger side (see Chapter 14).

One may go still further and point out that the Fundamental Pattern may be altered in other ways. Considered as a basic five-finger pattern, it may be altered harmonically and modally to function as a *secondary* pattern, as first discussed in Chapter 5 and later in Chapter 7 (the formula for diatonic double third scales). Recall that the distinguishing feature of a secondary pattern is the *absence* of a fourth finger black-key pivot.

As Chopin set it forth for the RH, it also represents the first five tones of the Lydian mode (in other terms, the E major scale with a raised subdominant), the mode most characteristic of Polish folk music. Perhaps this was simply irresistible for Chopin: its raised fourth degree typically abounds in his Mazurkas, that generic, collective title given for the three distinct folk dances represented therein. But the point remains that the Fundamental Pattern is rife with possibilities of all kinds. It may be viewed in many ways.

Chopin's pattern is now generally taken to be that of a whole tone scale. But as he laid it out for us, it would be considered as a proxy for the D-flat major scale in the LH and for that of its mirror, the B major scale in the RH. These are the very distinctions Chopin himself made in advocating these scales as the ones that should be first introduced. But except for smaller hands, the whole step between the fourth and fifth fingers is more natural—and surely this was so for the sizeable span of his own hand.

One can make the fair speculation that Chopin chose these keys to illustrate unmistakably their mirrored symmetry as major keys with the same number of sharps or flats. For surely G-flat and F-sharp (six flats and sharps respectively), representing the Fundamental Pattern as they do, mirror likewise. But a Fundamental Pattern representing these keys would not accommodate the thumb as naturally—except for very small hands (see Chapter 14).

Again, Chopin's *méthode* was left to us incomplete and rather vague in many important respects. We must defer to his students' varying accounts in these and many other matters; infer from his own imprecise language in some cases; and extrapolate, in other cases, in order to reap the full benefit of his groundbreaking approach. But as we have noted earlier, what is fundamental is the topographical arrangement; the exact interval taken by the fourth and fifth fingers—thumb and second also—is easily altered to accommodate the individual hand.

In addressing other alterations of the first and fifth tones of the Fundamental Pattern, the two white keys taken by the thumb and fifth finger, there is much to be gained by first considering their white-key relationship to each other before then turning to their relocation to black keys. A deeper analysis and understanding of the mutually opposing actions of thumb and fifth leads us to further appreciate the implications of this basic white-key to white-key relationship. Whether *dynamic* (muscular contraction does not result in a change of position: *cross tension* or *modeling* for example) or occurring as a repositioning in space, this movement in their diagonal, or *transverse*, plane is the fundament for all octaves and all patterns involving thumb and fifth finger.

Chopin himself (and later Busoni) did not eschew the pivoting of thumb and fifth, as his compositions readily attest.[1] Indeed, an extraordinary wealth of passagework from the Romantic Period onward otherwise defies classification in terms of a more rational, more natural and more pianistic approach to fingering.

As the movement axis from thumb to fifth, the positioning or location of this transverse plane is the key to proper placement of the hand vis-à-vis the keyboard (Appendix 10) and relevant to any specific group of keys. Optimal alignment and efficient, effective shoulder joint/shoulder complex stabilization follows from this since radial, length and ulnar axes must be in proper relation to an inwardly rotated humerus. Lateral adjustments can then be well coordinated with *all* pivoting actions and with all movement involving a transfer of weight or downward force. And in this way the fundamental conditions for coordinated curvilinear movement—as action and reaction—among all units of the playing mechanism are established.

The natural elevation of the hand in any of its movement away from the thumb (one must otherwise purposefully contravert it) takes place primarily in relation to this diagonal, transverse axis. Because of this and a resulting close proximity to the black-key plane, the fifth finger quite naturally finds its place on a black key. The altered Fundamental Pattern, now BBBBW/WBBBB, is in reality quite as comfortable as with the fifth on the white key—and for a very great many pianists, even more so.

This natural orientation, with thumb remaining assigned to a white key and fifth on black, is encountered with remarkable frequency once one becomes aware of it and recognizes it as a *bona fide* keyboard pattern. Along with the pattern altered for the thumb on a black key, WBBBB/BBBBW, it will not be foreign to pianists who have included cadences in their practice regimen from their earliest years. Both of these orientations also typify double note topographies with an abundance of black keys, and their fingerings follow from this (Chapters 7 and 8).

But in the realm of extrapolation, there are other topographical possibilities worthy of exploration in addition to those of white- to black-key alteration, pattern reposition (translocation) or interval reconstruction. The Fundamental Pattern (WBBBW) may also be inverted. In this case the long fingers adjust for key depth rather than key length (BWWWB). And both thumb and fifth may be altered (BBBBB), positioning the hand entirely in the black-key plane.

In these arrangements resides the key to fingering figurations and combinations that do not seem to squarely fit, or to obviously derive from, basic keyboard patterns that are harmonic or modal. Topography remains the chief determinant and the Fundamental Pattern the origin, the *Urgrund*.

That the long fingers will be found to ideally adjust for key depth rather than key length if the Fundamental Pattern is inverted is the reason that chords and basic five-finger positions on many black-key tonics are generally found to be quite comfortable, differences in key resistance notwithstanding. Again, it is only the topographical issues surrounding thumb-hand pivoting that are, on the whole, problematic.

If the whole-tone Fundamental Pattern is converted from WBBBW to BBBBB, the resulting pattern is now pentatonic. In Chopin's well-known "Black Key" Etude (Opus 10 No. 5), the fingering of this altered pattern is by far the superior solution (see below). And in extending both patterns beyond the range of an octave, fingering options are necessarily limited, though all essentially involve diagonal movements of thumb and fifth along their transverse axis (Appendix 10). With these topographies, the pivoting action of thumb and fifth is unavoidable. But, surprisingly, the movement is most natural—*if* this axis is respected.

The conjoining of Eschmann-Dumur's discovery of major scale symmetry and Chopin's insight into the pianistic principles represented by his Fundamental Pattern inevitably leads us to reconsider the generally accepted (standard) fingerings for the scales. Even when approached only from the standpoint of keyboard symmetry, topography becomes the key player in a rational reappraisal and reordering of scale fingerings first for the left hand; those for the RH logically follow from this. The pianistic security and comfort emanating from this newfound consistency cannot help but invite further analysis and consideration of the implications. "But why do they work?" we must ask. And long-held "maxims" and misconceptions are inevitably challenged.

The issues surrounding the fourth finger are not only indicative but uppermost. In reconfiguring the fingerings to take in the full implications of Chopin's and Eschmann-Dumur's contributions, they simply may not be avoided—and indeed, it has never been possible to really do so. But there have been conscious, albeit misguided, attempts to ignore or dismiss the matter. Symptoms of misuse, overuse, over- and underdevelopment, as well as poor or inadequate training, have themselves—singularly or all together—been taken as evidence of some negative inherent nature regarding the hand's ability to accommodate itself to the keyboard. The "individual hand" and "individual preference" have thus become the last refuge of an archaic approach with severely limited underpinnings.

Such arguments are a red herring, in the absence of a deeper investigation of finger choice and healthy technical solutions; there remains plenty of room for individual choice within the realm of a resolution of pianistic problems that nonetheless manifest a sounder physiological and kinesiological foundation. The full range of the fourth finger's natural function and movement potential is better explored and its unique role better exploited, for example, than dismissing it as "weak" or resignedly submitting to what has even been referred to as its "perverse but necessary usage."[2]

The realization that the fourth is the preferred pivot finger for thumb-under actions in movement away from the torso is a transforming one. So too, is realizing that its structure, strength when properly enlisted, and movement proclivities are designed to coordinate with the thumb's opposing action—all in the support and transmission of the powerful capabilities of the upper arm in its role as the generator and transmitter of force. Optimal alignment, ulnarly balanced movements and requisite shoulder complex stabilization are the indispensable cooperatives within the playing mechanism's entire kinetic chain—from the tips (base) of the shoulder blades to tips of the fingers, operative from one end of the keyboard to the other.

Such a reevaluation applies to the fifth finger as well: it is no "little player," even if its role in scale, arpeggio and trill fingerings is necessarily limited. But its use is unavoidable in large chords, double sixths and octaves. And we have seen that the search for a more balanced solution to fingering double thirds lies precisely in enlisting the fifth finger to enable consistent deployment of the prehensive—the gripping, grasping, seizing—abilities of the entire hand. This is absolutely essential for a healthy, more effective and more secure double note technique. In this regard it is highly worth noting that a German connotation for double note technique is Doppelgriff=Spiels.

Likewise, the key to the cooperative functions and movements of the hand reside in its own symmetry. Our everyday use obscures its remarkably functional architecture with an assumed familiarity. Even as pianists, we generally tend to see it in a rather limited context, although we place demands on it that far exceed those from any other profession, even from other instrumentalists. It must receive and transmit force, either of its own effort or with that of the lower and upper arm, the rest of the shoulder complex, or the torso. But the hand with its fingers is the premier connection, the first line of contact with the keys. The keyboard's topographical symmetry and the hand's own functional symmetry will each have their way—cooperatively or not, with either positive or negative impact.

This is where a deeper look at the physiological and kinesiological implications of Chopin's Fundamental Pattern takes on a life that goes far beyond simplistic and limited recognition or acceptance of it as a merely useful combination for finger exercise. Its topology is more than representative of an "ideal position" for the hand—and even more than signaling a rationale for generating topographical solutions for scale fingerings and other patterns and passages. In pursuing the movement potential of the hand and its digits as they relate to it, we discern this fuller potential as a true fundament. We are then privy to still further insight into the means for active assembling of key groups, distribution of force and production of tone.

We have already noted—and everyone is well familiar with—the unavoidable prevalence of thumb and fifth in the (planar) organization of white-to-white-key and black-to-black-key forms, such as octaves or chords of three or more voices. But where do these fit in our "natural fingering" scheme? Do they deserve or require any particular consideration from a topographical perspective? If so, how should this be done?

SYMMETRY AND SIMPLICITY

It is a rather curious fact that the keyboard is usually viewed as symmetrical only by virtue of the regular ordering of its black and white keys. But it is even more curious that some authors of technical treatises have (even recently) bemoaned its group of two black keys as "asymmetrical" vis-à-vis that of the three black keys.[3] Such an extremely limited and rather strange sense of what it is that constitutes keyboard symmetry is proffered while at the same time purporting to celebrate a defining aspect of this very same symmetry: what Ernst Bacon calls the "two centers of symmetry" (D and A-flat/G-sharp).[4] Although this should be taken as a sincere though confused attempt to bring topography into the equation in discussion of keyboard orientation, it fails unequivocally with its (literally) superficial appraisal.

Instead, the "foot is cut to fit the shoe" and old fingering usage is merely applied to the surface (planar) topography. In such an approach, individual topographical characteristics do not have a notable impact on the genesis of fingering solutions. Applying consistent finger patterns continues to take precedence over all other considerations, which is simplistic in light of a topographical symmetry that will not go away. Arm shifts therefore take precedence over a fundamental orientation of the fingers to the keys—but their differing lengths also will not go away. The individual functions of each finger and its unique relationship to the lower (hand and forearm) and upper arm are also given no significant importance.

But deeper investigation into topography and symmetry reveals a fundamental organization that is far more relevant and practical. A true simplicity is to be found in the confluence of the keyboard's symmetrical design and the hand's functional architecture, this architecture sporting a symmetry of its own as it navigates the keyboard's *topology*. It is an innate simplicity that supports rational keyboard organization in matters of fingering. From this follow clarity of comprehension and ease of execution.

In Chopin's presentation of the Fundamental Pattern, the third and longest finger is assigned to G-sharp in the RH (B major scale) and A-flat in the LH (D-flat major scale). Seen then as representative scale fragments—i.e., as four-finger groups beginning with the thumbs—analysis shows that they mirror exactly in interval and topography. This is, of course, very interesting but perhaps of no particular account in itself at first (recall that Cortot never did get the point). We all know that both scales share all five black keys and each is characterized theoretically by five sharps or flats.

Whether the Fundamental Pattern is taken to be a whole-tone five-finger pattern or seen as a basic finger group of either of those scales is also of little moment for our present purpose. We have already noted that, on the whole, the major-minor five-finger patterns bear little or no relevance to the fingerings for the scales whose modes they are supposed to represent. Degrees other than, or in addition to, the third must be altered before any significant relation to the actual scale fingerings—standard or topographical—is achieved. And these alterations chiefly involve the fourth finger of either hand. It is most important to keep in mind that the interval relationships of major scale degrees four through seven (the four notes of the topographical "four group") are all whole tones. No doubt our attention to the essential, defining half-step leading tone function of seven to eight obscures this other important fact.

Moving, then, the fourth finger "down" (RH) or up (LH) one black key of the Fundamental Pattern—a whole step, and a rational interpretation of Chopin's dictum—we are privy to some interesting observations and a rather astounding conclusion. The whole-tone series of the four fingers now assigned to a BBWW topographical arrangement is that of degrees 4, 5, 6 and 7 of the A (RH) and E-flat (LH) major scales respectively—each having three sharps or flats and three black keys. They too mirror as to interval and topography. But in either hand, the thumb is now assigned to D and the fourth finger to A-flat/G-sharp—both points of symmetry!

This is all the more important in that we have already observed that a key signature of three sharps or flats represents a certain de facto "line of demarcation," beyond which topography trumps other influences. Recall the genesis of the diatonic double third fingerings from a core topographical perspective. And most significantly, recall that Chopin's compositions are largely written in key signatures of three or more sharps or flats. Or with three or more black keys: B minor, for example, has a key signature (D major) of two black keys, but the harmonic and melodic forms own three and four black keys respectively. In this light, key signatures are deceptive indicators of a topographical imperative.

Moving down or up (each hand) yet one more black key—RH to F-sharp and LH to B-flat—reveals the most surprising relationship of all. With each thumb now on either side of point of symmetry D (RH below it and LH above), we see that the major scale of one flat (F) exactly mirrors that of one sharp (G). And with RH on B-flat and LH on F-sharp—altered for diatonic scale degrees—vice versa! It begs the question as to whether this inverse relationship is true of the other major keys as well. It takes but a short leap to discover that this is indeed so with all major scales, whether proceeding by whole step or by fourth or fifth.

The lowered sixth degree (parallel minor) is characteristic of the harmonic minor form. The requisite alteration of the respective whole tone four groups for G and F (in both cases involving the third finger of either hand) displays a topographical symmetry similarly available for consistent application in the fingering for other harmonic minor scales as well (see Chapters 2 and 13). The process toward symmetrical solutions invariably proves to be not only a rational one but a simple one as well.

This characteristic augmented second (2+ of the altered sixth and seventh scale degrees) is also an enharmonic minor third. Recall that the fully diminished seventh (o7) is constructed entirely of minor thirds, the octave being divided equally into those intervals. Also, that there are only three diminished chords comporting with topographical fingering when they are extended as arpeggios: only three in which the leading principle of "fourth on black, thumb on white" is manifest. We also observed that these very same chords consequently mirror each other in their topographical construction (Chapter 3).

Now taking the full-diminished seventh chord built on the white key tritone—that defining interval of equal temperament! (remember that points of symmetry D and A-flat/G-sharp are tritones, and that the tritone divides the octave in half)—F in the LH and B in the RH with thumbs equidistant from point of symmetry D, we note that the fourth finger of each hand is assigned to point of symmetry A-flat/G-sharp). Moving the fourth finger by a perfect fifth—down in the RH, up in the LH—we arrive at the other two "topographically correct" full-diminished seventh chords (all minor thirds). All mirroring implies symmetry by definition, and examples of such keyboard relationships are legion.

TOPOGRAPHY AND TOPOLOGY

The upward or downward whole tone shift of the fourth finger brings with it an accompanying shift of the fifth finger. It is a transposition of the Fundamental Pattern, its sequence of whole tone tones merely beginning and ending on a different pitch. But the topographical sequence of black and white keys has changed, and therefore the pattern's topology: the hand must now relate to, orient and adjust itself to, different points on the keyboard surface. *Although the intervals remain the same, the hand's orientation does not.*

This is most notable when the fifth finger is shifted upward to B-flat in the LH and downward to F-sharp in the RH: thumb and fifth are now exclusively assigned to the black keys, the three long fingers to the white. Remarkably, this shifting and transposing of the whole tone pattern results in a symmetrical *inversion* of the Fundamental Pattern. The third finger is again assigned to a point of symmetry, but this new assignment of long fingers to the white keys reveals their new adjusting function: to key depth rather than key length.

The point of symmetry at which this now occurs is at D instead of A-flat/G-sharp. With thumb and fifth now taking B-flat and F-sharp, we are at that very area at which a certain amount of controversy has always existed: the four-part chord and arpeggio fingerings for LH B-flat major and RH B minor (Chapter 3). Recall, too, that for both hands the major and minor triads for B-flat/B are topographical anomalies compared to the black-white construction of the other major-minor triads. Liszt was obviously aware of this particular arrangement since he makes consistent use of it in arriving at his double third fingerings for the enharmonic keys. For him it serves as the core, to which he allocates the sole five-finger group of his fingering sequence.

With the long fingers now compensating for key depth instead of key length, this arrangement too is "topographically correct" and is a model for like topographies. Its most important significance, however, is that it is the model for the hands' ideal orientation in the *black-key plane*—just as the Fundamental Pattern serves as the model for that in the white-key plane. But a symmetrical focus on D rather than the A-flat/G-sharp-centered Fundamental Pattern also leads to other implications residing in Chopin's Fundamental Pattern, owing in particular to issues of thumb-hand pivoting.

Execution of patterns and figurations in the black-key plane can now be seen in a new light: some fingerings are more natural and topographically accommodative, and some passages are more amenable to a natural resolution. This new whole tone group (B♭-C-D-E-F♯ and its enharmonic equivalent) is the inversion of the Fundamental Pattern, the "flip side of the coin," so to speak—an apt metaphor too, perhaps, for much else pertaining to Chopin and Liszt: in their art, lives and work.

As noted with other seemingly extraordinary and unusual fingerings, we can make a case that Liszt *did* consider topography and key choice for some of his most challenging passages. They have most likely entered into Liszt's calculations far more consciously, and far more rationally, than is often believed.

Example 11.1

Liszt, *Spanish Rhapsody*

Allegro animato

Example 11.2

Liszt, *Spanish Rhapsody*

[Un poco meno allegro]

sempre animando

One does not have to conjure up imagined scenarios of a caricatured Liszt performing at the keyboard to fathom them, or execute them.[5] It is also most noteworthy that his monumental Sonata is written in B minor, with all its potential for harnessing the topographical advantages of related keys.

Some, such as Franklin Taylor, ultimately found it impossible to ignore this symmetry in certain of their calculations (double thirds, for example), but still fewer recognized its revolutionary effect on the standard approach to fingering. Even Moszkowski, who understood and did more than anyone else to disseminate Eschmann-Dumur's extraordinary discovery, ultimately failed to be influenced by Chopin's Fundamental Pattern to any significant degree, the full scope of its revolutionary implications still not yet realized.

But like a horse and carriage, you can't have one without the other, if topography is to have the enormously positive impact on the fingering process that it can and should. And it is the whole tone pattern that is the key to unlocking this relationship of keyboard symmetry (Eschmann-Dumur) to pianistic fingering (Chopin).

A FUNDAMENTAL PATTERN

From the standpoint of keyboard symmetry, Chopin's pattern may indeed be seen as fundamental—in the truest and best sense of the word. And from the standpoint of topography, it may be seen to reflect the keyboard's inherent suitability to the hand's natural architecture. Conversely, the hand with its natural adaptability—its wondrous ability to *manipulate*, to assume the shape of forms outside itself—is the facilitator for these *fixed* topographical characteristics and their manifold manifestations as they are constantly encountered in the course of keyboard travels.

But fundamentally, these manifestations—these patterns, these topographical shapes—are fewer than generally recognized, obscured as they are by the enormous wealth of harmonic resources now at our disposal and the distractions of the technical difficulties themselves. Paradoxically, simplification of the tuning system, and therefore the keyboard, is what permits this. The earlier chapters have addressed the remarkable simplicity of determining fingerings by linking core topographies. These core topographies derived from the Fundamental Pattern are, essentially, core structures—"plastic" though they are (see Appendix 9: "Modeling").

We have also explored further application of the five core topographies when extended beyond the hand's natural position: the larger intervals correlating to lateral extension of the fingers or horizontal distribution of the arm—all as manifest in arpeggiations of all kinds. This too may be first considered from the standpoint of the Fundamental Pattern, from expansion of its range to encompass the octave. Thumb and fifth now take the octave D, the third finger on A-flat/G-sharp—the two points of symmetry. The two tritones thus effected mark the two halves of the octave, its overall division into twelve equal semitones.

In parallel fashion, the architectural symmetry of the hand is respected: the third finger (length axis of the arm) represents the symmetrical division of the hand into two parts. Note, though, that anatomists also divide the hand into thumb and "hand" (fingers two through five). The diagonal path of the thumb and fifth (their oblique, transverse axis of ulnar opposition) intersects the length axis of the third finger.

This is the key to understanding the movement implications of the Fundamental Pattern as a fundamental orientation. And it is critical to understanding its alterations as an organic, evolving outgrowth of the application of its basic, underlying principles. Some of Chopin's most difficult passages—along with those of Brahms, Debussy, Scriabin, Ravel, Szymanowski, Barber and so many others—will no longer be seen as keyboard anomalies necessitated by innovative harmonies and their extended figurations. The key to their successful execution will be seen instead as residing in this fundamental orientation all along, to have its place in the scheme of things.

To recap somewhat: The arpeggios may be seen as represented by, even derived from, *translocations* of the Fundamental Pattern. Translocations cannot be called "transpositions" since the interval relations of the long fingers change when shifted upward or downward to successive groups of three black keys (octave on white keys, long fingers on black keys). Only the white-key tonic root position four-part chords and their arpeggios for the RH (excluding the full diminished chords) may appear to be unrelated, to lie outside this model—but only at first. Here too, interval and topographical alterations consistently conspire and coincide to reveal the same black and white key groupings that are reflected in the core groups for the diatonic scales.

When translocated, this "octave representation" of the Fundamental Pattern results in the topological scheme seen here (note relevant enharmonic equivalents).

For each hand, thumb and third on tritone *except* on that of F and B (again F and B!), reflecting the consistent impact of symmetry:

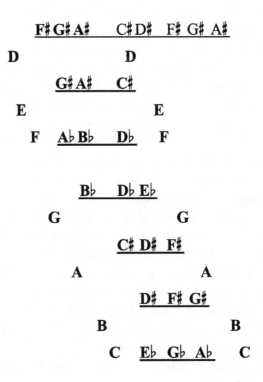

Chords of four or more parts and their arpeggios are found herein via the alterations of the three black keys. Going still further, others may in fact be related to a translocated model in which the three black keys taken by the three long fingers are not consecutive. Consider, for example, the M-M-m seventh and M-m-M seventh on D.

W	B	B	B	W:	D	F♯	A♯	C♯	D
W	B	W	B	W:	D	F♯	A	C♯	D

Here, however, there are two topographically correct options for the arpeggiation of this M-m-M seventh chord. Like the B and E harmonic minor scales, any core pattern of BWBW/WBWB may be repositioned: a more "negotiable" grouping—one that minimizes lateral "stretching"—is the usual result. In this case, repositioning to core groups C♯-D-F♯-A (LH) and A-C♯-D-F♯ (RH) will afford the superior fingering. Nonetheless, even this topographical resolution can be seen to derive, in fact, from an alteration of the translocated Fundamental Pattern with long fingers on C♯-D♯-F♯ (above).

As with the scales, arpeggios are extended by the thumb-under, hand-over pivoting action. But as already noted above, the interval/topographical construction of some seventh chords does not satisfactorily permit extension (arpeggiation) by this means. The only practical resolution is one in which harmonic extension of the pattern is achieved by what some call a "shift" (although Chopin was said to pass the thumb "under" the fifth). In any case, the upper arm as prime motor must inevitably be involved and the transverse axis of thumb and fifth adhered to. The more deliberate and kinesiologically sound their cooperation and coordination, the better.

The later literature is replete with passages consisting of note groups whose extension does not in any important way benefit from the thumb-under pivoting action involving any of the long fingers. In these the key actions involve thumb and fifth, the so-called short fingers. This is also the case with groups of notes—"handfuls" of notes—reflecting new, unusual interval relations and harmonic constructions that also do not readily comport with patterns most commonly encountered.

Certainly such an "extended" enlistment of thumb and fifth is not new to pianists with long experience in playing series of multivoiced chords, octaves, broken octaves, and tremolos of wide interval; even simple triads and their inversions require this. But as any accomplished pianist will confirm, there is definitely something different here. The new figurations clearly pose something beyond the technical challenges normally encountered. Yet they are intrinsic to the compositional style and implied sonorities.

Is there some application of the Fundamental Pattern that can in any way serve to provide some insight into execution of such passages?

What is unique about the Fundamental Pattern is the fact that the thumb-under pivoting action has no practical relevance in its own extension in horizontal keyboard space. Because of this, it is a prototype for all such passages. No application of this pivoting action, in any combination of notes or fingers—even if the grouping would be inconsistent throughout the pattern's extension—results in a more facile, more satisfactory execution than the "shifting" movement of the pattern intact. We have already observed this in the excerpts quoted from Liszt's "Mephisto Waltz." And the literature abounds in them—the later repertoire in particular.

As touched on above, the upper arm mechanism is the primary motor and the primary control for the horizontal movement distributing the lower arm and hand. Yet here this is only part of it: the opposing action of thumb and fifth along their transverse axis is the essential cooperative component at the keyboard end. This relative placement of thumb and fifth—*en diagonale*, so to speak—is discussed at greater length in Appendix 10. But I invite you to experiment regarding any finger-to-finger, key-to-key extension of Chopin's fundamental whole tone pattern. Compare the impact of this hand placement—thumb and fifth laterally oblique, fourth finger aligned with the ulna—with the still prevalent notion that, ideally, thumb and fifth should be placed at the ends of the white keys. The latter pales in execution.

A FUNDAMENTAL ORIENTATION

Regarding the contention that we often see only what we look for (a problem with an overreliance on videos) and that "old ideas die hard," I offer this revealing example. The great Leopold Godowsky often espoused the principle that the thumb should not take a black key unless absolutely necessary, though his extant interviews are silent on the issue of the fifth finger. Yet a first-hand recounting of a master class given by Godowsky attributes to him the statement that a pianist should avoid using the fifth finger on a black key (it must obviously be assumed he did not mean for chords and octaves).[6]

Nevertheless, a photo of Godowsky at the piano in a preceding companion article is revealing in its portrayal of the oblique relationship of white key thumb to black-key fifth in his hand position on the keyboard.[7] And going back to Chopin, the excerpt in Example 11.3 not only speaks to this issue (thumb on white keys, fifth on black keys) but is an exemplar of translocation of the Fundamental Pattern. From this perspective security, comfort and ease of execution are easily attained.

Example 11.3

Chopin, *Prelude in C# Minor, Op. 28 No. 10*

At this point in our discourse, it is worth making a few statements about photos, all of which I hope will shed a bit more light on the eternal issue of hand "position" or "shape" (both of which terms are useful and in use but have really quite different connotations). One can see, and determine, a great deal from photos. In regard to matters of alignment, many blatant incongruities are so obvious that one must indeed wonder.

This is evident in *most* photographs of both hands at the keyboard: the LH is entirely out of whack. The thumb makes contact midway on the white key and the second knuckle is inordinately arched, with the consequence that only a straightened fifth finger can contact and activate the key (first joint flexion is no longer an option). The shoulder joint and hand are both passively rolled (rotated) outward—quite a different dynamic from that usually portrayed by the RH in the same picture. After more than forty years, I continue to be astounded by the photo on the Dutton reprint of Ortmann's classic study, or the cover photo of Malwin Brée's *The Leschetizky Method*.

Such visual impressions do little to reverse long-held misconceptions or point the way to a more effective approach. In fact, they do much harm. That most left hands operate this way only speaks to the extent of the problem, to a status quo—not to natural movement potential. As noted at several points in this discussion, certain ingrained habits of orientation or training in the earliest stages have a negative technical impact when a wider range of movement, increased key resistance, speed, stamina, and biomechanical requirements for transmission of greater force compound their effect. And all that in addition to compositional complexity!

This matters greatly in that, whether "closed," "open," or contracted, there are really only four basic hand orientations (just below) in continual play at the keyboard. All are determined by the relevant positions of thumb and fifth as they are assigned to their four possible black-white key combinations. Each orientation fundamentally affects the movement dynamic potential within the topological parameters established by its "position" on the keys. Lines of action, represented by the individual axes of the hand as they relate to alignment; curvilinear movement and its kinematic representation as curves; and the mechanics of the upper arm are subtly yet substantially affected (Appendix 10).

Easily comprehended aurally and conceptually, the physical orientation to a simple whole tone passage from Debussy (Example 11.4) is demonstrative of this on a rather basic level.

Example 11.4

Debussy, *L'Isle joyeuse*

[Modéré et très souple]

Plus animé

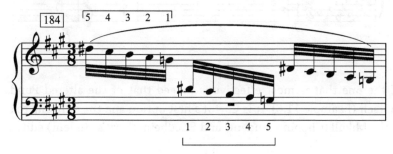

Once again, we will find a model—and some interesting associations—by taking a look at the Fundamental Pattern in a still different way. Altering the assignment of the thumb and fifth fingers, we arrive at four orientations of those fingers in relation to the long fingers on the black keys. For each alteration, there is a new topology: the spatial relationship of hand to keys is altered, as is the dynamic of the linking movements. In terms of topographical combinations they are WW, BB, WB and BW (the enharmonic equivalents should be assumed):

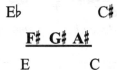

What is interesting, perhaps even highly significant, is the fact that repositioning thumb and fifth in the black-key plane reveals the ideal fingering combination for what is now a pentatonic rather than a whole-tone pattern. Like the whole-tone Fundamental Pattern itself, adhering to the five-finger pentatonic sequence as represented by this alteration proves the best fingering solution for horizontal extension in keyboard space.

It is difficult to encounter a better example than that found in Chopin's "Black Key" Etude, Opus 10 No. 5. Various fingerings are recommended in the several editions, among them what is seen in Example 11.5.

Example 11.5

Chopin: *Etude in G-flat, Op. 10 No. 5 ("Black Key")*

Yet the one that is most effective is indeed that of the altered Fundamental Pattern itself (Example 11.6). It is Cortot's first option and the only one to be found in both the Mikuli (Chopin's student) and Friedheim (Liszt's student) editions.

Example 11.6

Chopin: *Etude in G-flat, Op. 10 No. 5 ("Black Key")*

In addition to the Chopin (Example 11.3) and Debussy (Example 11.4) excerpts, other examples of the two WB and BW orientations of thumb and fifth abound. In fact, they are not at all new, even to students at the earlier levels. As noted repeatedly, the B and B-flat major-minor triads necessarily "reorient" the hand in executing a chromatic sequence of triads. What has been referred to as an anomaly vis-à-vis the others is again demonstrative of that very telling area of the keyboard,[8] the BWWWB inversion of the WBBBW Fundamental Pattern centered on point of symmetry D.

These four orientations of thumb and fifth are increasingly encountered in compositions of heightened chromaticism and new harmonic, modal and serial constructs. Fingerings for the inversions of triads and basic solutions for most double sixth scale patterns unavoidably require them.

In addition to these four possible orientations of thumb and fifth, further altering the topographical arrangements of the three "inside" tones (F♯-G♯-A/G♭-A♭-B♭) of the Fundamental Pattern to reflect requisite tonal alterations expands our earlier topographical perspective enormously. The conceptual expansion may be represented by this construct:

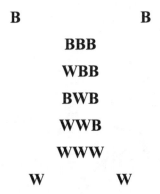

Permutations of the schema reflect all possibilities for *all* five fingers in any combination of black and white keys. Chopin's final movement (Finale: Presto) of his Sonata in B-flat Minor, Opus 35, is the exemplar *par excellence* in the advanced repertoire. And surely it remains the most daunting of challenges in matters of fingering. But the key to a truly pianistic solution to this supreme test resides exactly in the options to be found within the four orientations of thumb and fifth.

Passages *seemingly* outside any consideration of topographical influences as represented by Chopin's Fundamental Pattern can now be seen differently: they are intimately related. And there is nothing mysterious or "magical" about it. Keyboard symmetry reflected in a topography that conforms to the natural shape of the hand supports an approach to fingering that is first and foremost a natural one.

Chopin recognized this, humbled himself before the "genius" responsible for the keyboard's symmetrical design, and went from there. The key to successful technical solutions for many of his most vexing combinations is therefore similarly rooted in these orientations—albeit there is obviously a certain hierarchy of more pianistic to less pianistic, as we have seen in the topographical solutions to the scale and arpeggio fingerings.

Once again, you are invited to explore, analyze and consider from this new, expanded perspective. I am confident that such an inquiry will result in a deepened sense of the keyboard's topographical organization and a heightened appreciation of its symmetry. The repertoire excerpts are offered in further support of this undertaking, as well as to provide specific guidance in matters of fingering.

THE TOPOGRAPHICAL ADVANTAGE, EXPLORATIONS IN KEYBOARD SPACE

4

As the chief mechanical difficulty in pianoforte-playing, we now lay stress upon the unevenness, resulting from the local relations of black and white keys, of the field forming the scene of action for the performer's fingers.
—Hans von Bülow

Particularly detrimental is the principle: "The more difficult, the more useful" because it hinders the automatization of the correct fingerings.
—József Gát

WE HAVE BEEN CONSIDERING the demonstrably superior advantages of a fundamentally topographical approach as it applies to the fingering of scales, arpeggios and other basic patterns—and by extension to the fingering of passages in the repertoire—over those afforded by the more traditional, generally accepted approach. Conceding these advantages, one must then wonder why it is that such a consistently coherent and physiologically beneficial approach to fingering has yet to be adopted overall.

The "standard" scale and arpeggio fingerings remain so pervasively entrenched that the syllabi and requirements of numerous competitive as well as noncompetitive student auditions and examinations now merely refer to them as "*the* fingerings." Such is the ready assumption of what has become a kind of unassailable doctrine. We recall the concert pianist's shocked comment: "How can there be any other fingerings than the ones we use!" For all the conveniently dismissive talk about fingering being a purely "individual matter" and that all depends on the "individual hand," such vague thinking obviously doesn't extend to scale and arpeggio fingerings—or any slavish adherence to a particular fingered edition. Here groupthink and dogma hold sway.

That the C major fingering should remain enshrined as the supreme model for all scale and arpeggio fingerings defies both common sense and experience. The black-key tonic scale fingerings are considered unavoidable aberrations by many, or fathomable exceptions by most. And given the repertoire requirements of the early years—"readability" being rightly an essential concern—they are generally postponed for quite some time, with scant attention paid to them at best. The theoretical focus therefore on those key signatures having no more than one flat (C and F) or three sharps (G, D and A) is standard fare, and many years go by before it is deemed necessary or advisable for a student to move beyond them.

The consequent difficulty that students usually have in transitioning from these relatively few favored white-key tonic scales to black-key tonic scales—and introduction of black keys generally—is not a new concern, but one that teachers have continued to voice repeatedly. Absent abandoning "beloved C," this state of affairs is now taken as pretty much par for the course. Still, it attests to a problem of "method" time and again, all the while (remarkably) failing to receive any meaningful examination.

We should keep in mind that any fingering for an all-white- key "organization" is wholly arbitrary, given the absence of topographically defining black keys—or "no pivot," as Chopin would say. The leading rationale of the standard fingering for C is that the thumb, as first finger, should be assigned to the scale's first degree (RH ascending and LH descending). Based on a logical finger sequence and, presumably, the influence of C major's position as the theoretical starting point in the Circle of Fifths, such a giant as Liszt himself also enthroned it as a model for transposition to keys having black-key tonics.[1]

Artur Schnabel's thinking on the standard fingering for C major (" which is still adhered to with reverence") is rather interesting, and unique, in this regard. He considers the standard pattern "ingenious" but "musical only for the left hand; musical by accident." He takes issue with the fact that the RH fingering assigns the "strongest" finger, the thumb, to the subdominant; it should therefore be altered to reflect assignment of the thumb to the dominant, to be in accord with the LH. As do most, he discusses the patterning only for one octave. For the RH it would now be 1-2-3-4/1-2-3-4; the LH would be unchanged. Barring this "the subdominant might easily get a musically unintended accent on it, and thus lead to a crime against the harmonic system of centuries and make music the victim of standardization."[2] But such passionate pleadings yet again beg further questions as to the potential for and advisability of an overall consistency of scale form fingerings—certainly of great pedagogical concern—as well as their application in the repertoire. They are, nonetheless, implicit of just how far one can stretch the rationales of scale fingering when all-white-key C is held as prime exemplar.

But advantage of the hand's natural orientation to the scales of the enharmonic keys was disregarded, and pattern prevailed over topography. The C major fingering was thereby secured as the fundamental, "ideal model" for the generations of pianists and teachers that followed despite the many topographical and biophysical incongruities encountered in the white-key tonic scale fingerings that derived from it. Most commonly presented and considered for a range of one octave only—of great value in the repertoire of the early classics (sonatinas for example)—it does indeed appear "ingenious." And so it singularly serves throughout the pedagogical literature for any discussion of scale playing—unfortunately without discrimination. Its relative awkwardness and ineffectiveness when applied beyond the range of an octave to those descending left-hand scales having white-key tonics (excepting E and B) is obviously of no account.

No doubt any prevailing prejudice toward left-hand use in favor of right-hand dominancy has also done much to dismiss this failing as a "problem of the left hand" and not a problem of the fingering itself. Readers of my generation, at least, will remember very well forced discouragement of left-hand use, particularly in writing; "lefty" was not a welcome label, embarrassment a "motivating" tactic.

As for all-white-key C, one can only speculate as to any influence of all the age-old connotations and cultural representations of black versus white, not to mention the many fears of what left-handedness itself—or the "Left"—might represent. To be seated on the "right hand" is the ancient place of honor; "right" also equals "correct." And we need only look further to our language itself for many others: their etymologies notwithstanding, *adroit*, *gauche* and *sinister* are but a few.

Fortunately, we are now much more enlightened by a broad swath of relatively recent research into the correlation of left-hand, right-brain and right-hand, left-brain activity—or more correctly, left side (of body)–right brain and right side–left brain. The ongoing research and subsequent understanding of their creative and intellectual interplay has already yielded much, and promises still more.

But that the training of the left hand required special attention—for many reasons, including its general neglect—is also attested to by the extraordinary amount of concert and pedagogical literature by composers of both great and lesser renown. Theodore Edel notes that "in the nineteenth century almost everyone was right-handed; that is, until recently the small amount of individuals who were born left-handed were discouraged from using the left hand and forced to conform to the majority." Long before the several concerti and forty-some well-known commissions by and for the renowned pianist Paul Wittgenstein (1887–1961), there was already a wealth of recital repertoire for the left hand alone.[3] That this development can be concretely connected to right hand injuries or other trauma is indisputable. But one must also acknowledge the breadth of etudes and other studies for the left hand specifically geared to its technical training and virtuosic development.

Throughout the technical and pedagogical literature, one is hard put to come up with any serious attempt at a discussion or analysis of scale playing that does not set forth C major as exemplar. But it is really quite remarkable that Ortmann, given the intent and scope of his treatise, chose the C major scale as his "lab" model despite long-prevailing recognition of the superior comfort to be found in those scales having a predominance of black keys.[4] Perhaps his choice was predicated on the awareness of the peculiar difficulties and disadvantages of this all-white-key scale. But I do not think so, and he does not tell us.

It is, rather, a further reflection of the peculiarly singular position of the C major scale in pedagogical thinking and pedagogical practice. Even scales such as A harmonic minor and B-flat or D major having only one or two black keys, certainly not a preponderance of them, would have been far more revealing and instructive for the purpose at hand. Although his is an extraordinary and distinguished attempt at a comprehensive study of the biomechanics of pianism, other assumed or unchallenged—limited, and even false—premises nonetheless form the basis for more than a few of Ortmann's conclusions.

Among them is the underlying assumption throughout his impressive and valuable treatise that the basic action of the pianist's finger is that it should be raised preliminary to the playing of each key ("finger stroke"). Although valuable primarily as *training*, such a concept is an obvious holdover from a less enlightened approach to pianism that, unfortunately, continues to the present day. Ortmann does allow that such an action is but one of several available to the pianist, and he discusses the relative advantages of several of these "non-percussive" and "percussive" actions.[5] But too many of his conclusions are nevertheless predicated on "stroke" or "striking" from an elevated preparation, the least biomechanically and kinesiologically efficient overall.[6] Of course, Ortmann has never been alone in this, and such unmusical terminology remains very much in use to the present day. Other nontechnical, though imprecise, terms such as "swing," "press," or "fall" imply varying approaches to imparting acceleration to the key that are far more appropriate, useful and effective. And one finds yet again that some of the pianist's most basic "everyday" movements are simply assumed, escaping substantive analysis. Significantly, his conclusions and recommendations as to the "correct" action of the thumb in scale or arpeggio playing suffer from several incorrect a priori assumptions, resulting in an incomplete and seriously flawed discourse on the matter.

Ortmann's research and analysis is also notably deficient in addressing the correlative, coordinated role of finger flexion and *dynamic* joint stabilization—particularly that of the shoulder joint/shoulder complex within the biokinetic chain of the pianist's playing mechanism. And although he occasionally refers to the rotation of the humerus (upper arm), he does not distinguish between inner and outer (*medial* and *lateral*) humeral rotation, unlike Schmitz. Consequently, one is left with vague, inconclusive and impracticable analysis in this regard. But Ortmann's meticulous findings, though often not fully developed, do support Schmitz's more rationally organized—and, I submit, more far-reaching—methodology (see Appendix 9). On the whole, they are mutually supporting and reinforcing.

Although there are a number of other significant oversights in his study as well—and Arnold Schultz has already taken issue with several of them[7]—a full critique is not the present intention; nor can it fall within the scope of this work. Neither is it necessary beyond pointing out some of the conceptual gaps that have contributed to an ongoing impact on attitudes toward fingering choice. And it should not be taken that such commentary is in any way an indictment of this invaluable, groundbreaking, and enduring work.

Unfortunately, Ortmann's work is often mentioned but rarely read. And for all the adulations garnered, *The Physiological Mechanics of Piano Technique* remains, for the most part, unavailable. Ortmann's remarkable treatise should be studied incessantly and with great attention to its enormous detail. It is a stellar contribution to a body of works attempting at the time (mid-1920s to late 1930s) to establish a soundly scientific basis for pianism, and it remains an invaluable treasure trove of copiously documented information. His monumental study deservedly holds a place as one of the preeminent resources for pianists and their teachers.

But conceding this, one finds a most substantial and fundamental failing in Ortmann's laboratory method itself. And this must also be taken into serious account when considering many of his conclusions. His electrographs of the playing movements of (unidentified) "expert" pianists are oftentimes presented as evidence in support of certain predetermined physiological and kinesiological "facts." By itself, such a selection of the subject pianists based on any perceived merits of their playing would at best have to be founded on a *subjective*, personal aesthetic in the absence of an already known or established biomechanical "standard." At a time when the *objective* of such research was exactly that—scientific establishment of such a standard—the cart has been put before the horse, so to speak. Fortunately, movement study has come a long way since then. But even in his time, others were making far better use of available techniques to document and analyze movement.[8]

A more objective, dispassionate study of the *movement potential* of the pianist's playing mechanism could have revealed such a standard. Such a correlation to the parameters of keyboard space, as affected by the laws of physics and the body's own complex physiology and structural design for purposeful spatial accommodation, could have resulted in a far more lucid, cohesive, comprehensive and systematic approach. The particular influence of the keyboard's *biplanar* topography and the extent of its horizontal range in relation to the performer's fixed seated position would not then be significantly discounted in any truly scientific search for answers to some of the problems still plaguing pianists and teachers. Nor would the arm's own anatomical center.

It was left for Schmitz to do much of this, and *The Capture of Inspiration* remains the incomparable result. Though also imperfect, this singular work is nonetheless rooted in a scientific approach that is thorough, disciplined and precise: it is a model of scholarship and creative thinking. Moreover, he grasped the yet to be fully explored significance of assignment of long and short fingers to black and white keys, as well as some of the other implications of Chopin's iconoclastic approach to fingering relevant to the keyboard's biplanar topography and extensive horizontal range.

And so, it was Chopin all along who, with his Fundamental Pattern and choice of key for his compositions, had essentially got it right—who intuitively grasped the far-reaching topographical implications of the enharmonic keys (courtesy of equal temperament!) and their related symmetry. Sadly he did not live long enough to harvest the full genius of those preliminary insights to their logical, inevitable conclusions.

But as noted earlier, some of the greatest teachers and pianists of the hundred and more years that followed Chopin have been in the forefront of those pleading for serious reappraisal and revision of these now-standard fingerings for the fundamental forms. Implicit therein, too, is a plea for reconsideration of keyboard pedagogy, from the ground up, toward one that is topographically based. Chopin's thinking is reaffirmed as we call into question the very basis for these fingerings specifically and keyboard solutions generally.

One cannot help but again be reminded of Neuhaus's own iconoclastic conclusions regarding Chopin's Fundamental Pattern and a prevailing "tyranny of C major" as voiced by him at the end of a long and distinguished career. We can now, unfortunately, only wonder what the mind of such a great pianist and artist teacher might also have done with those realizations had he come upon them—or written more about them—earlier in his career. But he passionately decried the "hundreds and thousands of exercises, etudes and educational pieces that have been written in that beloved C major." For Neuhaus there was no compelling logic or mitigating rationale in this, and he goes on to protest that "except for an excessive love of ivory and a contempt for ebony it would be difficult to find an explanation for this one-sided approach."[9]

TOPOGRAPHY AND PEDAGOGY

The black keys upon the keyboard are "terra incognita." Consequently at the very start the child has an incorrect view of what music really is.
—Alfred Riesenauer

B major is easier to play than C major for the fingers fall naturally into the required groups, and the joins are in each case from the third or fourth finger on a black note to thumb on a white note, which again conforms to the natural relationship of the thumb and fingers. . . . It is hardly more difficult to remember to play all the black notes and the lower of each pair of white notes, than it is to remember to play all the white notes. B first is my advice!
—Ambrose Coviello

IN DEVELOPING A COMPREHENSIVE TOPOGRAPHICAL PERSPECTIVE in matters of fingering, it bears repeating yet again that the keyboard is not merely constructed of white and black keys, but that the rows of each are positioned in their respective horizontal planes. Therefore it must always be kept in mind that—in terms of where the individual notes lie—any scale, arpeggio or other passage consisting of both black and white keys is, in fact, *biplanar*. C major and A natural minor are the only scales occurring solely in the white-key plane; the chords and arpeggios of F-sharp/G-flat major and D-sharp/E-flat minor (including its m-M-m seventh) are the only fundamental forms exclusively lying in the black-key plane.

The vertical movements of the keys and their exclusive role in tone production notwithstanding, all distributive movements occur within and among these two horizontal planes. Assigning long fingers to short keys and short fingers to long keys obviously minimizes the necessity for inward and outward adjustments of the arm from plane to plane. But there is more to this.

Judicious application of the long fingers should be enlisted to help establish, as well as preserve, an optimal orientation of the arm in keyboard locations more distant from its anatomical midline. And relative finger lengths should be employed to "neutralize" interplanar disparities of key depth whenever possible. Fingering choices that serve to accommodate lateral distance (interval) within the movement range of the hand itself are better served with this in mind.

Any conclusion that a satisfactory scale or arpeggio fingering application that works without "obstacles" (the black keys) should be nonetheless appropriate for one with obstacles—that is, the impact of fixed, unavoidable topographical attributes— surely flies in the face of all logic and common sense. In practice, it is at best merely a trans*positioning* (not *transposing*, as in the theoretical sense) of an encoded, reflexive finger pattern. There is little benefit of sensory recognition or sensorial reinforcement of key contact or key resistance that is already familiar, the ground shifting as it does topographically and the upper arm shifting the hand accordingly.

The degree to which any meaningful aural connection is thereby maintained, enhanced or similarly reinforced is likewise highly questionable given the distracting potential for overriding sensations of "negative" tension (unnecessary and inappropriate muscular contractions) and movements that are inherently awkward—to say the very least. To plead only that the solution to overcoming these consequent difficulties would be found in assiduous practice—a matter of just "getting used to them"—is simplistic at best.

Seymour Fink, in his chapter "Fingering: The Key to Arming," contributed to *A Symposium for Pianists and Teachers*, resurrects von Bülow's view.[1] He acknowledges the unavoidable yet supreme challenges of topography, but at the same time he advocates for all-white-key "diatonic C major" as the indomitable ideal in matters of fingering:

> They must learn to play their longer fingers on the narrow part of the white keys, and in general to negotiate the uneven, crowded terrain of the black key area. Chromatic transposition (playing almost entirely in the black key area) is the best method for obtaining these skills. . . . Playing black-key scales with C-major fingering is another useful way to acquire this readiness. Soon we are disposed to finger all passages as though they were in diatonic C major . . . and translate all our newly developed skills to the bumpy real world near the fallboard. The resulting inconvenience is more than made up for by the simpler, more direct mental effort, and the expressive power of the arms that is unleashed."[2]

This view is, of course, exactly what has impeded progress toward fuller appreciation of the keyboard's topography and symmetry all along. From a more informed, enlightened topographical perspective, such a narrow goal—to eventually become "disposed to finger all passages as though they were in diatonic C major"—is not only pointless and inefficient but physiologically harmful as well. And as an attempt to impose some kind of order, some unifying rationale on the seemingly disparate organization of the "regular" or "standard" fingerings, it is quite wanting on the whole.

Certainly we must learn to deal with that "bumpy" terrain near the fallboard, where topographical factors such as key depth and height, playing surface and resistance (leverage)—not to mention the spatial restrictions of the fallboard itself—hold great sway. But this only when an exclusively black-plane excursion is demanded of the passage at hand; it is not the real world where we spend most of our playing time. Resolution does not reside in a victory of pattern over topography. Nor should a more unified, systematic approach to the challenges posed by the keyboard's topography be founded on it.

Expressive power does not unreservedly reside in (upper) arm movements any more than expressive (musical) content can be said to be inherent in a composer's fingering. Both are further examples of the incongruity of thought that typifies discussion of these matters. As with scale fingerings, the "every hand is different" argument seems not to apply when deferring to the composer, no matter that individual training and technique—not to mention hand size (Chopin's and Rachmaninoff's, for example)—render such arguments inconsequential. Expressive power manifests a far more exquisite engagement and integration of biophysical, energetic, intellectual, emotional and spiritual forces than such magical thinking implies.

Although needlessly and unwisely deferring to C major in his experiments, Ortmann nonetheless strongly disagrees with von Bülow, Fink and others before them in the matter of transcending the challenges posed by topography. He presents quite compelling validation, replete with electrographs and other supporting arguments, for a fingering of sequences that is adjusted to neutralize topographical disparities. This to avoid unnecessary arm movements, and thereby minimize the risk for incoordinate movement generally. In comparing the relative advantages of two fingerings, those of pattern versus topography, he asserts:

> The value of one fingering over another rests, or should rest, in the greater ease and smoothness of the requisite movement in so far as it can meet the musical demands of the passage. . . . A change of movement of a single finger may mean a considerable change in the movement itself. . . . The forward and backward shift of the hand . . . adds nothing to the tonal result, and must, therefore, from a purely muscular standpoint be considered superfluous movement. The advantage . . . in the slightly greater simplicity of fingering, 4-3-2-1 being uniformly repeated . . . is outweighed by the loss in accuracy of dynamic control which normally accompanies a shift of hand. The inequality can, of course, be overcome with practice, but often some vestige of it remains. . . . The forward and backward shift [in this case] . . . is an arm movement, occurring only when the thumb plays a black key. But it covers also the time during which the other fingers are playing. It adds, therefore a difficulty in finger control. *And a sufficiently sensitive dynamograph will record such variations even after prolonged and apparently successful practice* [emphasis added].[3]

On this argument the incomparable and now legendary Wanda Landowska weighs in further, chiding and chastising those who hold to such an approach:

> What an error it is to believe that fingering should remain identical in sequences! The fact that in sequences a musical design is reproduced on different degrees is one thing. But fingering is only concerned with the *topography* [emphasis added] of each phrase as it appears on the keyboard. When the disposition of the black and white keys is modified because the motive is repeated on another degree of the scale, it requires a different fingering.[4]

The "shape," or more aptly the contour, of a motive or other musical pattern—and this includes the phrase—is fundamentally determined by the parameters of its *intervallic range*. Any calibration of dynamic range follows from this, but emotional and musical content is quite another, entirely subjective, matter. For pianists, musical shape is, in fact, reflected in the curvilinear movement of the *upper* arm that responds and corresponds to it, at the same time unifying all movements of the lower arm and hand. "Curves" represent the paths of that movement, its "shape," which does not therefore depend on strict adherence to a finger sequence that is primarily of the hand.

As with all movement at the keyboard, optimal orientation and coordination of the arm must also take into account the relative distances and direction of any sequences from its anatomical midline as well as their distant location at the extreme registers. But musical shape also implies scope of movement as well as intervallic range and pattern contour. It therefore connotes and encompasses height and depth in addition to length and breadth: the vertical as well as the horizontal. The keyboard's topography surely cannot be ignored in any consistently proportionate execution of a musical pattern's shape.

That fingering pattern should trump keyboard topography is not the simple solution. It is a simplistic solution.

Here it is useful to consider a still current and frequently espoused—again, one might even say "standard"—argument. This holds that such transpositioning not only is the key to transposing but at the same time neatly controverts topographical considerations, including symmetry, as the defining attribute for keyboard fingering. The strong inference is that the C major scale is, with good reason, the exemplar of sensible fingering and should remain so.

An example is usually given at the elementary level, with the clear intent to dismiss and disparage a topographical approach as one that is obviously and patently ridiculous. The transposition of a simple tune such as "Merrily We Roll Along" ("Mary Had a Little Lamb"), encompassing a perfect fifth as it does, benefits from assignment of a five-finger position of the right hand. How silly it would be, we are told, to transpose this tune from the key of C major to the key of D-flat, fingering it then as we would the major scale for that key, with thumb on the white key and long fingers two and three on the black keys. Surely one would simply transpose the same pattern on the new tonic with the same five fingers. And of course we would!

The argument makes sense and, on the face of it, would seem to be a strong one—especially if the transposing exercise were given to the left hand. Until one really thinks about the illogic and the lack of topographical awareness—even pedagogical inappropriateness—represented therein:

First: The fingering for the C major scale is not used in playing the tune—only a five-finger pattern on tonic C. Strictly applied, the C scale fingering for the RH would prove even more awkward than that for tonic D-flat, in which the long fingers are assigned to the short black keys.

Second: The argument, if followed logically, would therefore compare the tune played with the five fingers, thumb on D-flat—not with the fingering for the D-flat scale.

Third: A five-finger pattern on D-flat is, in fact, a more comfortable and physiologically efficient transposition of the melodic pattern for transposing the tune. In the black plane now, longest third finger compensates for the key depth of the sole white key.

Fourth: Pedagogically, a comparison of patterns would prove far more beneficial. For example, the tune played yet a half-step higher, on D—with the longest third on the only black key—would represent the topographical inversion of D-flat. This would afford further confirmation of topographical application, not refutation.

Fifth: Five-finger patterns have an important place in any sound, practical pedagogy. But they bear comparatively little relation to the scales and their fingering sequences unless altered otherwise than the usual major/minor third. Five-finger patterns with altered seconds and fourths as well as thirds ultimately have far more practical relevance to the fingerings of scales themselves.

Sixth: One of their most useful applications is indeed as tool for introducing and exploring principles of transposition at the elementary or even well into the intermediate level. But in the cited example, or other such tunes like it, a transposition of C to D-flat is of no particular theoretical relevance at such an early stage. Even though the root relationship is stepwise (adored by Prokofieff) or may be considered harmonically that of the Neapolitan (creatively exploited by

Chopin) of C major, the benefit is really only a conceptual and aural one. More fundamental relationships of root (dominant, subdominant and mediant), key and mode change, as well as those of topography and symmetry, are better served by a deeper, more serious and more open approach to all the possibilities at hand.

Yet the foregoing typifies the entrenched bias toward C major as fundamental model. Founded on a stretched effort to compare apples to oranges—a five-finger pattern to a scale fingering—it further evinces the ongoing resistance and persistent failure to fully comprehend, or even admit, the defining impact of topography and symmetry on all keyboard patterns and their fingering.

TOWARD AN INTEGRATION OF THE THEORETICAL AND THE PRACTICAL

The Spanish pianist and teacher Alberto Jonás does not appear to have had any particular knowledge of Chopin's fundamental use of a mirrored position (as represented by his Fundamental Pattern spelled both as flats and sharps). Nor does he seem to have been aware of Chopin's preferred practice of initiating his students' scale study with the favored D-flat and B major scales that follow from it, five flats and sharps respectively. But in his unique and extraordinary seven-volume *Master School of Piano Playing and Virtuosity* (Vol. II, 1922) Jonás cites Theodore Wiehmayer, who, in his *Tonleiter-Schule* (School of Scales), was one of the first proponents of the advantages of a topographical approach to scale fingerings:

> The scale may be looked upon from two entirely different points of view,
> namely, from the standpoint of the musical ear and from that of the fingers. . . .
> The ear distinguishes the various scales only by the . . . so-called tonic of the
> scales. The fingers . . . distinguish the characteristic difficulties of the various
> scales solely by the nature and construction of the two positions [the four- and
> three-note/finger groups] . . . without in the least concerning themselves about
> the tonic, or the order of the whole and half-tones of a scale.[5]

Consistent with Chopin's approach, he then proceeds to recommend that the major scales should be studied beginning with those of the enharmonic major keys.

But Jonás counters: "All this may be true, and yet the teacher who would try to teach the scales in the order just mentioned runs a decided risk of confusing the pupil's *mind* [emphasis added]. It is better . . . to employ first a tonality that has neither sharps nor flats and to proceed in accordance with the circle of fifths, which introduces them gradually . . . very helpful, however, remains the considerations of the groups . . . in all scales as given by Wiehmayer."[6] Jonás presents these "new" fingerings concurrently with the "old" ones and is a strong advocate of them:

> Comparatively few pianists are aware of the similarity of construction of all the
> major scales in the keys of equal sharps and flats. . . . The result of this
> similarity is that the best fingering for a scale with one or more sharps must
> also be the best for the opposite scale with the same number of flats. This
> brings to light that the scales of G, D, A and F major as we play them are *badly
> fingered* for the left hand, if we admit that the fingering of the right hand is
> better (and it is so), in the opposite scales of F, B♭, E♭ and G major. *And indeed
> the l.h. will play the scales mentioned more fluently* [emphases added].[7]

Jonás also agrees with Moszkowski (*Écoles des Gammes et des Doubles Notes*) that the thumb on a white key is best immediately after the third and fourth fingers on black keys. But for the minor scales he applies this sequence to the harmonic form only and dismisses the melodic minor as an "antiquated, illogical and undeserving musical feature." He is in agreement with Josef Hofmann, who also dismissed the melodic minor, but on different grounds: that it did not afford the pianist's fingers any "new intervals" and was therefore superfluous for training.[8] But it is noteworthy too that C.P.E Bach felt exactly otherwise: he did not include fingerings for the harmonic minor in his famous essay, only the melodic minor form.

Though clearly favoring these new fingerings, Jonás does not go further than practical but nonetheless consistent observation, which he subsequently applied to all major and harmonic minor scale fingerings.

What still had to be done was to go beyond recognizing mirrored patterns and generally recommending assignment of the fourth finger to a black key, and this is the chief goal of *Natural Fingering*. Even to compile a manual of topographically adjusted scale, arpeggio and double note fingerings simply would not do it. Without deeper exploration and explanation of the underlying principles, the pure weight of so many years of standard fingering usage would continue to dwarf any demonstrable merits of a more broadly based, topographically oriented approach.

And the very knowledge of so many failed attempts within the last 125 years, several by some of our most outstanding artists, teachers and pedagogues, to provoke and promote a new approach to our methods of fingering would still loom very large indeed. So it is that even more recent attempts to somewhat tactfully present them as "alternatives"—still without adequate in-depth analysis or more specific principles or guidelines for their broader application—have done little to sway such entrenched conviction or alter conventional practice. It is rather encouraging to note that the Canadian Royal Conservatory of Music syllabus requires only a "logical fingering" for the performances of those scales that constitute this particular aspect of its "Technical Tests."[9] Overall, though, the standard fingerings remain "the" fingerings.

But it will be seen that such a "topographical approach" allows far more practical integration of the sensory *and* theoretical at a much earlier stage than might first be apparent. There need be no conflict between Wiehmayer's then-revolutionary recommendations and Jonás's conservative reservations. The simple resolution is to continue to employ C major—but not as the model for scale *fingerings*. It would serve, instead, as a *visual* model for diatonic major scale construction (its two half steps are white keys only, no black key between) and an *aural* model for developing a sense of tonality. It would also rightly retain its position as a *theoretical* basis for scale study proceeding through the Cycle of Fifths. The C major diatonic construct would remain enormously valuable as the practical basis for sequenced patterning at the elementary to early intermediate levels precisely because of the absence of black keys and the immediate proximity of its white-key plane.

It also seemed equally important to show a way for the individual teacher to adopt and adapt to this topographical approach. To whatever degree it would be "user friendly," it must be "teacher friendly" as well. It is otherwise wholly unrealistic to expect abandonment of certain key principles and guidelines that have for so long comfortably served established methods of providing a foundation in the formative years of study—however limited and unsupported in their broader practical application at increasingly advanced levels of difficulty.

Fortunately, we can imagine a progressive methodology to this end. With guidelines for a logical sequence that is inherently flexible, it would serve as a general framework to be adjusted or altered by the teacher as deemed appropriate for age, level, individual style and pedagogical intent and suitably adhered to, in its entirety or in part, *over time*. One should always keep in mind that the element of time is the significant factor in all kinds of integration. And to enlist variety toward that end ensures vitality as well as aural and intellectual engagement.

Any instrumental technique ultimately consists of movements that are both responses to patterns (seen, heard, envisioned) and *patterns of response*. Any sequence of notes to be played therefore implies a sequence of movements. Although what follows may be rightly taken to offer guidance in early development of many important areas of piano technique, it must be emphasized that it is presented primarily in the context of achieving topographical *orientation* in a most natural, biomechanically healthy way. Indeed, that is the chief topographical advantage.

To whatever degree such a topographical methodology is embraced, the rational basis in which it is grounded will become ever more apparent. Its roots go deep, its underpinnings are secure, and its advantages far-reaching and long-lasting.

FROM THE BEGINNING: A PRESERVATION OF THE "NATURAL" SENSE

In any rational search for suitable fingerings there must be some real sense of where to begin. It certainly cannot be the all-white-key C major scale that, along with the A natural minor, must be considered an anomaly.

Neither is it reliably an initial or accustomed use of a playing mechanism that may be overdeveloped in some ways and underdeveloped in others, one in which habitual actions and responses are therefore physiologically and kinesthetically inefficient. *Chronic* tension is, by definition, already "structured"—deeply internalized and largely out of conscious awareness.

And it also cannot be one in which keyboard topography and points of key contact, the very points at which key movement is initiated, are not adequately considered, and even ignored. It is not usually appreciated that specific movements involved in playing a specific key or groups of keys must likewise take into consideration the goal of quite specific points of key contact. Otherwise, the movements practiced will not be consistent in all the factors that are at work. Any long-lasting benefits of repetitive practice (drill) that would culminate in a reflexive response (automatization) cannot then accrue efficiently and reliably.

Daniel Gregory Mason (1873–1953) was of the same illustrious New England family of musicians that includes Lowell, William and the Mason & Hamlin piano makers. He was quite influential as a composer, author, teacher and critic in his day. His extraordinary memoir, *Music in My Time—and Other Reminiscences*, makes for reading that is captivating as well as informative. But his little-known *A Neglected Sense in Piano-Playing* also holds much that is extremely valuable; early on the book pointed to some of the concerns addressed herein. In speaking of this "neglected sense," Mason distinguishes between a "tactile sense proper" and a "space sense." The first is that "sense of touch in the finger-tips by which they ceaselessly explore the keyboard, finding their way about by *observing the landmarks of the black keys alternately grouped in twos and threes*" (italics added). Second is "the sense of space, either spanned by the fingers or traversed by the hand . . . [that] enables us to measure intervals without feeling of the keys."[10] The first points to *topography* as the arbiter of keyboard space. The second points to *topology*, the quantifiable measure (interval, distance and range) of that topographically defined space.

Tobias Matthay (1858–1945) early on warned of the dangers of prematurely forcing certain kinds of patterning on the individual fingers before a fuller sense of the arm and the hand is awakened and further developed. In other words: arm first. To that end, he devised and recommended for the most elementary stages what he set forth as "The Aiming Exercises—for the study of accuracy in 'aiming' or directing the Act of Touch."[11] He exhorts: in learning to "depress keys into sounding, instead of at once trying to do so with *individualized* fingers (a most complex matter) . . . after one has learnt in some measure to give motion to the key *in the proper way*, only then to proceed to the simpler exercises for the individualization of each finger [italics in original]."[12]

Taken together, Mason's and Matthay's pronouncements clearly acknowledge and advocate the greater role of the upper arm as prime negotiator of keyboard space while at the same time drawing attention to the intrinsically invaluable role of the black keys as arbiters—the defining characteristic—of that space. They also constitute a strong plea to go beyond what was already deemed "traditional" in pedagogical circles and to seek out better ways of introducing and adapting the natural playing mechanism to the keyboard from the start.

Clearly, any effective approach to fingering must be one that is comprehensive. It must go far beyond mere finger patterning, intellectual "grouping," or individual idiosyncrasy if it would also serve as a positive, even *determining* factor in technical development, and ultimately tone production.

The preservation of that "natural sense"—to whatever degree it resides in him or her—must ever be foremost in bringing the student to the keyboard. If no longer fully operative or seemingly unavailable, it must then be reawakened or restored. And beyond that, such appreciation and awareness of it must be so developed that any future absence will immediately signal the need for attention and conscious intervention. Physiologically and kinesthetically, choice of fingering is therefore most important at this early stage.

Coordinated movements will most likely proceed from fingering that best orients the upper arm in keyboard space. But proper orientation of the hand and its fingers to the keyboard also follows that of the upper arm. For this reason the thumb is at first avoided in alternate hand (cross-hand) patterns. Incorrect, unnecessary and excessive use of the radial (thumb) side of the hand at the expense of the ulnar side ("end" fingers four and five) is one of the main factors contributing to incoordinate movement at the keyboard. Consequent physiological debilitation and even severe injury are the unfortunate and all-too-frequent manifestations at the more advanced stages.

From very early on, then, it is the sense of the fourth finger's connection to and participation with the ulna, and thereby to the upper arm (shoulder complex), that should be enlisted and awakened, then preserved and further developed. This *ulnar orientation* is not to be confused with *ulnar deviation*, which partly arises from that unhealthy and potentially damaging misuse and overuse of the radial side of the hand. Such deviation, eventually chronic, is a consequent misalignment of the hand in the *direction* of the ulna in which lateral adjustments of the hand at the wrist do not assist in its proper alignment with the forearm. The lower arm (hand and forearm), rather than the upper arm, incorrectly takes the initiative in horizontal movement ("leads"). This common tendency is particularly manifest in approaching more distant locations away from the torso beyond the arm's midline, this midline determined by its "anatomical position" ("neutral position," for some, is often less forbidding).

In regard to the arm's anatomical midline, it is not generally recognized that the keyboard area immediately in front of the pianist's torso is already a "distant location" for both hands, requiring certain rather sensitive adjustments for correct alignment and coordinate use. It is therefore most important that the beginning pianist's introduction to the keyboard should not be confined, nor his or her movement restricted, to this middle C region.

Proper shoulder joint/shoulder complex stabilization and control of the humerus (the single bone of the upper arm) plays a determinant role in all movements at the piano; but this is a technical aspect best not isolated or focused on at this primary stage. What is most important is consistent employment of the longest fingers instead of the thumb in movement farthest away from the midline of the arm: in front of the torso and beyond. Apart from other matters of alignment, key depth and distance are thus most efficiently negotiated. Fortunately, this too is an innate tendency, a natural sense, of most children. After just a little encouragement and experimentation, children quite naturally continue to gravitate to such finger choices when moving throughout the keyboard range in locating keys more distant from the arm's midline: toward the right for the left hand, toward the left for the right hand. This important "hook-up" of the arm to the keyboard and its topography is not to be underestimated.

A teacher's well-grounded grasp of topographical principles and their biophysical underpinnings increases her ability to recognize and appreciate fingering attempts that may in fact be optimal, even if contrary to long-standing thought or habit. Especially in the early stages of study, it is important that some movements toward key depression be left alone, with others encouraged and further developed, and still others supplanted to enable and engage a more natural and efficient orientation to the keyboard. This requires knowledge, experience and discrimination. A developmental sensitivity is always in order.

There has been tremendous growth of interest in the field of piano pedagogy, and piano teaching has made enormous strides overall. But a deeply prevailing challenge to acceptance of a topographical approach to fingering persists in the ever-increasing, and I believe mistaken, efforts to achieve higher quality through standardization of approach. Standards are one thing; standardization is quite another. One does not necessarily include or require the other.

The now-traditional fingerings and attendant misconceptions have become ever more entrenched as "standard," and their influence resolutely persists in the vast array of methods and teaching repertoire currently available and forever flooding our studios. Even granted that it is not easy to give over to an unfamiliar approach—no matter how convincing or appealing—wholesale adoption of a topographical approach to fingering will surely not be furthered without guidance for teachers of students at the elementary and intermediate levels.

What first follows, therefore, is a suggested approach along general lines for beginning students. Although geared primarily for the early ages, it is easily adapted for maturing young people and even adults. Within this broad framework there is much latitude for specificity, such as may be deemed appropriate for the individual student and the particular learning situation. Again, the chief aim is a topographical orientation from the very beginning and the earliest introduction of those concepts that will form the basis for fingering considerations specifically and a biomechanically sound technical development overall. All patterns should be presented as below: without notation.

THE BLACK KEYS FIRST

Without the black keys, the white keys would be an undifferentiated maze; it is the black keys that define and organize the white keys. This initial perception of the keyboard already goes a long way toward a topographical orientation.

And if we hold that the generally accepted form of the *pentatonic scale*[13]—its five tones represented on the keyboard by the five black keys (**BB BBB**)—is in one very important sense fundamental to the diatonic scale (its two minor thirds later becoming the whole-step and half-step intervals of the third-fourth and seventh-eighth degrees of the major scale), then the black keys are indeed the ideal introduction to the keyboard. *Visually* this relationship is readily apparent.

Aurally, this pentatonic scale affords its age-old advantage: the absence of half-steps. With its whole tones and characteristic minor thirds (idiomatic of street and peddlers' calls, for example), it is most naturally singable and engaging, even "exotic" in appeal. The remarkably successful Kodály Method is based on this melodic "archetype" transposed. Also applied instrumentally, cultural adaptations of this universally famous approach to sight-singing and ear-training now go beyond Hungarian and other Central and East European folk tunes to include those of the Celts and Southern Appalachians (United States), among others.

Spatially, this pentatonic form is a keyboard pattern that immediately occasions movement throughout the breadth of the entire keyboard, ascending and descending. And *physiologically*, the use of the longest fingers (third and fourth) in distant location promotes the sense of a balanced and supported arm moving through keyboard space. Excessive "thumb orientation" is avoided from the first.

The following may—even should—be introduced over a period of several lessons and revisited over time.

First, the student should locate these key-group hands separately, the LH ascending only and the RH descending only. It is best if these groups are first located in key "blocks" (played simultaneously), although individualized finger action should be allowed if the student is so inclined. In either case, these should first proceed *without a specified fingering*.

Next they are to be played ascending and descending in each hand, followed by the cross-hand sequence of L-R-L-R etc. and R-L-R-L etc.

Examples:

    (1) BB
    (2) BBB
    (3) BB BBB

Second, these patterns are now to be played with LH **4-3/4-3-2** and RH **3-4/2-3-4** for the respective black key groups. Because these fingers encourage and preserve the ulnar orientation of the balanced arm, they are best for moving through keyboard space.

Half-steps are next introduced to the student as the smallest interval that will be encountered, both aurally and spatially, in their use of the keyboard. The **chromatic scale**, a scale of half-steps, is most simply introduced *in each hand* using only the third finger (again, thumb is to be avoided) beginning from any key, ascending and descending. This involves use of the entire arm rather than groups of fingers; these smallest divisions of keyboard space are more keenly sensed and appreciated in this way. The longest third finger best orients the arm for the white keys, their key bottom deeper relative to the black keys.

Because the two- and three-group black-key patterns of the pentatonic are constructed of whole steps, one may logically proceed to introducing the scale of whole steps: the **whole tone scale**.

Beginning with the group of three consecutive black keys, ascending or descending—

(a) BBB WWW, cross hands (and reverse hands) using **4-3-2/2-3-4**

—and then beginning with the two-black-key group—

(b) BB WWWW, as above using **4-3/2-3-4-5**

—the stage is set for diatonic fingering patterns starting from middle C. Reading should not be delayed.

MIDDLE C, DIATONIC PATTERNS AND THE "TYRANNY OF C MAJOR"

From a reading standpoint, the so-called middle C approach has much to recommend it.[14] Aurally it is most practical; hearing is engaged in the middle range of the keyboard. Visually it is likewise accommodating since it demands little of the peripheral—the range being challenging enough if attention to the page is also required. Also, the notation for middle C is common to both hands in treble and bass clefs, and note patterns are mirrored contrariwise from it, usually beginning with the thumb of each hand. The basic fingering patterns employed are therefore symmetrical. In all-white-key C, this poses a distinct advantage at the very beginning of the reading process.

But for students of any age, this middle-C approach physiologically requires use of the arm beyond its anatomical midline, in front of the torso—a distinct disadvantage. This alone can already constitute the beginning of a fundamental biomechanical orientation to the keyboard that is far from ideal. To counteract such a "positioning" that is fraught with potential difficulties down the road, the teacher should become skilled at guiding and positioning the arm. To this end, it is important that (1) *inward* rotation of the humerus is sensed and maintained, and (2) finger use is properly aligned with the forearm and predominantly ulnar-oriented, as opposed to thumb-oriented. In this way, the teacher aids in eliciting even further the student's natural sense.

Since it is usually too early at this stage to instruct in the subtleties of adjustment for optimal alignment, it is therefore imperative that students be led to make use of the widest range of keyboard space from their first keyboard encounters (left on their own, they usually do!). The reading may sensibly require only a limited playing range, but technical development and keyboard exploration may—and should—employ the largest range practicable. In this way, an appreciation and awareness of the proper alignment of the entire playing mechanism as it engages and accommodates the keyboard *throughout the several playing registers* may be preserved, encouraged and further developed from the outset.

The white keys of the C scale are indispensable as a *diatonic model* for the whole- and half-step construction of the major scale precisely because there are no black keys between the third-fourth and seventh-eighth scale degrees. The successive intervals of this diatonic construction are thus most easily visualized in terms of C, and the scale degrees of these distinguishing half-step intervals are most easily remembered and referenced when transposing to major scales constructed on other tonics.

With patterning taught by a combination of rote and written finger numbers, a great deal of time may therefore be profitably spent in C major at this very elementary stage. After single fingers, patterns based on groups of two to five fingers and sequenced on each scale degree increase the range of keyboard use beyond the limitations of middle C region five-note/finger groups and expand keyboard comprehension. Because the successive harmonies are implied in such sequencing, a strong basis for tonal familiarity and recognition is introduced.

For all of the above, absence of notation frees the student for sharper hearing, keener visualization, and heightened physiological and kinesthetic awareness. However, it is most important that reading be introduced from the very beginning, concurrent with all of this—and the student must be so impressed.

But the C major scale itself does not need to be introduced *theoretically* at such an early stage; the student's experience with its diatonic construction can, and should, remain practical. And in regard to the technical aspects of extended-range scale playing, it definitely should not the first scale to be encountered for this, as Chopin clearly understood. Any scale with a black-key pivot for the fourth finger, the placement of the longer third finger naturally compensating for the difference in W-B key depth, is far more preferable. Moreover, it is usually quite some time before piano playing itself is significantly dependent on scale study. Nonetheless, there is an enormous amount that the teacher can do preliminary to this (see Chapters 13 and 14)—and all of it far preferable to introduction of scales requiring the thumb-under pivoting action at such an early stage.

What remains most essential is that a diatonic major scale, in this case C, is being *used*, that its whole- and half-step arrangement is being *heard* as it relates to a particular tonality or tonal center (key note). With the sequencing of five-finger patterns, the implied harmonies of C major as heard in stepwise progression are emphasized. Varied and, later, even transposed to other keys, these further develop and reinforce the student's *tonal sense*, that sense of tonality and familiarity with its basic building blocks.

Though useful in the early stage of reading, the five-finger position beginning with each thumb on middle C, ascending in the RH and descending in the LH, should not be dwelt on for too long. Besides being a position for a less-than-ideal orientation of the hand and arm to the keyboard, an all-too-easy reliance on finger numbers develops—a tendency that all experienced teachers will readily confirm, and a habit that is extremely difficult to alter. Focusing on these rather than the note heads themselves is fostered, and visual recognition of *note patterns* is also thereby discouraged.

Far more important is that specific notes are identified and located (in fact, "*Where* is this?" often supersedes "*What* is this?") regardless of fingering. Overemphasis on fingering in the early stages of reading is too often a chief detriment to reading progress. Absent this, the notes are located primarily with arm movements, and a stronger spatial and kinesthetic—even aural—sense is developed as a result. Development of the smaller motor reflexes needs attention, but it should not be prematurely forced since this is tension-producing, as Matthay recognized very early in his teaching career. Eye-hand coordination and processing of images are affected by muscular tension, whether in the ocular segment or the playing mechanism itself.

At this point, it is worthwhile to briefly address the matter of rhythm and "count-ing" as it may potentially affect reading and recognition of note groups and patterns. It is rare that a young student, regardless of age, does not respond to the rhythmic impulse; the body itself is rhythmic in nature. This is evident in any rote patterning that is unencumbered by the necessity of the reading process itself. Even in the case of relatively complex patterns, the student will be seen and heard to give them some kind of regular and consistent rhythmic sense or organization, usually reflecting the rhythm of their most readily available biomechanical response. And this is also most true in regard to reading and sight reading.

More often than not, the naturally gifted reader, as well as the "slow" reader, will develop reading skills only—or seemingly—at the expense of "counting." Put another way: counting, as commonly taught, will often impede the process of grouping notes into rational, identifiable patterns. Just as excessive emphasis on a note-by-note reading process may discourage natural recognition of otherwise more-or-less-obvi-ous relationships, so may insistence of a "beat by beat" approach in the early stages. What must be recognized and appreciated is the very likely possibility that such a student will group notes and recognize patterns if left to the rhythm of his or her own responses—even the rhythm of the eyes as they encounter and travel the page. The teacher's strategy must therefore be very calculated and well balanced as to the most necessary and effective aspects of the student's own reading "style" that ought to be encouraged and strengthened. It is not solely a matter of addressing perceived deficiencies and then setting out to rectify them.

Nonetheless, as with all reading, the reading of music is very much an intellec-tual process in that it requires the ability to first recognize and only then translate a learned system of symbols. But a natural keyboard orientation and comfortable key-board visualization is essential to this translation. Both keyboard and aural pattern-ing should therefore not be underestimated—nor should singing. Sight reading certainly most benefits from a biophysical, kinesthetic and tactile response that is natural, familiar, and secure.

It is very much a matter of hearing and speaking the language before reading it, not the other way around. Beginning with pentatonic and whole-tone patterning that focuses mainly on a black-key orientation, such as was suggested earlier, that is then followed—or even accompanied—by the convenience of C major for diatonic patterning strikes a very necessary and practical balance at the elementary level. Pentatonic, chromatic, whole-tone, and diatonic scale constructions are established as the foundation from the very start.

PRELUDE TO THE TOPOGRAPHICAL SCALE
FINGERINGS: C♭, C, C♯

Building on the student's earlier experience with the black-key pentatonic scale groups is a useful way to introduce a theoretical origin of the diatonic scale. That is, the minor thirds of the pentatonic scale/series are "filled in," so to speak, to create a stepwise pattern (it may later be noted that this is similar to the early rationale for the ascending melodic minor form). Transposing C major, having no sharps or flats ("seven naturals"), to C♯ (seven sharps) and C♭ (seven flats) makes a very important, but often overlooked, connection regarding these keys. It also clearly sets forth the function of sharps and flats in note spelling, especially helpful in introducing the enharmonic spellings of the white-key half-steps (B/C♭-B♯/C and E/F♭-E♯/F).

As with all the enharmonic major scales, placement of the half-steps is the real challenge, since the topography remains the same throughout. Employing the Fundamental Pattern as they do, C-sharp and C-flat constitute a very logical introduction to the major scales proceeding from the black keys first. And note that these are enharmonic D-flat and B, Chopin's preferred keys for preliminary scale study. But introduced as C-sharp and C-flat, they have the advantage of serving as a theoretical and practical link to C, one that transitions from a predominantly black-key orientation to the all-white-key patterns first encountered at the elementary reading level.

C-sharp and C-flat (enharmonic D-flat and B) might also be considered as alternative starting points of the Circle in Fifths, particularly useful for our purposes as keyboard players. The circle is then inverted, from F-sharp/G-flat, if you will, with C major being the transition point, rather than the starting point, of sharp to flat keys and vice versa (see Chapter 1). This might be approached in several ways.

C-sharp may be introduced first since the half-steps of scale degrees 3-4 and 7-8 (1) are marked by white to black keys—each white key immediately preceding the black-key groups. With alternating hands two to four octaves ascending and descending, the pentatonic fingering as suggested above, and a long finger playing the white key:

B	**B**		**B**	**B**	**B**		**B**	**B**
C♯	**D♯**		**F♯**	**G♯**	**A♯**		**C♯**	(etc. 2-4 octaves
		E♯				**B♯**		ascending,
		W				**W**		descending)

And then similarly for C-flat major, in which each white key immediately follows a black key group:

	B	**B**		**B**	**B**	**B**		**B**	**B**
	D♭	**E♭**		**G♭**	**A♭**	**B♭**		**D♭**	(etc. as above)
C♭			**F♭**				**C♭**	
W			**W**				**W**	

Next, the thumbs are employed in a full three-black-key Fundamental Pattern. Attention should be drawn to the fact that the core four group in each hand, all whole steps, is mirrored exactly (is reflected contrariwise) in terms of interval, topography and fingering. The student thus becomes acquainted early on with this application to diatonic scales throughout his or her studies.

Here it is important to recognize that very small hands may have difficulty grasping the Fundamental Pattern, mostly because of the height of the black keys rather than hand span. At this point an individualized, detached (nonlegato, as opposed to staccato) finger action backed up by the arm suffices in most cases for successful implementation. It may of course be introduced later on instead, once the hand can more comfortably take hold. But it is also worth remembering that Chopin himself did not insist on a legato connection when initially introducing this pattern. He was correctly concerned that the student might not otherwise be inclined to permit the freedom required to experience a fuller sense of the arm, the *horizontal* position of the hand (which he maintained was essential), and the dynamics of the key action itself.[15]

For C-flat:

```
(3)        1  2  3  4  5         1  2  3  4  5
Cb         Fb Gb Ab Bb Cb        Fb Gb Ab Bb Cb
    Db Eb                   Db Eb
     4  3                    4  3
```

For C-sharp:

```
  3  4                3  4
  C# D#               C# D#                      C#
      E# F# G# A# B#       E# F# G# A# B#
      5  4  3  2  1        5  4  3  2  1
```

Altering the four- and three-note groups accordingly, one may now proceed to C major from either C-flat or C-sharp. The RH core group can be seen as deriving from that for C-flat, and the LH from C-sharp. Each hand is consistent with the altered Fundamental Pattern:

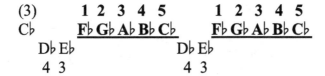

```
(a)            1 2 34        1 2 34
               FGAB          FGAB
        CDE            CDE             C[DE]


(b)
        CDE            CDE             C[DE]
               FGAB          FGAB
               4 3 2 1       4 3 2 1
```

An important note: many students will continue to find 4-3-2 (LH ascending and RH descending) as a more comfortable alternative for the three-note group for some time, but with 1-2-3 quite comfortable for the reverse direction (LH descending and RH ascending). Since the key fingering issues center on the altered Fundamental Pattern, there is every reason not to discourage this very common and natural inclination. As always, the student is guided in properly engaging the thumb and aligning the arm in the more extreme registers; a wise alternative is limiting the playing range to two octaves in the area of the arm's midline.

With the beginning student now well on the way to appreciating the logic and innate comfort of a topographical orientation, more attention can then be focused on the mirrored Fundamental Pattern. Its usefulness is unique as the basis for extended scale and arpeggio fingerings, and its inherent advantages in furthering a more natural approach to keyboard technique are unmatched (Chapter 14). To this end, other cross-hand scales employing the topographical core groups are introduced next (Chapter 13).

TOPOGRAPHY AND TONALITY

13

Please do not think that I am so naïve as to ignore the logic of the circle around which our scales are built and the center of which is C. I merely stress that the theory of piano playing which deals with the hand and its physiology is distinct from the theory of music.

—Heinrich Neuhaus

Playing a melody in C major feels very different under the hand from playing it in F-sharp major. We are physically in a different realm.

—Charles Rosen

CHOPIN'S CHIEF PEDAGOGICAL CONCERN was development of a basic keyboard *orientation* as manifested in and ideally represented by the Fundamental Pattern. His own admonition, and pedagogical practice, that students begin scale study with the D-flat and B major scales, as well as his preference for compositional keys favoring a host of black keys, reflected this sensitivity to the hand's natural accommodation to the keyboard's topographical symmetry. Absent this realization (we recall that the great Chopinist Alfred Cortot, though eventually acquiring Chopin's manuscript, nonetheless missed this essential point entirely), several convoluted—romantic (small r)—explanations for Chopin's key choices have appeared, none of them convincing.[1] It is clear that Chopin put a premium on pianistic comfort, for him a *sine qua non* if artistry were to be the ultimate goal.

Chopin never did manage to finish, further expand, or clarify his *méthode* before his death. And so we have been left with only the sketch and certain vague—sometimes rather cryptic, even contradictory—comments that, seemingly at first shed relatively little light on the evolution of his determined attempt to resolve matters of fingering rationally and systematically. The accounts of some his students are often not in agreement, sometimes revealing only their own limitations of analysis or perception. Mikuli's well-known report regarding Chopin's often very individualized and idiosyncratic approach to fingering serves as one example. But Schumann's apt remark, that Chopin's music could be likened to "cannons hidden beneath flowers,"[2] perhaps has its counterpart in the Fundamental Pattern. Its power is indeed belied by its simple but elegant beauty.

The scale fingerings later proposed as alternatives to the "nontopographical" standard ones reflect, and are rooted in, the Fundamental Pattern. But their connection to it was not recognized, and the fuller implications of symmetrical relationships and other underlying principles remained to be realized. Again, it certainly would be most illuminating to know just what it was that so moved Neuhaus to ultimately designate Chopin's pattern as the very key to a pianistic pedagogy. How did he see its fundamental simplicity, its fundamental utility? What did he see beyond the obvious? What potential power did this "egg" hold for him?

That many understood the good sense and appreciated the demonstrable ease of these alternative fingerings but were nonetheless of two minds as to their implementation in pedagogical practice was noted earlier. It was of particular concern that the accustomed theoretical approach might be threatened, and that there could be none to supplant it. But topographical orientation as well as theoretical conceptualization and *functional application* go hand in hand. They are not in conflict—indeed, quite the contrary. They are mutually reinforcing.

Fully explored and fully understood, keyboard symmetry is hard to ignore. And its theoretical underpinnings, first as they relate to the major keys of the Circle of Fifths, point to an even deeper fundamental relationship. Chopin, with his enharmonic spelling of the Fundamental Pattern in D-flat and B major, clearly intuited the far-reaching implications of this relationship, and they are repeatedly reflected in the key schemes of his compositions. In retrospect, there can be little wonder that he held the "genius" of the keyboard's design in unceasing awe.

TOPOGRAPHICAL MIRRORS: REFLECTIONS OF SYMMETRY

Architecturally, structurally and physiologically, the body abounds—and revels—in symmetry. Basically, whatever we have one of is found at its center; what we have two of are each found at or toward its periphery. Arms and eyes aside, the hands are, from the pianist's standpoint, most likely the first to be thought of in terms of symmetry as it may be applied to the keyboard. In terms of long and short fingers, the hand's symmetry is readily apparent. And viewing both hands, thumbs touching, we encounter "mirrored" symmetry: all aspects are reflected in their entirety but oppositely—as if in a mirror.

The middle C approach to reading employs another kind of symmetry, and owes its long-standing success to it. This *notational* symmetry is likewise mirrored in that all notes as they proceed from middle C in opposite directions are reflected visually in all respects. The assignment of the thumb of each hand to middle C with the stepwise positioning of each finger thereafter forms the basis of this enormously successful approach to reading. Although the interval relationships—the sequence of whole and half-steps—do not mirror, this is of no particular import since, initially, the topography is that of all white keys. The enormous advantage of this elementary keyboard approach lies in such a synthesis of physiological, topographical and notational symmetries.

At first all patterns are symmetrical, proceeding as they do contrariwise from middle C. But since they are all white keys, they are least accommodating to the varying finger lengths. And as frequently noted above, the orientation of the arm—at *distant location* from its anatomical midline, even though immediately in front of the torso—is rather far removed from its most natural, most comfortable position relative to the keyboard. Most of the extant methodology then introduces altered tones: B-flat to the second finger of the LH and sometimes the fourth of the RH to F-sharp, though usually shifting all five fingers up a whole step to D, giving F-sharp to the third finger.

Such rational employment of these altered five-finger patterns is basic as well as practical. But topographical and intervallic symmetry is not encountered in these first experiences with the major tonalities of F and G. Further exploration of the symmetrical relationships that are inherent in the keyboard's remarkable design is abandoned early on. So it is that the fledgling pianist has no meaningful encounter with them until much later acquaintance (though indirect) with the five-black-key enharmonic major scales—or directly, through Chopin's Fundamental Pattern.

At this early stage, the real heart of the problem of a natural orientation—of engaging and preserving that natural sense—resides in moving beyond the immediate but temporary advantages of such a five-note/five-finger symmetrical introduction to reading. Put another, perhaps better, way: the challenge from the start is to provide a larger keyboard and theoretical context for this approach and, at the same time, to "defuse"—in a very real sense—its inherent topographical and physiological disadvantages.

BEYOND C MAJOR

It is a wise maxim that development of requisite keyboard skills and technical proficiency should always be pursued *in advance* of the difficulties and complexities to be encountered in repertoire. If repertoire-specific challenges are anticipated, and the student is consequently equipped for independent discovery, he or she may then better move forward with a far more secure, natural, and integrated response. To this end, there are several ways for *progressively* incorporating diatonic scale study into a student's regular technical regimen.

A topographical, or *black-key*, evolution of the C major scale, presented as in the last chapter, is excellent preparation for the early-age beginner; there remains the distinct advantage in forgoing any patterns requiring thumb-under pivoting at this crucial stage. And it is best that upper arm "locating" movements continue to be favored throughout the broad ranges of the keyboard. In this way, visual and tactile groupings are reinforced without the added complexities of thumb-under action, and optimal coordination of the entire playing mechanism is methodically introduced and purposefully developed.

Indeed, the hand-over-thumb pivoting action (RH descending and LH ascending) is best introduced *before* the thumb-under action in any case; the correct relation of thumb to fourth or third is most readily and naturally enlisted, most easily coordinated and sensorially reinforced. The Classical-era composers of the sonatina are noteworthy in their preference for employing scale patterns in this pedagogically astute fashion.

But the teacher may easily continue the alternate hand approach to this same advantage, while systematically introducing the sharps and flats as they occur according to the Circle of Fifths. Initially, elementary-level students would obviously concentrate on scales in those keys that they are presently encountering or will soon encounter in their reading and repertoire.

The alternate (cross-) hand scale groups presented in this chapter should all be extended to a range of two or more octaves and rhythmically approached in an individual manner best supporting patterning, the main focus at first. As with reading, the student's own internal rhythmical inclinations can be most revealing, serving as an excellent starting point for scale patterning that adheres to a more specific and intentional (conscious) rhythmic structure later on.

Individual fingering choices for the three-note groups should also be allowed. Fingering for these would not be fixed but fluid, and much will be learned about the student's hand and overall coordination in the process. It will be observed that finger groups will often be exchanged or interchanged, ascending or descending, to adjust for keyboard range and proximity to torso. But where there is not a strong inclination otherwise, the long fingers (4-3-2/2-3-4) are to be preferred and encouraged, as these best preserve the sense of a balanced arm while avoiding overemphasis and overreliance on engaging the thumb (radial) side of the hand. What is not negotiable, of course, is the topographical fingering for the core groups—the very point of this process.

The Major Scales

Because the major scale of any number of sharps exactly mirrors that of the same number of flats, and vice versa, there is a distinct advantage in first presenting them that way. The mirrored core (four-note) groups all lie comfortably in the hand and determine all scale fingerings. But they consist of *whole tones* only for the flat keys in the LH and the sharp keys in the RH and are therefore favored for initial presentation.

Example 13.1

		(2 3 4)	(2 3 4)	(3)
F:		FGA	FGA	F(GA)
		B♭ CDE	B♭ C DE	
		4 3 2 1	4 3 2 1	

		1 2 3 4	1 2 3 4	
G:		C D EF♯	C DEF♯	
	(4 3 2)	(4 3 2)	(3)
	GAB	GAB	G(AB)

The major flat scales of the RH also mirror those of the LH sharps, but the interval arrangement for their mirrored core groups now reflects the *diatonic* (whole and half-step) alterations of the Fundamental Pattern necessary for each scale.

Those alternate hand fingerings easily follow from the four- and three-note groups of the C scale for each hand. Because the student can more easily relate the F scale to C major by visualization, it would be introduced first, rather than G as is customary. The RH four group is constant, but B must be lowered to form the first tetrachord of a diatonic scale pattern beginning on F:

Example 13.2

C: CDE **FGAB** C

F: **FGAB♭** CDE F

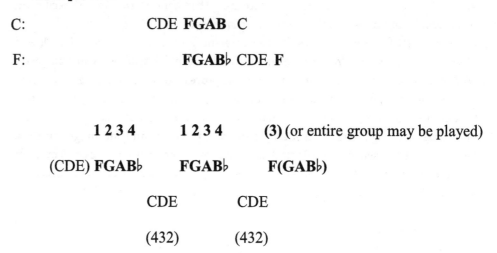

	1 2 3 4	1 2 3 4	(3) (or entire group may be played)
(CDE)	**FGAB♭**	**FGAB♭**	**F(GAB♭)**
	CDE	CDE	
	(432)	(432)	

B-flat is the lowered seventh degree of C major but now the fourth degree of F major. The *fourth* finger is lowered. The *tendency* of flats to resolve downward in the direction of the half-step (the fourth degree to the third here) is encountered.

For G major the altered tone F-sharp is the raised fourth degree of C major, now the seventh degree of G. The *fourth* finger is raised. The tendency of sharps to resolve upward in the direction of the half-step (leading tone to tonic) is now encountered.

Example 13.3

	(2 3 4)		(2 3 4)	
	CDE		CDE	
G:	(F♯)GAB	**F♯ GAB**	**F♯ G(AB)**
	(4) 3 2 1	**4 3 2 1**	**4 3 (2 1)**

In both instances, the distinguishing scale degree alteration is associated and correlated with the fourth finger. As the center of the ulna's axis, the direction of the alteration is experienced in the direction of the torso with this key finger: sharps up, flats down. Tonal alteration is reinforced kinesthetically.

The topographical patterns and complementary mirror groups are noted and analyzed for B/W keys and intervals. For G and F, the order of crossed (alternate) hands is reversed. The student observes that the core group of one scale exactly mirrors that of the other.

As with their single-hand counterparts, the student encounters partial groups in executing the alternate hand major scales from tonic to tonic: for the sharp keys in the LH (as in Example 13.3), and for the flats in the RH (beyond F). The mirrored core groups made up exclusively of whole tones are therefore the basis of the alternate hand scales as presented below in the Circle of Fifths.

Drawing attention to the mirroring of note groups is not merely imparting interesting information; nor is it even a matter of interval analysis. Very early on, it introduces the fundamental rationale and determinant for an approach to scale fingering that attends to topographical factors (already the *key depth* principle may be noted in regard to the longer third on the white key and shorter fourth on the black, for example). Moreover, keyboard visualization is encouraged as a real part of the process, further demystifying the keyboard while revealing another aspect of its extraordinary organization. To spark or further fuel a student's fascination with the keyboard is certainly a worthy goal—and no mean feat.

The Tonic-Dominant Relationship and Primary Chords

Concurrent study of the major scales of C, G and F affords an excellent opportunity for the more capable student, of whatever age, to begin to grasp the important relationship of the dominant to the tonic: that of a perfect fifth or its inversion, a perfect fourth. Whether pertaining to scale degree or root movement with implied harmony, it is manifest and heard in the relationship of C-G and C-F and is fundamental to our Western concept of tonality. The origin and meaning of the terms *dominant* and *subdominant* are explained as the perfect fifth *above* and *below* tonic C, the relationship exemplified in the Circle of Fifths.

*Sub*dominant		Tonic		Dominant
F	-	C	-	G
IV	**-**	**I**	**-**	**V**

The very young student would do best to become familiar with this relationship by playing the roots of each chord in the following progressions, first with single fingers (which finger will the student favor?) ascending and descending, and eventually with alternate hands and later transposed.

C - G - C   (authentic [cadential] relationship: I-V-I)

C - F - C   (plagal [cadential] relationship: I-IV-I)

C - F - G - C   (primary triad progression: I-IV-V-I)

Two-voiced chords are introduced next, root and third being the essential tones of any harmony. At first the LH plays the root, the RH the third of the chord. Next, each chord is played cross hands in four "places" (a four-octave range). Initially transposed to F and G, the student thereby touches on the differing harmonic functions of the same chords—their specific role in a given tonality.

Although these are more manageable than three-voiced chords at this stage, they also have the advantage of being ideal for introducing the *distant location principle*, in which the longer fingers best align and orient the playing mechanism when proceeding past the arm's midline in the direction of the torso. 4-2/2-4 cross hands is again preferred in order to engage the full arm and thereby avoid a less coordinate or excessive radial orientation. The progressions given here are also transposed to the minor modes.

Later, triads (root-third-fifth), first as I-V-I then I-IV-V-I progressions, are likewise transposed. Also played cross hands (ascending and descending), they too afford greater use of the keyboard's range. When played as broken chords (easier at first), they also serve as an early aural model for arpeggios.

Though eventually suitable for placing the intervals within a five-finger group, employing LH 5-3-1 and RH 1-3-5 is not recommended. If this fingering is not insisted upon initially, it will be observed that, in most cases, the student will naturally use fingers that favor the arm's ulnar orientation, i.e., avoiding the thumb when crossing the torso for "distant" locations. And they should be allowed to do so. Indeed, I have observed that some of the *most* gifted students, those with the most natural and comfortable sense of the keyboard, avoid entirely the use of the thumb when first finding and playing triads in distant locations—particularly if a black key is involved. And they do this instinctively, and comfortably, for quite some time.

Again, preserving and encouraging this natural sense of alignment with the "back-up" of the upper arm is what is most important at this early stage. There is time later for insisting on specific fingering patterns that "fit the hand," which is to say, corresponding to chord root, third and fifth (5-3-1/1-3-5). Time later, when the necessity for more finely tuned adjustments will be better appreciated because they can be referenced to this accustomed natural orientation.

The Melodic Minor Scales

With their respective thirds, major and minor chords of two and three voices readily lend themselves to an aural and theoretical introduction to these modes. The melodic minor (the "hybrid" form, that of melodic ascending and natural minor descending, is not meant here) is best introduced prior to the harmonic minor. Because the lowered third degree of the scale is the distinguishing tonal alteration from major to any of the three minor forms, it is therefore a more appropriate focus of the student's attention at this very early stage of musical foundation. The tetrachord structure of the major scale is major-major; for the melodic it is minor-major.

We might recall that Josef Hofmann did not consider the melodic minor form significantly important because it introduced no new intervals to the hand, preferring instead the harmonic minor with its characteristic augmented second (2+). But it is precisely for this reason (there are no "new" intervals, only whole and half-steps) that the melodic minor is recommended here as the first minor form to be studied and practiced. This is especially important for the early-age elementary student for whom managing the 2+ will, in most cases, be found rather awkward.

The Harmonic Minor Scales

The harmonic minor form of the scale can also be presented, for variety as well as aural challenge, even if not yet encountered in any of the current teaching material. But because of the 2+, the core patterns do not permit so consistent a mirroring of topography or interval (though mirrors are plentiful; see Chapter 2, Example 2.25). The student should therefore be thoroughly grounded in the mirrored core patterns of the major and melodic minor forms before moving on to the harmonic form. This ensures the maximum benefit of early initiation into the unsuspected wonders of keyboard symmetry.

ALTERNATE HAND DIATONIC SCALES

For the earliest-age beginner, any theoretical discussion must normally be limited at best. Apart from its advantage for the smaller hand, the major-melodic minor-harmonic minor study sequence as presented below for alternate hands satisfies the need for a more simplified, yet appropriately focused, introduction to the necessary alterations characteristic of these minor forms. These scales progressively derive from the diatonic major forms, in which the core groups are composed exclusively of whole tones. Such a progression from major to melodic minor (before the harmonic minor, contrary to the usual practice) has the superior benefit of employing the same whole-tone core groups throughout *both* modes.

Reinforcing even as it builds on the symmetrical equivalents of the whole-tone Fundamental Pattern, it is that "major connection" developed earlier in Chapter 2. At the same time the distinguishing alteration of the major to minor third—of the first three scale degrees—is consistently encountered in the initial three group, just as it was in the two-voiced chords introduced as above. And the core patterns employed exactly represent those later encountered by each hand in playing the full scale individually.

Moving on to the harmonic minor, the emphasis is on the lowered sixth degree, and the altered core patterns reflect this (note LH F-B♭-E♭). This is a far more rational and progressive approach to the altered tones of the minor scales for the young pianist, even as topographical core patterns are reinforced sensorially.

Example 13.4

Major

	Flats		Sharps	

RH: 2 3 4
       FGA   **B♭ CDE**   F   1 2 3 4
                                   GAB   **CDEF♯**   G

LH: 4   32 1   4 32

      2 3 4   1 2 3 4
    B♭ CD   **E♭ F GA**   B♭   DEF♯   **GABC♯**   D
         4 3 2 1   4 3 2

      2 3 4   1 2 3 4
    E♭ FG   **A♭ B♭ CD**   E♭   ABC♯   **DEF♯ G♯**   A
         4 3 2 1   4 3 2

      2 3 4   1 2 3 4
    A♭ B♭ C   **D♭ E♭ F G**   A♭   EF♯ G♯   **ABC♯ D♯**   E
         4 3 2 1   4 3 2

      2 3 4   1 2 3 4
    D♭ E♭ F   **G♭ A♭ B♭ C**   D♭   BC♯ D♯   **EF♯ G♯ A♯**   B
         4 3 2 1   4 3 2

Example 13.5

Melodic Minor

      2 3 4   1 2 3 4
    FG A♭   **B♭ CDE**   F   GA B♭   **CDEF♯**   G
        4   32 1   4 32

      2 3 4   1 2 3 4
    B♭ CD♭   **E♭ FGA**   B♭   DEF   **GABC♯**   D
         4 3 2 1   4 32

      2 3 4   1 2 3 4
    E♭ FG♭   **A♭ B♭ CD**   E♭   ABC   **DEF♯ G♯**   A
         4 3 2 1   4 32

      2 3 4   1 2 3 4
    A♭ B♭ C♭   **D♭ E♭ FG**   A♭   EF♯ G   **ABC♯ D♯**   E
         4 3 2 1   4 32

      2 3 4   1 2 3 4
*   C♯ D♯ E   **F♯ G♯ A♯ B♯**   C♯   BC♯ D   **EF♯ G♯ A♯**   B
         4 3 2 1   4 32

*D♭ minor could only be a "theoretical" relative minor key since there is no F♭ major.

                NATURAL FINGERING

Example 13.6

Harmonic Minor

```
 2  3  4                                      1 2 3 4
F G A♭  B♭ C D♭ E   F              GAB♭  CDE♭ F♯   G
      4  3  2  1                   4 3 2

 2  3  4                                      1 2 3 4
B♭ C D♭  E♭ F G♭ A   B♭            D E F  GAB♭ C♯   D
      4  3  2  1                   4 3 2

 2  3  4                                      1 2 3 4
E♭ F G♭  A♭ B♭ C♭ D   E♭           A BC   D E F G♯   A
      4  3  2  1                   4 3 2

 2  3  4                                      1 2 3 4
A♭ B♭ C♭  D♭ E♭ F♭ G   A♭          EF♯ G  A BC D♯   E
      4  3  2  1                   4 3 2

 2  3  4                                      1 2 3 4
C♯ D♯ E  F♯ G♯ A B♯   C♯           BC♯ D  E F♯ GA♯   B
      4  3  2  1                   4 3 2
```

Related tonally (harmonically), topographically, or both, these cross-hand scale groups provide broad opportunity for a strong elementary grounding in diatonic scale construction. The student is also served well by this early experience of the B/W key core patterns as they consistently apply to scales and, later—literally by extension— arpeggios.

The unique advantage of the cross-hand scale groups is that they represent exactly the topographical groups of the full scales for each hand while not requiring the thumb-under pivoting action. This systematic, progressive presentation pro- motes a rational, *visual* organization of the scales, and a natural, topographical orien- tation to the keyboard is further developed. In this way, a sure foundation for more advanced scale study is firmly established. At the same time, fundamental theoretical aspects are broadly encountered and richly applied.

Suggestions for such a rational approach have been specifically presented or clearly implied in the foregoing. But even at this early stage of study, the knowledge- able and creative teacher will surely find a great number of other ways to enhance the student's keyboard experience and to secure his or her technical development through such a logical but flexible approach. A topographically informed, imaginative partner- ship of scales and repertoire in the formative years can only serve to deepen the ben- efits of a more natural pianistic orientation—and the pleasure that comes with it.

A PENTATONIC ORGANIZATION

As has been noted, Neuhaus's endorsement of the whole-tone Fundamental Pattern as the cornerstone of a pianistic methodology is accompanied by his recommendation of abandonment of C major as a pedagogical basis. For him, as for Chopin, physiological and keyboard considerations must trump theoretical ones. In his remarks, Eigeldinger tells us that "the distinguished Russian teacher pays tribute there [*The Art of Piano Playing*] to Chopin as a pioneer of a revolutionary teaching concept, one radically disassociating piano apprenticeship from the basic principle of the theoretical *solfège* system."[3]

But as asserted throughout this discourse, the topographical supports the theoretical, and in a remarkably more creative way. Because of its inherent relationship to the keyboard's equal-tempered symmetry as well as the Circle of Fifths, one of the beauties of this approach is the natural ease with which any number of important tonal and harmonic relationships may be introduced and explored topographically.

We have also noted that the keyboard's topographical symmetry is in fact negatively characterized by more than a few as "asymmetrical." This asymmetry is ascribed to the groups of two and three black keys in (regularly!) recurring alternation—as opposed to regularly recurring groups of only two *or* three, one must suppose. In some instances, this keyboard asymmetry is bemoaned at the same time that its points of symmetry are acknowledged. But remember that examination of the relationship of the two black-key groups to point of symmetry D also reveals the topographical inversion of the whole-tone Fundamental Pattern. Taken together, the third finger is to be found on both points of symmetry: D and G-sharp/A-flat respectively.

Yet another interesting symmetrical—even mathematical—phenomenon suggests itself in examining further the topographical underpinnings of the fingerings for the major scales, and from which the fingerings for the minor forms evolve. We may consider that BBB, as a group of *three* black keys, therefore represents an *odd* number; and that BB, a group of *two* black keys, represents an *even* number. Working contrariwise from point of symmetry D, we will number the black-key groups accordingly and, comporting with Chopin's notation and practice, assign flats to the LH and sharps to the RH:

Example 13.7

B B	**B B B**		**B B B**	**B B**
4 2	5 3 1		1 3 5	2 4
D♭ E♭	G♭ A♭ B♭		F♯ G♯ A♯	C♯ D♯

[D]

Key of: Ab Bb Db Eb F			G A B D E

The numerology is quite fascinating. With the fourth finger assigned to each of the black keys shown in Example 13.7 (thumb on white), we will construct the whole-tone core groups; recall that these constitute the major scale degrees 4-5-6-7. Beginning with the mirrored core groups LH B♭-C-D-E (F major) and RH C-D-E-F♯ (G major), and from them constructing the diatonic major scale sequence descending, the reader is invited to enjoy a little discovery.

Remarkably, as represented in Example 13.7, each number represents exactly the number of flats or sharps in its respective key signature up to five black keys (the enharmonic major keys of G-flat/F-sharp, C-flat and C-sharp likewise have five black keys). And going further still, it is even more fascinating to learn that in ordering these very same numbers sequentially their occurrence (as whole-tone core patterns) is now that of the major keys of the Circle of Fifths!

Example 13.8

5	4	3	2	1		1	2	3	4	5
D♭	A♭	E♭	B♭	F	**[point of symmetry D]**	G	D	A	E	B

This suggests a very user-friendly approach to introducing scales topographically. Such a *pentatonic* organization is an interesting alternative to the more traditional method of presentation according to the Circle of Fifths. And later, as is advocated in Chapter 14, introducing the pivoting action "hand over thumb" before "thumb under" comports with such an exploration and presentation of the diatonic major scales at the outset.

As seen in Example 13.7, this is, admittedly, an unabashedly topographical organization, even though unified pentatonically. But reflecting keyboard symmetry as it does, it is one that also has the virtue of furthering visual and sensorial clarity. At the same time, it affords variety and welcome simplification in several important respects, as it invites a revealing comparison of related keys and topographies. This pentatonic arrangement also suggests other novel sequences for grouping scales—of all forms, particularly the harmonic minor (see Chapter 2, Example 2.25)—for presentation and study.

A RELATIVELY MINOR MATTER: THEORY AND TOPOGRAPHY

Early-age students may—and should—continue to *experience* minor scales as introduced here in this limited functional manner (that is, only as it relates to altered scale degrees) for quite some time, without benefit—or burden—of theoretical explanation or analysis.

This is particularly true in regard to the harmonic minor, in which its theoretical derivation involving the matter of related major keys and shared signatures (but differing tonics) would otherwise present unnecessary, even insurmountable, complexities. Experienced teachers commonly observe in their students a confusion that persists well into the more advanced years of study because of it. At this elementary stage it will be the physical, visual and aural aspects of these major and minor scales that are most important and most useful. Practical and functional, the topographical approach is ideal.

Introducing the harmonic minor is fairly simple when its derivation is approached functionally. Just as the raised fourth (for sharps) or lowered seventh degree (for flats) is of significance in regard to *successive* major scales in the Circle of Fifths, attention is here drawn to the function of the raised dominant (5+) of a major scale. Its tendency to resolve upward establishes the sixth degree as the new tonic of a minor scale. With this raised (augmented) fifth degree now serving as the leading tone of a new tonality, there is a change in its *function*. And because this was effected by means of tonal alterations within the formerly major key, the key signature does not change. The new minor key is *related*, or derived from it, and is therefore said to be its *relative* minor.

Example 13.9

C:	C D E F G A B C
A hm:	G♯ A B C D E F G♯ A

Apart from the matter of key signatures, A minor being the *relative* minor of C may be of theoretical significance only to the older beginner. But with its leading tone the raised fifth degree of C major, a functional significance of this tonal relationship may yet be more meaningfully noted and understood, even heard, by the younger beginner as well. And already one of the most fundamental *agents* of modulation, that of altered tones rather than key notes, is practically encountered at an early level. Appreciation for key relationships is further instilled.

The derivation of A harmonic minor serves particularly well as the first relative minor scale to be introduced theoretically and practically. The function of tendency tones and their innate tendency toward upward or downward resolution is readily recognized and easily visualized within the context of the all-white-key C major scale.

Example 13.10

```
          1 2 3 4 5 6 7 1

C:        C D E F G A B C

            1 2 3 4 5 6 7  1

A hm:     G♯ A B C D E F G♯ A B C

            I       V       V/V
```

What was formerly the half-step relationship of leading tone to tonic in the relative major (C) now occurs between the second and third degrees of the new relative minor (A). A strong tonal relationship to the relative major is thereby maintained while at the same time establishing the definitive third degree, essential to all forms of the minor mode.

Though now constituting that "unstable" minor third (recall the cadential function of the "Picardy Third"—a major third in early music), the former tonic C remains, in a very important sense, stabilized and *tonality-related* nonetheless.

This may be further understood in terms of tonally "anchoring" the "instability" of the minor mode. The tendency of the lowered third degree to resolve downward in the direction of the half-step at the same time reinforces the second scale degree of the relative minor. Formerly the leading tone of the relative major, its relationship is now that of the dominant of the dominant (V/V or V of V). The tonality of A minor is more definitively established, more firmly secured.

The major scales of C, F and G and their relative minors A, D and E are highly useful in exploring this theoretical relationship. These scales are also those of the keys (tonalities) almost exclusively encountered in the repertoire of the early-level piano student.

The earliest grasp of altered tones and tonal relations has profound implications for the strongest, most comprehensive foundation for musical growth. Although essential for all phases of musicianship, the implications in regard to future development of improvisational skills are especially noteworthy. That the topographical fingerings early on reinforce and secure the practical and aural experience of these functional relationships is an enormous advantage beyond that of consistency, pianistic comfort, or the playing mechanism's biophysical health.

EARLY REPERTOIRE

Piano teachers and their students are extremely fortunate in the wealth of clever, tuneful and engaging material available for early instruction. By and large, the repertoire found in beginning-level methods and collections makes pointed and extensive use of the five-finger/note groups and their transposition as a means of keyboard organization and—in various ways and with varying degrees of success—as a systematic method for developing reading skills. And this is rightly so.

But early topographical scale study employing the cross-hand core groups is far more in sync with these aims than early introduction of standard scale study that employs the pivoting action from the start. Topographical symmetries are far more easily coordinated with musical patterns at hand, where "positions," fingerings and divisions between the hands are often found to be less than ideal. There is, therefore, great potential in reformulating early teaching material that serves to build on the very practical advantages of a middle C contrariwise approach to reading, in which notation is mirrored but fingering reflects the hands' symmetry only.

As presented in Book One of her *Belwin Piano Method*, June Weybright's overall approach to fingering is the rare model for just such a rational presentation of the challenge of fingering as keyboard strategy. Mostly, there are no printed fingerings and the score is uncluttered and appealing to the eye. But solutions are suggested by the material itself: the charming tunes and clever arrangements are logically and skillfully presented with the aim of inviting the student to rationally deduce the fingering logistics, even writing them in at key points of strategy. It is a thoroughly practical and commonsense approach. But what is notably most worthwhile is the introduction of F major and G major, in that order. Correlating these topographical mirrors (F for the RH, fourth on B-flat; G for the LH, fourth on F-sharp), the user-friendly fingering naturally follows.

In *The Joy of First-Year Piano*, Denes Agay enriches and enhances the student's early musical experience enormously. A wealth of original compositions interspersed with authentic folk tunes and his creative and imaginative use of modes—with the attendant "positioning" required of the hand—is purposeful, pleasurable and thoroughly appropriate. Agay follows in the footsteps of fellow-Hungarian Béla Bartók who, in writing his six-volume *Mikrokosmos* for his son Péter, uniquely grappled with the challenge of contributing a more comprehensive, progressive, and musically rich method for young pianists. Creative enrichment and expansion of the pedagogical repertoire was a particularly cherished goal of Soviet composers at the time, and the compositions for students by Kabalevsky, Khachaturian, Samuel Maykapar, Prokofieff, Shostakovich and others are especially well known.

Bartok's compatriot Miklós Kocsár is one among several others who have been similarly motivated in the wake. His *Games with Intervals* (Editio Musica Budapest, 2005)—entirely unfingered—is a unique contribution to the contemporary pedagogical literature. Also noteworthy are the compositions of American composer Vincent Persichetti,[4] in which mirrored symmetry is the featured compositional device, echoing fellow composer Ernst Bacon's espousal of its potential in the realm of composition.[5]

There are, of course, many other fine collections of age- and level-appropriate repertoire. Today's teachers have ready access to a vast array of compositions that have long enriched the musical experience of the elementary-level and early-age pianist. But suggested fingerings in them are often far less than ideal, and profuse to a fault. However, the topographically and biomechanically aware teacher can easily come to the rescue with more natural fingerings. And note redistributions will often facilitate matters enormously.

In any case, repertoire and keyboard work must always be intelligently balanced and creatively supplemented. As the student advances, the most imaginative compositions will present him or her with a wide variety of melodic, harmonic and embellishing patterns. Contrasting compositional styles of an appropriate emotional level may also offer related, reinforcing, or complementary technical and rhythmic challenges within their stylistic limits. But a clear, rational approach to the most natural orientation of hand and arm to keyboard will never fail to promote and inspire progress along these lines.

INTIMATIONS OF SYMMETRY

14

With these five notes one must begin the whole methodology and heuristic of piano playing. . . . This small formula is truly weightier than many heavy tomes. . . . You cannot find anything more natural on the keyboard than this position.

—Heinrich Neuhaus

Symmetry! Everything has to be symmetrical.

—Sviatoslav Richter

THE TRANSITION FROM what is generally considered the "late" elementary to "early" intermediate levels is one of the most challenging for teacher and student alike. Varying degrees of talent and diverse learning styles notwithstanding, repertoire continues to move from complexity to complexity: visual, intellectual, aural and physical. An assigned composition's style should be of interest and its emotional content, in some way, meaningfully relevant if one is to enlist engaged study. Technical ability, cognitive skills and personality must be wisely matched. Fortunately for pianists, and their teachers, there is a wealth of literature to draw on.

Having arrived at the early dances of the Baroque and Classical periods, the young pianist progressively advances to the short sonatas, or *sonatinas*. The predominant model for Classical expression,[1] the sonatina/sonata typifies the period's emphasis on form. Proportion and balance constitute the esthetic ideal, but harmony is the germinating force. Even melodies, themes and motives are harmonically inspired and intentionally crafted, for later development within the tonal and structural framework of the composition.

What has heretofore been primarily a matter of finger patterning, keyboard familiarity and introduction of theoretical and harmonic fundamentals now becomes increasingly obvious as "building blocks" in the comprehension of a compositional style and advancement of reading skills. The fundamental forms—scales, chords, broken chord patterns (Alberti Bass in particular); chord inversions and extensions (as arpeggios)—are of paramount importance hereon. The need to expand and improve the requisite technical skills for achieving a successful and satisfying musical experience is likewise made plain. As ever, the music makes its own demands.

The student now typically encounters a melodic range that is normally expanded beyond the usual five-note/five-finger pattern or its extension one step above (a fifth with an added sixth) or below—a range of a major or minor seventh altogether. Transitional passages and embellishing figures are extended to a range of an octave or more. Repeated and double note patterns are also frequently met: short passages of thirds and sixths abound, but octaves, in passages of any challenging length, less so.

New means for shifting or extending the basic five-finger position must necessarily be employed. Chief among these is the pivoting action of hand over thumb and thumb under hand. There is clearly a technical transition to be made here as well, and Chopin's Fundamental Pattern will be seen to be a formidable tool toward this end.

At the beginning level, important technical emphasis is on preserving and encouraging the upper arm's natural orientation in keyboard space. Apart from any tendency toward stabilization that is naturally provided by its physiological structure, voluntary movements of the *lower* arm (which includes the hand and its fingers) depend on the distributive actions and *dynamic* stabilizing of the shoulder *complex* (upper arm and shoulder girdle) throughout keyboard space. Less attention to the hand in its pronated position at the keyboard is purposefully intended to tap the beginning pianist's natural sense of a unified playing mechanism: his familiar everyday arm use. A focus on the long fingers and their black key assignment proves ideal.

But the nature—and the allure—of piano playing is such that the entire hand's orientation to the keyboard cannot and should not be put off for long. Even if a teacher willed it to be so, the student will not have it that way. After all, the natural prehensile, grasping action of the hand is likewise familiar and everyday.

The hand and its fingers are the ultimate recipients of the purposeful actions of the upper arm, while the keyboard with its topographical symmetry is the place where the rubber meets the road. The hand's natural orientation to it is therefore of prime importance. Especially as the student advances, the Fundamental Pattern holds the highest potential for positive impact, as a rich resource and practical pedagogical tool.

Chopin's rational recognition of the definitive role of the enharmonic keys (scales), the pedagogical implications of his Fundamental Pattern and his extraordinary insights into topography and pianism as reflected in his compositional key schemes remain, even to this day, nothing short of revolutionary.

CHOPIN'S PATTERN AS FUNDAMENTAL TOOL

The Fundamental Pattern should be introduced concurrently with scale study—even earlier, if at all feasible. But since very small hands may have some difficulty grasping the higher black keys (it is less a matter of actual hand span), the whole-tone Fundamental Pattern may be adjusted. Alterations to encompass a perfect fifth (illustrated in "a" below) or even the tritone (b) make it uniquely suitable as a tool to facilitate, encourage and develop this all-important prehensile key contact even for the youngest students. For the smallest hands, the fifth finger may be omitted entirely, focusing only on the remaining core group.

	Left Hand	Right Hand
	(E) F♭ G♭ A♭ B♭ C	E F♯ G♯ A♯ B♯ (C)
(a)	F G♭ A♭ B♭ C	E F♯ G♯ A♯ B
(b)	F G♭ A♭ B♭ B(C♭)	F F♯ G♯ A♯ B

In contrast to the cross-hand scale patterns, work with this five-finger pattern is relatively static—but potentially more plastic. Assigning long fingers to short keys and short fingers to long keys, it immediately occasions use and development of the entire hand, as well as attention to the support and alignment requisite for correct finger action and arm balance. As Chopin understood very well, the all-important pivoting actions later encountered in extended scale and arpeggio patterns for each hand depend on ensuring this basic physical (horizontal) orientation for lateral adjustment at the wrist.[2] Preliminary work with the Fundamental Pattern is indispensable for introducing and developing them.

Building on the student's initial black-key experience (Chapter 12)—and presented as the fundamental pattern (lowercase)—it also offers a number of valuable opportunities for synthesizing the theoretical and the practical.

First, the concept of raising and lowering tones (sharps and flats) may be more fully developed and clarified here since the Fundamental Pattern is presented alternatively in sharps or flats. Although Chopin's own symmetrical notation for it comports with his prescription of the D-flat major scale for the LH and B major for the right, it should be first presented in sharps for the LH and in flats for the RH.

In this way, altered tones are physically experienced and perceived as movement in a direction toward the torso: sharps upward in the LH as higher pitches are encountered, downward in the RH for lowered pitches. Moreover and equally important, this spelling represents it early on as the fundamental core pattern from which the major scale fingerings derive.

Second, intervallic alterations of the Fundamental Pattern are the foundation for the diatonic scale fingerings. Only five topographical *core* patterns represent the tonal alterations and topographical organization for *all* major and minor scales. Symmetrical fingerings are therefore readily deduced from them. The student may— even *should*—be initially grounded in them before commencing more extended patterns, cross hands or otherwise.

Third, the leading topographical principle assigning "fourth on black and thumb on white" is consistently encountered and experienced—emphasized though not necessarily explained at first. Even though the repertoire at hand may not yet require thumb-under pivoting (scale and repertoire assignment would ideally enlist hand-over-thumb pivoting initially), topographical orientation and awareness is further promoted nonetheless, and the ground is laid for all future work in the fingering process.

Fourth, the teacher may work from the Fundamental Pattern to introduce or develop:

- Cross-tension modeling (see "Modeling" in Appendix 9)
- Fingerings for the chromatic scale within the range of the Fundamental Pattern
- Diatonic scale and arpeggio fingerings
- The physiologically correct pivoting actions of thumb/hand and other co-functioning fingers

Fifth, variants applied to the core patterns afford almost limitless opportunity for further technical development at the same time they foster a topographical orientation and further their sensorial reinforcement. Repeated notes, trills, broken or double thirds and combinations of these basic patterns are excellent for individualizing finger action (as so-called finger independence or finger isolation exercises). At this stage, it is particularly useful to work with patterns in which the first joints (terminal phalanges) of the fourth and fifth fingers lightly flex to sustain the keys at the keybed (the "bottom" of the key) with a properly aligned arm poised behind them. Variants are then assigned to fingers 1-2-3. This has the advantage of working from a more balanced ulnar orientation of the arm and avoiding any excessive gripping (usually a misguided and inefficient attempt at stabilization) or overworking on the radial (thumb) side.

Wisely appointed and progressively assigned, the pedagogical advantages of newly encountered patterns and compounds have long been recognized. Again—and it cannot be emphasized too strongly—practicing with variants further intensifies and reinforces sensorially the core topographical patterns deriving from the Fundamental Pattern. In this way an exceptional foundation for later scale and arpeggio study is secured, the arpeggios essentially reflecting lateral distances of larger intervals.

A PROPER PRELUDE TO THUMB-UNDER PIVOTING

Before commencing the study of scale playing *away* from the torso and the attendant complexities of thumb-under pivoting, the student should first concentrate on the pivoting movement of the hand *over* the thumb. In this way, the all-important ulnar relationship of thumb and fourth finger is attended to more directly. The student is afforded an excellent opportunity to correctly establish their relative positions, discover and experience the requisite alignment of the arm, and consider the proper repositioning of the thumb. This is an invaluable preliminary to the far subtler yet more complex movement of the thumb under the hand.

Therefore, introducing single-hand extended scales that are limited to movement in the direction of the torso (LH ascending and RH descending) offers the best opportunity for each hand to first experience them in a range of more than one octave. A welcome and logical sequel to the cross-hand scale patterns, this serves as a transitional stage leading to the full ascending and descending scale patterns for each hand. Aural patterns are further cemented, even as technical development and keyboard skills progress in other ways.

To this end the Fundamental Pattern offers an ideal but now familiar point of departure—a secure springboard, if you will. There are three main ways to proceed.

First, the *transposed* core groups of the Fundamental Pattern are this time experienced in terms of flats for the LH (ascending) and sharps for the RH (descending). The fourth finger takes the black key a half-step from the thumb, easiest at first, the final crossing appropriately taken by the third finger (distant location and key depth principles).

Starting from the Fundamental Pattern at the lowest position of the keyboard, the LH ascends pivoting over the thumb, the fourth finger taking the black key one half-step immediately following. Topographically altered for *whole tones* and sequenced in this manner, the four-note core group in effect proceeds from the key of D-flat through the Cycle of Fifths to white key F (tonic of F major). The range is F to F.

LH (ascending):

FG♭ A♭ B♭ C/ D♭ E♭ FG/ A♭ B♭ C D/ E♭ FG A/ B♭ CD E / F
5 4 3 2 1/ 4   1/ 4   1/4   1/ 4 3 2 1 /3

The RH begins with the Fundamental Pattern at the next-to-last place on the keyboard. Similarly altered and sequenced descending, the four-note whole-tone core groups effectively journey through the Circle of Fifths, from B major to white key B (median of G major). The range is B to B.

RH (descending):

5 4 3 2 1/4   1/ 4   1/ 4   1/ 4 3 2 1/ 3
BA♯ G♯ F♯ E/ D♯ C♯ B A/ G♯ F♯ ED/ C♯ BAG/ F♯ E DC/ B

The logic of the patterns as they relate to the Circle of Fifths is appealing (and they are fun to do!). The mirroring of the LH (flat) and RH (sharp) core groups is easily seen, as are the relations of the closing tones of the sequence to point of symmetry D, each the interval of a third above and below it.

These visual mirrors for the major scales are unique to the keyboard, and their recognition contributes greatly to its demystification; the most should be made of them. As encountered in this exercise, it is another way in which the underpinnings of our harmonic system can be practically related to the keyboard's topography and symmetry, further appreciated and understood.

Second, following this, diatonic sequence for the complete major scales may be introduced, as sharps for the LH (ascending) and flats for the RH (descending). Now the Fundamental Pattern for the core groups is reversed. From B and D-flat through the Circle of Fifths to C, they are extended for a range of two to four octaves. Beginning with the core group and similarly altered, but ending on their keynote (tonic):

	LH Ascending		RH Descending	
B	E F♯ G♯ A♯ B		F G♭ A♭ B♭ C	D♭
E	E F♯ G♯ A B		F G A♭ B♭ C	A♭
A	E F♯ G♯ A B		F G A♭ B♭ C	E♭
D	E F♯ G A B		F G A B♭ C	B♭
G	E F♯ G A B		F G A B♭ C	F

Fingering is easily learned and applied since it is constant: core groups derive from the Fundamental Pattern and the finger sequence for these major scales (4-3-2-1/3-2-1) follows from it. Now *diatonic*, the necessary half-step alterations are, as noted earlier, taken without changes of fingering. Attention is properly and efficiently focused on the necessary tonal alterations. This also reflects the intent of Chopin's instruction, later to be expanded upon: "Start with the B major scale and work through them one by one to C major, *moving back one finger each time* [emphasis added]."[3]

Third, the major scales may be studied and practiced individually, as above—that is, all the consecutive sharp or flat scales for each hand from tonic to tonic. The LH ascending and RH descending patterns separately represent one-half of the full scale sequence that is eventually played in its entirety by each hand. But aurally, visually and kinesthetically, the student experiences the complete scale with its ascending and descending patterns. Meanwhile, the teacher postpones employment of thumb-under pivoting.

It is recommended that these also proceed from B major and D-flat major. Each scale is then reduced by one black key until arriving at all-white-key C major. In this way one fingering set is clearly seen to derive from the Fundamental Pattern (sharps for the LH and flats for the RH), while the other reflects consistent operation of the leading principle, *fourth on black, thumb on white* (flats for the LH and sharps for the RH).

Clearly, and implicitly, there are numerous creative options for valuable scale work that do not require thumb-under pivoting in the early years. If this essential action is isolated and progressively introduced, attention to the composition of its movements may be more appropriately focused—and with far more lasting benefit.

HALF-TONE AND WHOLE TONE APPLICATIONS
OF THE FUNDAMENTAL PATTERN

For introducing the thumb-under pivoting action, the whole-tone Fundamental Pattern may be "transformed" into a half-tone (chromatic) pattern. Beginning with the thumb of each hand, the spelling of the altered tones for each hand would correctly reflect the alteration of the descending and ascending chromatic tones—flats for the LH and sharps for the RH:

E F G♭ G A♭ A B♭ B C   E F F♯ G G♯ A A♯ B C

1 **1** **4** 1 **3** 1 **2** 1 1   1 1 **2** 1 **3** 1 **4** 1 1

From this, the fingering may be altered to include the basic pattern for the chromatic scale (French fingering, LH descending and RH ascending), while employing the all-important pivoting relation of black-key fourth to white-key thumb.

E F G♭ G A♭ A B♭ B C   E F F♯ G G♯ A A♯ B C

1 **1** **4** 1 **3** 1 **3** 2 1   1 2 **3** 1 **3** 1 **4** **1** 1

Augmenting the pattern, the thumb may take the half-step then whole step beyond the (sustained) fourth finger—even further for larger hands—to access and demonstrate the potential of inner humeral rotation and its essential role in the thumb-under/fourth-finger pivoting action.

All these exercises should first be practiced hands separately (HS) away from the torso. Later, contrariwise practice hands together (HT) is excellent not only for simultaneous coordination of both hands but as the foundation for the extended chromatic scale. Beginning with (LH) C and (RH) E, the following range is recommended for comfort, clarity and easy visualization. Topographical mirroring once again facilitates comprehension and a welcomed sense of organization.

1 2 3 **1** **3** **1** **3** 1 2 3 **1** **3** **1**

RH ascending: **E F F♯ G G♯ A A♯ B C C♯ D D♯ E**

Point of Symmetry **D**

LH descending (read from C):

C D♭ D E♭ E F G♭ G A♭ A B♭ B C

1 **3** **1** **3** 2 1 **3** **1** **3** 1 **3** 2 1

From here the student may easily launch its extension beyond this range. It is recommended that this be done to include each succeeding three-note WWB group at first. Initiating from points of symmetry D and A-flat/C-sharp is useful later on.

These may then culminate in a "hybrid" half-tone, whole-tone pattern (the term *half-tone scale* is to be preferred to "chromatic" in the early years, naming it for what it is and more suitably distinguishing it from the *whole-tone scale*). With this, the student's aural and spatial sensitivity to half and whole steps is heightened, even as the all-important alternate opening and closing of the hand is emphasized and developed.

CC#DD# <u>EF#G#A#</u> <u>CC#DD#</u> E

Point of Symmetry **D**

CD♭DE♭ <u>EG♭AbB♭</u> <u>CD♭DE♭</u> E

This pattern is best introduced ascending for the LH and descending for the RH, fingered 1313 /1432/ 1313 1; again, thumb-under pivoting is eschewed at first. The range is progressively increased to three or more octaves, and in both directions; HT parallel begins on C; contrary begins with the Fundamental Pattern on C in the LH and E in the RH. Note that this sequence also approximates the five-black-key enharmonic major scales in topographical orientation.

For the whole-tone scale, a chromatic-diatonic fingering is applied to the two possibilities available as a whole-tone scale sequence. Regrouping C-D-E F#-G#-A# (WWW BBB) and C#-D# F-G-A-B (BB WWWW) also reveals their relation to the Fundamental Pattern and the topographical core groups.

1 3 1 **2** 3 4   1 3 1**2** 3 4

For the RH: CD **E F#** **G# A#**   FG **ABC#** **D#**

For the LH: **G♭ A♭ B♭ C** DE   **D♭ E♭ FG** AB

4   3   **2**   1 31   4   3   **2**1   31

Even here, the underlying root relationships can be seen as a fifth (fourth). Viewed another way, the similarity to the fingering for the diatonic scale sequence is obvious. The solution may also be considered an exemplar of a *chromatic fingering diatonically applied*. And as with all topographical fingerings, organic transposition from any point—especially any black-key pivot—is remarkably facile.

    But both whole-tone scale sequences are in fact equidistant from points of symmetry D and A-flat/G-sharp. The Fundamental Pattern can also be seen here in its topographical inversion: B♭ C D E F# (BWWWB).

G♭ A♭ <u>B♭</u> CDE F#G#A#

G A B C#D# FG A

DIATONIC APPLICATION

Because they reflect the exact topographical arrangements to be encountered in all future work with scales and arpeggios, the five topographical core patterns derived from the altered Fundamental Pattern are obviously ideal for further development of the pivoting action of the thumb under the hand. Conversion of the Fundamental Pattern to a chromatic pattern permitted this action quite gradually; use of the core patterns develops this pivoting action throughout a larger intervallic range.

At the same time, the position is relatively static in that the horizontal distributing function of the arm is limited even though lateral adjustments must still be attended to (recall Chopin's purpose in recommending a detached, nonlegato touch for his Fundamental Pattern at first). But the lateral adjustments as applied here in thumb-under pivoting most clearly demonstrate weight and mass shift ("transfer"), in conjunction with the thumb's oppositional movement corresponding with rotation at its metacarpal base. This permits more focused attention to the pivoting and adjusting movements, without any particular adjustments for key depth in keyboard locations more distant from the midline of the arm. The Fundamental Pattern can still be translocated to distant ranges for those purposes if pedagogically suitable.

The core patterns are comprehensive of the topographical combinations found in *all* scale and arpeggio fingerings. And many are, in a very real sense, "short" forms of their corresponding scales, in that the range of the "four group" is inclusive of the "three group."

Such topographically "self-contained" core patterns can be easily identified for those scales having one black key (F, G and A hm) and those having two adjacent black keys (E-flat, A and G hm). The inquisitive student might even enjoy the challenge of identifying such core-group "assemblies" that represent the four and three groups making up the individual scales.

The pivoting actions, of thumb-under *and* hand-over, applied to the corresponding core pattern go far in preparing for a confident and comfortable approach to a specific scale. The pentatonic organization of core patterns as presented in Chapter 13 provides an excellent basis for such "preludes" to a later focus on pivoting for single-hand extended scale patterns in a systematic fashion.

Like the alternate hand (cross-hand) version of the diatonic scales presented in Chapter 13, those for the major keys should also be introduced *complementarily* in working with scale patterns extended for more than two octaves. That is, a flat scale would be followed by, or at the same time introduced with, its "mirrored" sharp scale or vice versa. An important factor to be stressed in all the above—and indeed in all the scales to be studied—is assignment of the fourth finger to all newly introduced accidentals (RH sharps and LH flats). There is consistent physical and visual identification; security and clarity are ensured.

All scales should be practiced hands separately for some time; there should never be a push toward scales in both hands simultaneously unless the repertoire studied will soon require it. Otherwise, facility and attention to technical detail soon suffers. Similarly, minor scales should be introduced for extended scale study only after a thorough grounding in the major patterns. Here too, the ascending melodic form (unaltered descending—*not* as in the hybrid melodic-natural minor) best precedes the harmonic minor.

As to the theoretical benefits of scale study, this approach is, in fact, far more systematic in all regards. The lowered leading tone for successive major flat keys and the raised fourth degree for sharp keys permit an unbroken, unified transition from flats or sharps from and *through* C major. Allied with topographically consistent fingerings (fourth on black, thumb on white), nothing could be more logical or rational—or more unifying. For the piano with its black keys and the pianist with his two hands, the Circle of Fifths moves beyond the theoretical to the practical.

But in addition to mirrored patterns and root movement by fifth (the customary pedagogical progression for scale study beginning with C major), there are several other relevant, revealing and interesting ways to move ahead with scale organization and introduction of new keys, their topographies and fingerings:

1. All scales, major and minor (parallel and relative), may also be ordered on a common core pattern or according to the number of black keys. As examples, F, G and A hm each have only one black key; taken together, they are the three black keys of the Fundamental Pattern: F-sharp, G-sharp and B-flat (!).

2. Scales—major and minor—may be presented in a pentatonic sequence (Chapter 13), by assignment of the fourth finger to the black key of a core topographical pattern, a process that is further revealing symmetrically.

3. Scale study may be further organized emphasizing root movement of a fifth, but without limiting it to the major key scales; introducing the minor key scales would not be confined to their parallel or relative major (upper case) and minor (lower case)relationships. The sequence F – C – G – d – a – e is but one excellent possibility; an interesting one is d – g – G – D – a – E – A.

4. Beyond the relative major/minor, root movement by third is of particular interest and of great value harmonically. Other mediant relationships that are topographically and theoretically in sync should be explored or presented. D♭/A, B/E♭ m-hm, E♭/G and C♯ hm/A include enharmonic mediant relationships and are among many good examples.

Although these are but a few, there really are countless ways of organizing the scales beyond the customary. Recall especially the inverted Circle of Fifths presented at the end of Chapter 2. But at more advanced levels, scale sequences may also incorporate and explore root movements by whole and half-step as well as the tritone (all of these considered the least "stable" in traditional harmonic practice). The possibilities for introducing and developing skills for transposing and modulating are therefore enormous. And from the standpoint of a rational fingering process for natural solutions, chromatic and other transitional groups (Chapters 4 and 5) are usefully employed in joining such scale sequences for seamless, fluent progression.

The advantage in all this is that topographical orientation may at the same time be tailored to the individual student's aural, theoretical and technical needs in an imaginative yet unstrained and informative fashion. And it is primarily experiential.

This is especially important in the matter of retooling, in which old, inefficient orientations (particularly of the LH) are to be studiously avoided while the newer, more pianistic ones supplant them over time. And as noted earlier, repertoire choice must be in league with such a goal. The creative, flexible teacher will find this approach rich in possibilities, even at a relatively early stage.

ARPEGGIOS

In arpeggios the issue of thumb-under and hand-over pivoting is considerably more involved because of the horizontal distance covered. The Fundamental Pattern is easily adapted for preliminary work.

The superiority of the commonly accepted fingering for arpeggios having a black key as their root was addressed in our earlier discussion of arpeggios. Four-part chord inversions that afford a black key for the fourth finger are therefore deemed more desirable than root position arpeggios that do not involve the fourth finger at all. The black-key fourth finger, white-key thumb pivots are demonstrably more secure, accurate and comfortable—more "natural" in every way. Of nearly equal length, the second and fourth fingers when assigned to two black keys optimally place the hand and balance the arm.

So it is that the Fundamental Pattern is ideally suited for introducing the mechanics of playing arpeggios, especially at an early age. In addition to the advantage of a relatively limited range of movement, the two black keys that are first taken here by the second and fourth fingers are at a lesser distance than later encounters with the major and minor arpeggios—more suitable for the smaller hand. And the situation of the white keys affords a progressive opening of the thumb on the one (radial) side of the hand and an expansion of its range of pivoting on the other (ulnar).

By simply disengaging the third finger, the Fundamental Pattern then reflects the model topographical combination for major and minor arpeggios. Because topographical orientation as it influences the pivoting actions is the chief concern, the pattern is not necessarily spelled out; this simplifies its use as an easy introduction to arpeggios and their mechanics. Introduced to them by way of the Fundamental Pattern, the youngest students may then be ready for the technique of extended arpeggios long before the specific requirements of repertoire. Here too, the smallest hands have the more comfortable option of taking the white keys, as shown in parentheses:

	1	2	4	1
RH:	**E (F)**	**G♭**	**B♭ (B) C**	
LH:	**E (F)**	**F♯**	**A♯ (B) C**	
	1	4	2	1

The usual problem with introducing arpeggios at too early a stage is the greater range necessary for both the pivoting and lateral actions than that previously encountered in playing scales. One obvious advantage in working with the Fundamental Pattern is that the student has several options corresponding to his or her individual hand span.

With this approach, the most favorable topographical orientation is enlisted even as the thumb need only very gradually pivot on the fourth finger to each successive white key. This means the student may profitably stay with this arrangement for quite some time before embarking on arpeggios extended through a range of two octaves or more. The requisite inner rotation of the humerus and the correlative rotations of pivot finger and thumb—indispensable fundamentals of a natural pianism—may therefore be properly attended to. Larger hands will ultimately be able to increase the pivoting range of the thumb to encompass an octave, the (thumb) span of an arpeggio:

1	2	4	1
D	**F♯**	**A♯**	**D**
1	4	2	1

From here the Fundamental Pattern may then be altered as to topography and interval, representing the core patterns of the following arpeggios.

LH					RH		
D	F♯	A♯	D		D	G♭	B♭	D
D	F♯	A	D		D	G	B♭	D
D	F	A	D		D	G	B	D

In translocating the Fundamental Pattern for major and minor arpeggios (see Chapter 11), the student is afforded the opportunity to apply the pivoting action to these three core patterns for quite some time (there is no need for the fourth, BBB—limited as it is to G-flat/F-sharp major and E-flat/D-sharp minor). Practice techniques with the usual variants will be especially valuable when applied to these "abbreviated" arpeggios.

These patterns are also later extended to a range of two or more octaves. And here too, arpeggios are best introduced LH ascending and RH descending to establish optimal orientation of the arm and to simplify control of the movements involved. Core pattern to core pattern—rather than tonic to tonic—is, in fact, most suitable. Single hand arpeggios ascending and descending are then best organized *topographically* as introduced above: all those with two black keys are introduced first, and so forth—always from more to fewer black keys.

RETOOLING AND REPERTOIRE

When students have for many years lacked the benefit of a topographical approach to developing natural habits of fingering, repertoire choice is crucial to their keyboard reorientation. This is especially the case at more advanced levels, in which keyboard range and compositional complexity challenge any and all technical foundations already long established. And it follows that those teachers who embark on integrating a topographical approach to fingering and keyboard studies should themselves "retool" for authoritative advocacy.

Any effective approach to retooling for a topographical orientation is balanced on three fronts:

1. Basic patterns and fundamental forms progressively assigned
2. Selected etudes in pianistic keys (signatures of three or more sharps or flats), all fingering adjusted as necessary for consistent topographical application
3. Repertoire in related user-friendly keys exclusively, fingering adjusted and applied according to topographical principles

The keyword is orientation. Throughout this discussion we have explored the keyboard's extraordinary symmetry of construction as the crux of all topographical organization, while repeatedly emphasizing that it is the hand's most natural accommodation to this fixed topography that lies at the root of a healthful, easeful technique.

We have pursued the implications of Chopin's Fundamental Pattern along with inversion, translocation, extension, alterations and permutations. As outlined in this chapter and creatively adapted, we can see that this promotes an enormous range of patterning specially designed to establish topographical familiarity and, at the same time, to ensure a more secure grounding in the pianist's essential responses to the keyboard. In retooling to establish the topographical basis for a natural fingering, it is indispensable that the Fundamental Pattern be employed as fundamental tool, while the fundamental forms—scales, chords and arpeggios, double notes, trills and octaves—are appropriately coordinated with repertoire.

We have also shown that the fingering for the fundamental musical forms may be represented by, derived from, or related in some way to Chopin's pattern, And mirrored by each hand in symmetrical resolution, the fundamental forms for the enharmonic major keys serve as exemplars. Not surprisingly, the road to retooling parallels the road to establishing an initial topographical orientation.

However, in this, one must be even more selective and sharply discriminating in matters of repertoire assignment. Ideally, all the related keys of a composition would also reinforce a natural topographical accommodation: "old" responses that would undermine establishing this as primary would thereby be avoided or minimized. The objective of the process is to reverse a predominantly white-key orientation with one that favors the black keys.

Fortunately we have Chopin's own extant repertoire favoring the more "pianistic" keys, along with a wealth of repertoire by Romantic and post-Romantic composers reflecting a similar topographical sense, to whatever degree it may have been conscious. In any case, key selection should always be a prime consideration in assigning repertoire, even if only to develop, strengthen and contribute to the student's sense of tonality along with understanding and appreciation of the related tonal affinities at the heart of a particular compositional structure.

But now we are also considering repertoire assignment for its potential as a prime means of keyboard reorientation. With attendant consequences to the playing mechanism itself, unwelcome former responses are in this way more likely to be newly and firmly supplanted with those that will be found to be more natural and productive. Since most tonalities having an abundance of black keys are often not new to the student at the later stages of study, reorientation would at first be more narrowly based on those the student already knows and has experienced.

It happens, though, that many of the most pianistic compositions—indeed many of the very compositions that inspire, interest and emotionally resonate with the advancing pianist—pose extreme reading difficulties by virtue of key, tonal and harmonic relationships as well as heightened chromaticism. Topographical comfort notwithstanding, a great deal of patience and skill must accompany even a large amount of motivation and enthusiasm.

It is to be expected that the wise teacher does not let the reading suffer from any premature or exclusive assignment of extremely complex (for the level) literature. But the familiarity and security of a topographical orientation lends support to such complexity in very large measure in any case. This is especially true when the tonal scheme of a composition revolves around keys of more than two sharps or flats. From this standpoint, therefore, an advisable approach to repertoire would most certainly be one of gradual and relatively comfortable progression rather than one of shock to all systems.

Taken for the most part from the well-known standard repertoire, the online excerpts are illustrative of the thinking behind a topographical approach to fingering from the early years onward. The topographical resolutions reflect the fingering principles and symmetrical relationships discussed in Chapters 10 and 11 as they specifically apply to repertoire of the late-elementary through intermediate and "advancing" levels of study.

EPILOGUE

Giving precedence to physiological considerations (the hand) and physical ones (the keyboard), Chopin is in effect the first to emancipate himself from "Tyrant C," ruler of non-pianistic tonality.
—Jean-Jacques Eigeldinger

Chopin . . . departed boldly on the road to discovery, especially in the matter of fingering. . . . One imagines that his ideas on fingering might have been revolutionary. . . . Unfortunately none of his pupils (not even Carl Mikuli) became famous enough to carry the torch of the Chopin method to future generations.
—Louis Kentner

CHOPIN'S FUNDAMENTAL PATTERN provides the rational basis for any comprehensive approach to fingering issues. It is not just an interesting practical alternative to the usual major and minor five-finger patterns; we have already observed how little related these actually are to the standard fingerings for white-key tonic scales—not to mention the black-key tonic scales. As a whole-tone pattern transposed and altered for interval, it yields the topographical fingerings for all the scales. As a topographical arrangement that may also be *translocated* (2-3-4 on any series of three consecutive black keys), it similarly yields the four-part chords, their inversions, and all the arpeggios that derive from them. Even chromatic fingerings are easily deduced from it, or applied to it, and those for diatonic double notes are consistently in accord.

Such a topographical approach to fingering is founded on Chopin's Fundamental Pattern and Eschmann-Dumur's analysis and exploration of the keyboard's organizational symmetry. But it is one that at the same time necessitates reappraisal of the still commonly held bias favoring the first three fingers, a technical approach that is mainly lower arm and oriented toward the thumb (radial) side of the hand.

A far more natural, topographical orientation recognizes and fully employs the opposition of the thumb and "end" (fourth and fifth) fingers as well as the coordinated pivoting action of thumb and relevant motor finger, especially in movement away from the torso. This orientation reveals, requires, enlists, supports and *encourages* a technical approach that is fundamentally upper arm (humeroulnar). The dynamic (not "fixed") stabilization of the entire playing mechanism is primarily that of the shoulder girdle/shoulder complex (which includes the humerus) and only secondarily that of the lower extremities. The primary motor for movement, distribution of weight and application of force is that of the upper arm at the shoulder joint. Keyboard symmetry and curvilinear symmetry (representing movement paths in keyboard space) harmoniously conspire in the properly aligned, coordinated movements of the playing mechanism's fully participating ensemble—its entire *gestalt*.

BEYOND THE FUNDAMENTAL PATTERN

From this, a topographical pedagogy is one that posits that natural orientation of the playing mechanism to the fixed but defining topographical aspects of the keyboard as a prime objective. It is one that thereby enables the teacher and student to sift through the vast catalogue of largely ineffective studies and exercises, inefficient and too often unrelated to the task at hand. Freedom from "a tyranny of C" enables one to appreciate C major in its proper theoretical perspective amid the keyboard's topographical influences from the first lessons forward. Such an approach represents economy of thought, time and effort. It is clear, direct and immediate as a means of fostering keyboard comfort and familiarity.

Topography and strategy must always remain the essential elements of a practical yet pianistic approach to fingering. As we have noted throughout, fingering is fundamentally a means of organizing the keys representing the notes of the score, and there are numerous possibilities for organization. But topography must take precedence owing to its physiological and kinesiological impact. And the influence and implications of keyboard symmetry in regard to coordination and a rational, *visually enhanced* organization are ultimately self-evident. Topography will always permit strategy, whereas strategy does not always purposefully encompass topography. A *topographical strategy* must therefore be in the forefront of our efforts to successfully resolve all matters of fingering. It is of primary, not secondary, concern.

In a very real sense, then, musical patterns have too often obscured our recognition and appreciation of keyboard patterns, with visual patterns on the page superseding those on the keyboard. That is, topographical patterns reflecting the unique topographical symmetry of the keyboard are largely overlooked—even though considerations of keyboard topography must unavoidably take precedence, one way or another, for the bulk of repertoire that is post-Classical.

I am advocating, therefore, an approach that more comprehensively reflects this vitally important characteristic of the keyboard. In refashioning, reordering and reorienting the playing mechanism's connection to the keyboard in a more natural and consistent way, there is ultimately more freedom, not less. It is the kinesiological equivalent of a literal reading of the score: one is enabled to eventually envision more, the concept is more plastic, and performances are more immediate and spontaneous. It is but another paradox yielding sweet fruit.

DEFINING KEYBOARD SPACE

With topography as the chief determinant, keyboard space is more properly defined and the keyboard surface is itself fundamentally ordered by applying the core groups and their tonal alterations instead of theoretical patterns. Their symmetrical and reciprocal relationships afford a more logical simplicity to the grouping of keys representing the underlying melodic and harmonic organizations.

These core groups are the fundamental "building blocks" of the fingering process, at the same time unifying what might otherwise appear to be an unwieldy mass of notes—even if comprehended compositionally in all other respects. The later post-Classical repertoire especially is replete with passages that may bear well under melodic, thematic, or harmonic analysis yet otherwise reveal little in matters of fingering. Debussy's dictum (that we must search for our fingerings) is certainly a wise one, especially absent a more relevant and efficient process.

Topography ends up being the chief influence and final arbiter. As laid out herein, such an approach to resolving seemingly obtuse fingering challenges is one that wholly conforms to how any matter of complexity is ultimately known and comprehended. As Edward Rothstein writes, in his brilliant *Emblems of the Mind*: "This quest . . . for mappings [that] reach the essential elements of the objects we study. . . deals not only with objects but with processes. . . . We must create metaphors as we work, exercising, in Aristotle's phrase, 'the intuitive perception of similarity in dissimilar things.'"[1] As to the nature and process of comparison, he admonishes that it is necessary that similarities be noted, characteristics defined and their *functions considered*. We must determine if there are any "significant similarities."

And then:

> Finding links and connections between different objects is only one of the ways we make sense out of any stream of phenomena we are exposed to, passing by us like notes in a musical score. . . . We try to find repetitions, similarities, ratios. Our search for pattern means dividing phenomena, grouping their constituent elements into smaller categories, constructing "phrases," seeing whether, when we do group them together, we recognize one element's relation to another. *We must also constantly decide what is important and what is negligible, which facts have significance and which do not* [emphasis added]. We do the same thing when we try to make sense of music.[2]

Surely this is what any fingering process is ultimately about. But at bottom, this very practical process is, for pianists, a matter of topographical organization and topographical orientation. It has been shown, I believe, that such an approach does not run counter to the fundamentals of musical organization but, rather, complements, clarifies, unifies and reinforces them. These may not be ignored any more than topographical determinants. All are operative and impact this process positively or negatively, obviously or subversively. The goal must ever be to enlist all elements of compositional and keyboard organization to the task at hand: to a pianistic resolution of the "artistic image."

It is my sincere hope that Chopin's Fundamental Pattern with all its "intimations of symmetry" will at long last be universally recognized for its revolutionary implications, and that they will be developed to more fully support the best of pianism and a truly pianistic pedagogy. It is my belief that such an approach is in the visionary spirit and the best traditions of his *méthode*—one that leads us ultimately to a natural fingering for a natural technique.

True science does not constitute a separate branch of knowledge from art. On the contrary, science, when envisaged like this and demonstrated by a man like Chopin, is art itself.
—Eugène Delacroix

NOTES

INTRODUCTION

1. Keyboard dimensions remain proportionate to human dimensions, remarking that these have necessarily changed over time (one need only note the dimensions of tables, chairs, beds, etc., of earlier periods). Also, dimensions frequently vary from model to model, somewhat better accommodating the hand span of younger players of spinets and consoles, for example. It is noteworthy that Josef Hoffman famously had a smaller-gauged Steinway specially constructed for his own smaller hands. And there is an effort currently underway to offer such optional scaled-down keyboards on grand pianos generally (but available on the Chickering 5'8" at least as early as 1970), emulating the practical advantage universally afforded to younger string players—a certain boon to piano manufacturers should it succeed.

2. James Freeman, "Fingering," in vol. 8, *The New Grove Dictionary of Music* (New York: Oxford University Press), 838.

3. Ibid., 839.

4. Jean-Jacques Eigeldinger, *Chopin: Pianist and Teacher As Seen by His Pupils* (Cambridge: Cambridge University Press, 1986), 40.

5. As further example: Chopin's fingering for the diminished seventh arpeggio on C—based on the root position chord, and his only for any arpeggiated sevenths—consequently does not employ the fourth finger as black-key pivot, as would otherwise be revealed by its inversion.

6. Two similar sets of notes were entrusted to pianist/composer and friend Charles-Valentin Alkan (Morhange) as well as Adolf Gutman, whom Chopin considered his most promising student. See Tad Szulc, *Chopin in Paris* (New York: Scribner, 1998), 409.

7. According to Marmontel, many of Chopin's "dearest students chose Alkan to continue the late master's tradition." See Eigeldinger, 134 n. 129.

8. Heinrich Neuhaus, *The Art of Piano Playing* (New York: Praeger, 1973), 84.

9. Significantly, Ruth Gerald holds that "the given standard fingerings form a basis of learning and help to establish the habits needed for fluent playing," while acknowledging "for some scales an alternative fingering system in common use exists and this is shown." See "Introduction" in Associated Board of the Royal Schools of Music, *The Manual of Scales, Broken Chords and Arpeggios for Piano* (London: Associated Board of the Royal Schools of Music, 2001).

10. Rudolf Ganz (1877–1972), the eminent Swiss pianist and dedicatee of Ravel's "Scarbo," employed this concept of mirrored symmetry in his published exercises. In them he also included five pages of exercises by Emile-Robert Blanchet. As legacies go, it turns out that Ganz had studied with Eschmann-Dumur, who was also his great-uncle! And his lessons were with Charles Blanchet at the Lausanne Conservatoire. Both Ganz and Blanchet later went on to study with Busoni, enjoying successful and respected careers.

11. A student of Anton Rubinstein and, by some accounts, Franz Liszt. In 1893 he made his orchestral debut under the legendary Walter Damrosch.

12. Otto Ortmann, *The Physiological Mechanics of Piano Technique* (New York: Dutton, 1962), 278–279.

13. Ibid., 256–259.

14. Thomas Fielden, *The Science of Pianoforte Technique* (New York: St. Martin's Press, 1961), 168.

15. Ibid., 157–158.

16. E. Robert Schmitz, *The Capture of Inspiration* (New York: Carl Fischer, 1935), 17.

17. Schmitz received permission to reproduce it from Leopold Binental, who had included it in his book *Chopin: On the 120th Anniversary of His Birth. Documents and Recollections* (Warsaw: Lazarski, 1930). In 1935 it was still in the possession of Marie Ciechomska and subsequently destroyed during the Second World War (ibid., 42).

18. In Cortot's book *Aspects de Chopin* (pp 56–66), Eigeldinger considers that "the illustrious pianist [Cortot] . . . underestimated and misunderstood the exceptional value of this document" (Eigeldinger, 90 n. 1). He strongly concurs with Neuhaus's wholehearted endorsement of the rationale underlying Chopin's "methodology." And he goes on to say: "These pertinent considerations also point out implicitly why Cortot misinterpreted the

Projet de méthode; great pianist though he was, the exercises in his *Principes rationnelles de la technique* almost all begin in C major—then to be transposed into all the other keys!" (Eigeldinger, 105 n. 47).

19. Seymour Fink's definition of *topography* is of peculiar interest: "The term used to denote the *irregular shape* [italics added] of the keyboard." *Mastering Piano Technique* (Portland, OR: Amadeus Press, 1992), 182.

20. E. Robert Schmitz's (1889–1949) publication of *The Capture of Inspiration* (1935) preceded that of his authoritative and best-known work, *The Piano Music of Debussy* (1950). Many of his most original ideas grew out of Debussy's music, for the express need to meet the technical and musical demands of this "new" music with its unusual challenges and revolutionary musical language. He was also a champion of the music of most of his notable contemporaries, presenting first performances or premiers of their compositions in France and abroad. These include works by Debussy, Honegger, Ives, Milhaud, Ravel, Roussel, Schoenberg, Szymanowski, Alexandre Tansman, Virgil Thomson, and many others. Schmitz was also highly esteemed as an interpreter of Bach and Mozart, in addition to Debussy and the "moderns." To that end he founded the Franco-American Music Society, New York Philomusica and Pro-Musica, which by itself consisted of forty chapters in Europe, North America, Honolulu and Shanghai. Schmitz was the one primarily responsible for arranging Ravel's first and only visit to the United States and Canada (four months in 1928), as well as tours by Bartók, Milhaud, Roussel, Prokofieff and many others through his organization Pro-Musica Inc. Ravel's own correspondence attests not only to his uniquely important role in promoting Ravel's music and artistic influence but also to their mutual respect and friendship. And Ives was extremely influential in the successful realization of these enterprising ventures.

    Schmitz was also determined to shed light on some of the most nagging problems of pianism and exert a meaningful influence on the teaching profession. This led to his establishing the Schmitz Council of Teachers, whereby he sought to advance Schmitz Pedagogy and to further disseminate his then rather iconoclastic ideas within the profession. Individual members of this rather extensive network of U.S. and Canadian teachers were specifically subjected to quite rigorous training in his principles and method, while more broadly influenced by his ideals and aesthetic—all toward certification as a "Schmitz teacher."

21. Her principal studies were with Paolo Gallico and Rosina Lhevinne.

22. See Gyorgy Sandor, *On Piano Playing: Motion, Sound and Expression* (New York: Schirmer, 1981), 55–57. Many professionals—including alumni of the so-called Russian System—currently credit their awareness of this important lateral adjustment to Sandor's treatment of it in his very popular and acclaimed text. But significantly, Schmitz's own published advocacy of same predates Sandor's by more than forty-five years!

23. For those who hold the performances of the late William Kapell in the highest esteem, as I do, the poignancy of his desperation is no doubt particularly hard hitting, as it certainly must have been to his devoted teacher, Olga Samaroff Stokowski. In his letter to her of June 13, 1944, he wrote: "I am terribly discouraged over my work. . . . My fingers become so tired when I play fast that I am now really alarmed and extremely discouraged. I don't know what to do . . . I don't know what it is." As quoted by Donna Staley Kline in *American Virtuoso* (Texas A&M University Press, College Station, 1996).

PART 1

1. Walter Robert, "In Defense of Scales," *Clavier*, 1(5) (Nov.–Dec., 1962), 14.
2. Schmitz, *The Capture of Inspiration*, 66.
3. Landowska was also a student of Moszkowski, as was Josef Hofmann and Vlado Perlemutter; Godowsky taught Neuhaus, who counted Sviatoslav Richter and Emil Gilels among his many students of renown.
4. Or "Tyrant C," as Eigeldinger so aptly and colorfully refers to it (Eigeldinger, 100 n. 30).
5. A state of affairs that Hummel clearly alludes to in his famous treatise.
6. Eigeldinger, 90 n. 2.
7. Stuart Isacoff, *Temperament* (New York: Vintage Books, 2003), 243–247.
8. Most recently, for example, Ross Duffin, *How Equal Temperament Ruined Harmony (and Why You Should Care)* (New York/London: Norton, 2007).

9. Margit Varró, *A Teacher in Two Worlds* (Budapest: Abraham/Varro, 1991), 511.

10. Referring to a story that has it that Christopher Columbus—to demonstrate the power of insight to produce what then seems obvious and immemorial—asserted he could make an egg stand on its tip. He did so by gently tapping the egg on a hard surface, flattening the tip. The story is also, however, attributed earlier, by Giorgio Vasari in *Lives of the Artists*, to Filippo Brunelleschi, creator of the dome of Santa Maria del Fiore in Florence.

11. Bruno Monsaingeon, *Sviatoslav Richter: Notebooks and Conversations* (Princeton/Oxford: Princeton University Press, 2001), 100. Richter also advises: "In a technical sense, I think the help you get from your hands is of great importance—at times on a purely psychological plane. If you meet a technical problem in one hand, the other hand's symmetrical movement may help solve it." Karl Aage Rasmussen, *Sviatoslav Richter* (Boston: Northeastern University Press, 2010), 208.

12. Ortmann, *Physiological Mechanics of Piano Technique*, chap. 22, "Individual Differences: The Hand," 311.

CHAPTER 1

1. Among these, the now legendary pianist and teacher Heinrich Neuhaus (1888–1964), whose teacher Alexandre Michałowski had studied with Karl Mikuli, the most well-known and influential of Chopin's students. His later studies were with Leopold Godowsky.

2. Kleczyński (1837–1895), although not a student of Chopin's, did study with three of his most outstanding pupils: Princess Marcelina Czartoryska, whose playing of Chopin's music was considered the standard to be emulated; Mme. Camille Dubois; and George Matthias. He consciously set out to experience and document the tradition of Chopin's teaching and later provided an edition of Chopin's works. At the Warsaw Conservatory, he was a teacher of Wanda Landowska, who also studied with Michałowski.

3. It is also noteworthy that Kleczyński refers to E-F♯-G♯-A♯-B as the "normal" position for the RH and F♭-G♭-A♭-B♭-C as the "analogous" position for the LH even though the symmetrical equivalent is F-G♭-A♭-B♭-C. The D-flat scale has F, not F-flat, as its third degree. No doubt this has contributed to later adoption of the whole tone E-F♯-G♯-A♯-B♯ as the fundamental five-note pattern. See Jean (Jan) Kleczyński, *The Works of Frederic Chopin, and Their Proper Interpretation* (London: William Reeves [undated]), 34.

4. In the "English" system of fingering the thumb is indicated by + and the fingers are numbered 1, 2, 3, and 4 from the index finger onward.

5. Kleczyński, 30.

6. Ibid. 34.

7. Schmitz, however, did advocate E-F♯-G♯-A-B as the *LH* corollary to Chopin's RH E-F♯-G♯-A♯-B pattern. And yet, in his espousal of a topographical approach to scale fingering, it is noteworthy that Schmitz too did not refinger these scales. He recognized that the standard fingerings for F major and G major needed revising but proceeded on the basis of an application of the longest third finger to the single black key—with unsatisfactory results. But it is also curious that he advocated LH fingerings for D and A, which favor the fourth finger on the black key F-sharp even though the third could be consistently employed. For these keys it would seem that Schmitz was influenced by his own proposed corollary to Chopin's RH pattern. Though uniquely promoting the concept of topographically based fingerings, Schmitz did not apply principles with clarity or consistency; this is even more evident in his suggested fingerings for the minor scales. He did not identify the fourth finger pivot as the "key player"; consequently the thoroughness and simplicity of the very approach he espoused eluded him. Schmitz considered the three-finger/note group to be the determinant; in suggesting alternative fingerings for certain scales he goes so far as to avoid use of the fourth finger altogether, obviously resulting in more frequent thumb shifts per octave.

8. Kleczyński, 34.

9. Heinrich Neuhaus. *The Art of Piano Playing* (New York: Praeger, 1973), 84.

CHAPTER 2

1. Richard Franko Goldman, *Harmony in Western Music* (New York: W.W. Norton, 1965), 15.

2. Ferruccio Busoni, *A New Esthetic of Music* (New York: G. Schirmer, 1911), 27.

3. One sees this manifest repeatedly in compositions by Chopin, Brahms and others, in which highly chromatic (unstable) passages—sometimes for pages on end—appear over repeated dominant pedals (pedal points), finally resolving to the tonic. Although such repetition is clearly meant for emphasis or reinforcement—of the dominant, for example—it also serves *functionally* to stabilize the sense of tonality in "the midst of instability": that is, the prevailing chromaticism. Likewise, dynamic shoulder joint/shoulder complex stabilization functions in the midst of the potential "instability" of swift and ever-changing keyboard position and movement direction.

CHAPTER 3

1. Goldman, *Harmony*, 20–21.
2. William Mason and W.S.B. Matthews, *A System of Fundamental Techniques for Piano Playing* (Boston: Oliver Ditson, 1878/1905), 179.
3. Goldman, *Harmony*, 111.

CHAPTER 4

1. Marie von Unschuld, *The Pianist's Hand* (New York: Carl Fischer, 1909), 48.
2. Eigeldinger, 37.
3. Ibid., as reported by Koczalski "after Mikuli," 106 (note 54).
4. Franklin Taylor, *Technique and Expression in Pianoforte Playing* (London: Novello, undated), 17.
5. Penelope Roskell, *The Art of Piano Fingering* (London: LCM, 1996), 41: "Tradition ascribes it to Liszt."
6. Frequency of thumb shifts is not unfamiliar to pianists; they are integral to the playing of all octave passages. But in these the hand is (potentially) more balanced in weight distribution. This is not to say that the French fingering is therefore inherently radially oriented. This would depend on whether or not a dynamic stabilization of the shoulder joint/shoulder complex participates in its execution; a counterbalancing ulnar orientation of the forearm would be favored here as well. That said, the natural ability of the second and third fingers for a quick "getaway" from the key (*retraction*, due to capabilities of extension) and their subsequent positioning is a prime factor in the speedy execution of the chromatic pattern. It is one not apparent in a more extended finger sequence, in which there is a lesser frequency of repetition. In the diatonic scales, for example, the fourth finger is called upon only once each octave—or once every seven notes. Moreover, the French fingering conveniently and systematically avoids the problem of playing between the black keys, the point toward which the white keys increasingly pose the greatest resistance to force and, for broader hands, problems of spatial accommodation. The thumb and third, playing as frequently as they do on the endmost points of the (white and black) keys, avail themselves of optimal advantage as to leverage.
7. Heinrich Neuhaus, *The Art of Piano Playing* (New York: Praeger, 1973), 150.
8. This double third fingering, one that Neuhaus treats as standard, is often attributed to Chopin. Chopin did not eschew glissando fingerings; his own fingering for the chromatic minor thirds employs glissando thumbs on the two consecutive white keys. This is as Chopin himself noted it in his Etude, Opus 25 No. 6. See Eigeldinger, *Chopin*, 37.
9. Neuhaus, *Art of Piano Playing*, 151.
10. Tobias Matthay, *Musical Interpretation* (Boston: Boston Music, 1913), 121–4.

CHAPTER 5

1. Roger Chaffin, Mary Crawford and Gabriela Imreh, *Practicing Perfection: Memory and Performance* (Mahwah, NJ and London: Erlbaum, 2002), 202–5.
2. Tobias Matthay, *Muscular Relaxation Studies for Students, Artists and Teachers* (London: Bosworth, 1908), 138.
3. Harold Craxton, a student of Matthay and a teacher at his school as well as the Royal Academy of Music, numbered Denis Matthews and Peter Katin among his outstanding students.
4. A first inversion major chord that is subdominant in origin and whose root is the flat second degree, the Neapolitan Sixth chord frequently plays an especially important role in Chopin's compositional language and structure. The introductory measures of Chopin's Ballade in G minor is but one particularly dramatic example.
5. Franklin Taylor, *Primer of Pianoforte Playing* (New York: Macmillan, 1890), 56.

PART 2

1. *Great Pianists Speak with Adele Marcus* (Neptune, NJ: Paganiniana, 1979), 61–62.

CHAPTER 6

1. Godowsky's transcriptions followed what was already a long line of transcriptions of Chopin, some even for the LH alone. Notable are several of Isador Philipp's transcriptions and etude studies which transfer some of Chopin's challenging RH passages to the LH. See Millan Sachania's interesting and informative Introduction to *The Godowsky Collection, Vol. 3* (New York: Carl Fischer, 2002).

2. Henri Herz, *Collection of Studies, Scales and Passages* (Miami: Kalmus/Warner Bros., n.d.; catalog no. K 03552).

3. Tilly Fleischmann, *Aspects of the Liszt Tradition* (Bryn Mawr, PA: Theodore Presser, 1991), 122–23.

4. Harriet Brower interview, *Piano Mastery: The Harriet Brower Interviews* (Mineola, NY: Dover, 2003), 94: "I believe in avoiding the use of thumb on black keys wherever possible, in order to keep the hand in a more natural position; this seems to me easier and more logical."

5. Malwine Brée, *The Leschetizky Method: A Guide to Free and Correct Piano Playing* (Mineola, NY: Dover, 1997), 42–43.

6. Editorial comments in the Preface to R. Schumann's *Studies on the Caprices of Paganini, Op.3* (Kalmus), 4 (26).

7. Frank Merrick, *Practising the Piano* (New York: Dover, 1965), 35.

8. This 3+1+3 solution was formerly unique to Hummel, who first presented it in his famous 1828 treatise. However, he employed it consistently for the RH ascending only. His fingerings for the enharmonic keys are telling, though, in that they fare much better. On the whole, fingerings are irregular but significant in that Hummel is clearly searching for solutions specific to the individual double third scale, and with a willingness to eschew the same pattern ascending and descending. He is apparently responding to topographical influences without yet having come upon the insights regarding keyboard symmetry that were to profoundly stimulate Chopin later on. J. N. Hummel, *A Complete Theoretical and Practical Course of Instruction on the Art of Playing the Piano Forte . . .* (London, T. Boosey and Co., 1829).

9. Moritz Moszkowski, *School of Scales and Double Notes for the Pianoforte, Opus 64* (London: Enoch & Sons, 1904): Second Part, "Remarks," 36.

10. Sachania, *Godowsky Collection* (Vol. 3), xvii.

11. Schmitz designates those "weight-bearing" fingers *motor fingers*. This is but a particular distinction in regard to the playing of any combination of double notes. In this instance the designation primarily reflects a differentiation of the articulation (the fundamental action for *legato*) of the fingers from their coordination with the pivoting action/movement of thumb under the hand, as repeatedly referred to in this discussion. As noted previously, the distinction is really not a fundamental one but rather of degree, complexity and function in a specific instance. However, the terminology is most useful.

12. Charles Cooke, *Playing the Piano for Pleasure* (New York: Simon & Schuster, 1941/1960), 120.

13. After many unsuccessful attempts to locate both treatises I was fortunately able to acquire Matthay's fingerings thanks to my esteemed colleague Beatrice Allen, who received them from James Friskin during her studies with him.

14. Cooke, *Playing the Piano for Pleasure*, 122.

15. Ernst Bacon, *Notes on the Piano* (Seattle/London: University of Washington Press, 1968), 46.

16. Alfred Cortot, *Rational Principles of Pianoforte Technique* (Paris: Editions Maurice Senart, 1928/1930), 40.

17. Ibid., 37.

18. The current overemphasis and widespread misunderstanding regarding the unique *but limited* role of "forearm rotation" has unfortunately led to a certain devaluation of the role of weight application and transfer in tone production. Usually referred to as simply "rotation," it is as if this were the only rotational action or component of the playing mechanism specifically and the body generally. This—one might quite fairly call it an obsession, even cultlike in some quarters—has also led to a limited understanding and appraisal of the full role of all rotations (plural!) in a comprehensive approach to inherent curvilinear movement in the service of piano playing.

One should also note that this concern was a burning issue with Levinskaya, Fielden (a close colleague of Matthay's), and James Ching (a student of Matthay's, as well as a very influential pianist and teacher in his time). All three have written extensively about it, and even Matthay did so in his later years, as he realized his thinking about forearm rotation was increasingly misunderstood and misapplied.

19. This is a not-so-veiled reference to an (in)famous statement by Josef Stalin, one that I hope will not be taken to be insensitive, offensive or glib by any of my readers. When asked how he deals with unwelcome opposition or seemingly intractable political and economic situations, he replied: "No people, no problem." The play on this quote is of course meant to make the same point, however, in regard to matters of legato: as one example, pianists often resort to staccato, rationalizing (even justifying) it musically and interpretively absent their successful efforts to find an alternative solution to the "problem" of legato.

20. Cooke, *Playing the Piano for Pleasure*, 120.

21. Although he allowed 3-2 as an option, this misaligns and overcontracts the hand, obviating its innate structural balance.

22. Walter Gieseking and Karl Leimer, *Piano Technique* (New York: Dover, 1972), 117.

23. Alberto Jonás, *Master School of Piano Playing and Virtuosity* (New York: Carl Fischer, 1925), Vol. IV.

CHAPTER 7

1. Charles Rosen, *Piano Notes* (New York: Free Press, 2002), 229.

2. Abby Whiteside: "They remain difficult and practically unplayable until they are produced in the easiest possible manner." *Indispensables of Piano Playing* (New York: Scribner, 1961), 51.

3. I had the good fortune to hear him many times over the course of many years, in concerts, private soirees and lecture performances. I will never forget the first time I heard him, in concert at Syracuse University. His program included a sonata by Clementi and numerous Godowsky transcriptions for the left hand of the Chopin Etudes—among them, of course, that for double thirds, Chopin's Opus 25 No. 6. But to top that, he performed Godowsky's incredible yet delightful juxtaposition of Chopin's Etudes, Opus 10 No. 5 and Opus 25 No. 9, a simultaneous delivery of the well-known "Black Key" and "Butterfly" Etudes, both in their originally composed key of G-flat!

4. In his definitive treatise *The Piano Works of Claude Debussy* (New York: Dover reprint, 1966) Schmitz instructs: "In the general technical aspects of the performance of double-thirds it will be found that the verticalization of finger work, and the maintenance of a supple but high bridge, *intimately webbed with arm action* [italics added for emphasis], will bring the clarity of even weight distribution on the two component notes in succession." In specific regard to *Pour les Tierces*, Debussy's Etude II of Book 1, he goes on to advise that "it will be found that the task of fingering is rendered much easier by the *basic assumption* [italics are again mine] of five black keys in the majority of sections, and the oft-repeated possibility of neutralized fingerings, i.e., bringing long fingers on short keys and short fingers on long keys"; p. 198.

5. "For all the reasons that a trill in double thirds is difficult, so are passages in double notes, fourths and sixths . . . practically all rotary action is shut out. . . . Rotary tilts the hand and that tilting makes for difficulty in the precision of the third. It is easier to maintain the third—to keep two fingers equalized in length under the palm than it is to adjust that length for each third, which is necessary if the rotary action tilts the palm." Whiteside, *Indispensables*, 95–96.

6. I will not say strengths, as it is more accurate and more productive to distinguish between relative propensities for flexion or extension and axial distinctions related to alignment. Any set or group or complex of muscles can be further developed or "strengthened"; or they may weaken or remain underdeveloped. Muscle strength and tone are dynamic in nature, not static. In any case, misalignment and insufficient, inefficient stabilization has a negative impact on *effective* "strength."

7. The physiological advantage is that of displacing the finger that is the center of the ulnar axis—the fourth—with the one at the center of the radial axis, the second. With the upper arm dynamically stabilized, control of the forearm's necessary adjustive movement in an oblique plane—momentary and temporary—is maximally and efficiently secured with

coordinated counter actions in the shoulder joint and within the hand. A swift lateral adjustment establishes the vertical plane for tone production.

8. Jonás, *Master School, Volume IV*. This combination was first published by Hummel (*Grand School of Piano Playing*, 1828), and Jonás tells us that Riemann recommends this combination (*Catechism of Piano Playing, 1888*). He also informs us that it is later advocated by Rosenthal-Schytte in their *School of Modern Piano Virtuosity*. As Jonás observes, "It is feasible in the direction towards the little finger, but its defects are manifest as soon as one tries it in the contrary direction, that is to say descending for the RH and ascending for the LH."

9. Walter Gieseking and Karl Leimer, *Piano Technique* (New York: Dover, 1972), 117.

10. In Jonás: Dohnányi was one of the "Master" contributors.

11. Moszkowski calls "transcendental" those diatonic double third scale fingerings that he devised for the purpose of eliminating successive repetitions of the third finger, while ensuring finger-to-finger legato connections in *both* voices for each hand to the greatest extent possible—which, he allows, is not always so. What is most interesting about them is the consistent occurrence of such "translocated" (as I have termed them) groups of three black keys, assigned 2-3-4 as in the Fundamental Pattern, in signatures of more than four sharps or flats. However, he eschews full use of them for the sake of thumb-under pivoting from a white to a black key—presumably for the benefit of a legato connection. The result is that they are far more awkward—and certainly less "transcendental"—than one might hope to expect, or than is necessary. Moszkowski was himself quite aware of this: "The superiority of these fingerings . . . is incontestable, and in many scales it does not even appreciably increase the difficulty. In other keys, however, the fingering becomes so complicated, that a very rapid movement is practically unattainable." *École des Doubles-Notes Pour Piano* (Paris: Enoch, 1901), 14.

CHAPTER 8

1. Neuhaus, *Art of Piano Playing*, 127.

2. Ernst von Dohnányi, *Essential Finger Exercises (for Obtaining a Sure Piano Technique)* (Budapest: Editio Musica Budapest, 1950), 44.

3. See especially Godowsky's fingering for his left hand transcription of Chopin's double sixth etude, Opus 25 No. 8, and the accompanying preparatory exercises in *The Godowsky Collection, Vol. 3*, 295–299.

4. Neuhaus, *Art of Piano Playing*, 150–152.

5. Roskell, *Art of Piano Fingering* (London: LCM Publications, 1995).

6. Note the inversion of the sequence, reflecting the inverted relationship of third to sixth.

7. See *Liszt Technical Exercises*, Julio Esteban, editor (Port Washington, NY: Alfred Music, 1971).

8. Jean Baptiste Cramer, *Fifty Selected Piano-Studies* (New York: G. Schirmer, 1899), ii.

9. In *The Russian Technical Regime* (Florence, KY: Willis,1991), for example, Alexander Peskanov admonishes, "It should be noted that the fingering is identical for all 24 scales." The rather odd but telling result is that the three group is placed variously for all three enharmonic major keys—despite their common topographies.

10. Gieseking and Leimer, *Piano Technique*, 117.

11. E. Robert Schmitz, *Capture of Inspiration*.

12. Schmitz, *Piano Works of Claude Debussy*, 201.

13. In successfully transmitting vertical force to the key (verticalization), the requisite alignment for ulno-radial counterbalances and counteractions, especially the counter-rotational stresses of pronation and supination, is especially subtle. Appropriate shoulder complex stabilization dynamically coordinated within the prescribed range of upper arm rotation (circumduction) must provide the necessary basis for adequate control.

14. The curvilinear movement paths (curves), particularly of the upper arm, should remain elliptical.

15. With half steps on either side of the three black keys (altered Fundamental Pattern), the major scale for G-flat/F-sharp strongly suggests itself as the preferred scale for early study. For each hand, the position of its characteristic black-to-white whole and half steps affords the easiest implementation of the thumb-under pivoting action, especially for smaller, inexperienced hands. The longest third finger "neutralizes" the greater horizontal distance of the whole step, the relatively shorter fourth that of the half-step.

16. As cited by Frederick Niecks in *Frederick Chopin, As a Man and Musician* (Neptune City, NJ: Paganiniana [undated]), Vol. II, 184.

17. Schmitz, *Piano Works of Claude Debussy*, 198.

PART 3

1. In this sense, *affect* refers to feeling, or an emotional response to or impetus for musical expression; emotions generate the response. Whereas *effect* refers to a mechanical, emotionally disconnected, cerebrally contrived attempt to convey an impression—even to create the illusion—of a feeling response; feelings or emotions surface, at best, only minimally or sporadically. "Inauthentic" and unintegrated, the response is lacking in spontaneity, and this is one not lost on an audience, whether at a deeper or a more superficial level. Even if invested with great energy (physically and energetically mobilized—or "cranked up," so to speak), movements are nonetheless divorced from authenticity of feeling or appropriate emotional response. In essence, *effect* is the very antithesis of *affect*.

CHAPTER 9

1. Wanda Landowska, *Landowska on Music* (New York: Stein & Day, 1969), 373.

2. Schmitz and more recently others have advocated scale fingerings consistently employing the third finger as the black-key pivot to a white-key thumb. Obviously, this is not possible in regard to the enharmonic keys having three successive black keys. But nonetheless curious is that all assign the fourth to a black key for E major. And yet, consistent assignment of the third as black-key pivot is entirely possible for key signatures of one through four sharps and flats.

3. F. Taylor, *Technique and Expression in Pianoforte Playing*, 15.

4. Neuhaus, *The Art of Piano Playing*, 149.

5. József Gát, *The Technique of Piano Playing* (London: Collet's Ltd., 1974), 242.

6. Gyorgy Sandor, *On Piano Playing* (New York; Schirmer Books, 1981), 52–53 and 58–59.

7. George Kochevitsky, *The Art of Piano Playing: A Scientific Approach* (Princeton: Summy-Birchard, 1967), 41–42.

8. This "swing," the fundamental rhythmic impulse manifested by controlled release of the upper arm (timing, release, path and parameters are the pianist's province), is the naturally efficient means for the application of weight and a prime source of momentum in piano playing. At the same time it is the object of gravity's effective pull. With its potential for acceleration and deceleration, it is this natural impetus that lends itself to musical line, "sweep" and the shaping of phrases. It is the chief determinant and *component* of the consistent direction of curvilinear, elliptical paths of movement. Rhythmic and coordinated "key swing" follows from this and occurs within it. It is "tucked in," as Abby Whiteside might have said. Such a controlled, well-timed release of the arm's mass (weight) and the *directing* of the kinetic energy of its swing is at the root of a technique that is biophysically sound. Alternation of contraction and release within complementary muscle groups governs this and is demonstrative of the basic "work-rest" principle underlying all that pulsates. At bottom, rhythm is pulsation, and such a technical approach is fundamentally and inherently rhythmic.

CHAPTER 10

1. Ortmann's extensive and persuasive analysis of the limitations—and distortions—of movement posed by the fallboard includes his (unheeded) call for piano manufacturers "to remove this limitation," a change that would "make the playing of octaves or mixed figures on black keys considerably less constrained." *Physiological Mechanics*, 280–282.

2. Schmitz's categorized system of in-out adjustments ("full," "half," etc.) evolves in part from this conclusion that *all* fingers should ideally engage each key at its end. A five-finger pattern of five adjacent white keys, in C major for example, would be optimally played on key edge aided by appropriate in-out and lateral adjustments. But a five-finger pattern in D major, the third finger now on a black key, would require that the second and fourth fingers engage their white keys midway, at a different point of resistance.

    However, having determined this ideal point of contact, Schmitz did not in fact fully deal with the implications of hand "placement" and subsequent points of varying key resistance. As example are most full-diminished seventh chords with white- or black-key roots encompassing the span of the entire hand (the reader will recall that only three of these chords for each hand are symmetrical and "topographically correct"). But stabilization as a dynamic function—particularly of the shoulder joint and shoulder complex—had then not yet come into its own, even in any of the related disciplines. In piano playing, Maria Levinskaya (*The Levinskaya System of Pianoforte Technique and Tone-Colour*; London: Dent, 1930) comes closest to it.

3. A word here about "key bedding" and any negative connotations regarding excessive pressure it may imply: there should be no confusion that this is what is implied or advocated in advancing the key depth principle. But weight transfer does not occur if weight is not applied. "Anchorage" at the keyboard end—or better, the articulating action of the motor/pivot finger—is a requisite for true legato action. This articulation is necessarily with the key at its bottom—from key bottom to key bottom. Note further that all *loco*motion involves a transfer of mass/weight, resulting in movement from place to place, point to point. At the piano, mass is trans*located* so that its weight may be subsequently applied as a factor in tone production, ideally in the vertical plane.

4. Otto Ortmann, *The Physical Basis of Piano Touch and Tone*, 44–45: "The more we deviate from the vertical the greater is the loss in force effect . . . the more we deviate from non-percussion [playing from the key surface] the greater is the loss in tone control."

5. *Articulation* (see Appendix 9) involves a forward displacement and an alternate rise and fall, elevation and release, of the weight of the playing mechanism mass. This alternating muscular contraction and release may be controlled as to intensity and timing. As the basis of playing with weight, this transfer—or shift of weight—depends on the hand's lateral adjustment at the wrist for proper alignment with the forearm and upper arm. The resulting curvilinear movements occur within the overarching full circular rotation (circumduction) of the upper arm in its shoulder (humeral) joint—its "swing" controlled for horizontal distribution and coordinated key depression and tone production to the extent necessary.

6. See Ortmann: *Physiological Mechanics*, 75–78.

CHAPTER 11

1. Jan Holcman, *The Legacy of Chopin* (New York: Philosophical Library, 1954), 12.
2. Bacon, *Notes on the Piano*, 50: "It is interesting that those fingers that carry the heaviest burden of playing should be the weakest, the fifth and the fourth, inasmuch as it is the melody and bass that mostly predominate." The pianist must then "habituate the hand to this perverse but necessary usage."
3. Seymour Fink, for example, refers to "its irregular shape" and "an arbitrary keyboard design" in *Mastering Piano Technique* (Portland, OR: Amadeus Press), 59 and 66.
4. Bacon, 47.
5. Neuhaus, *The Art of Piano Playing*, 143: "This fingering (with this music, of course) brings the whole of Liszt before me. I see his hands, his gestures, his eagle manner, I feel the breath of this demon in monk's habit."
6. Dale Haven, *Selections from* The Piano Teacher *1958–1963* (Evanston, IL: Summy-Birchard, 1964): "Notes from a Godowsky Master Class," 112.
7. Clarence Adler, *Selections from* The Piano Teacher *1958–1963* (Evanston, IL: Summy-Birchard, 1964): "Impact—Leopold Godowsky," 108.
8. For the white keys the tritone B-F is the "adjusted" fifth of equal temperament.

PART 4

1. More recently in "Fingering: The Key to Arming," by Seymour Fink, in *A Symposium for Pianists and Teachers*, 63.
2. Artur Schnabel, *My Life and Music* (New York: Dover, 1988), 129.
3. For an extraordinarily comprehensive catalogue and enlightening critical survey, see Theodore Edel, *Piano Music for One Hand* (Bloomington and Indianapolis: Indiana University Press, 1994).
4. Ortmann, *The Physiological Mechanics of Piano Technique*, chapter 18, "Scales."
5. Ibid., 231–234.
6. Though operating from an elevated "preparation," *Slap* differs markedly in these respects while at the same time affording an expansion of the tone-color palette; see Appendix 9.

7. Schultz, *The Riddle of the Pianist's Finger*, 292–310.

8. The cyclographs, for example, in Percival Hodgson, *Motion Study and Violin Bowing* (London: J. H. Lavender, 1934).

9. Neuhaus, *The Art of Piano Playing*, 88.

CHAPTER 12

1. See Hans von Bülow's *Introduction* to "J. B. Cramer, Fifty Studies for the Piano" (New York: Schirmer, 1875), ii.

2. Seymour Fink, in *A Symposium for Pianists and Teachers: Strategies to Develop the Mind and Body for Optimal Performance* (Dayton, OH: Heritage Press, 2002), 63.

3. Ortmann, *Physiological Mechanics*, 278–80.

4. Wanda Landowska, *Landowska on Music*, 374.

5. Jonás, *Master School*, 96.

6. Ibid., 98.

7. Ibid., 4–5.

8. Hofmann, *Piano Playing*, 110.

9. Royal Conservatory of Music, *Piano Examination Repertoire* (Oakville, ONT: Frederick Harris Music, 1972), Grade IX.

10. Daniel Gregory Mason, *A Neglected Sense in Piano-Playing* (New York: G. Schirmer, 1912), 20–21.

11. *The Act of Touch* was Matthay's first published essay on piano technique (London: Longman's, Green, 1903).

12. Matthay, *Muscular Relaxation Studies*: Introduction, v.

13. Numerous other "arrangements" of these five tones exist throughout the folk music of many, if not most, ethnic cultures. This five-note sequence, intact but begun on any of its tones and with the initial tone (as "tonic") doubled at the octave, may give rise to its reception and formulation as a six-tone scale; still without half-steps, it may be heard then as in a "major" or "minor" mode, depending on the position of the two minor thirds in the now "rearranged" pentatonic series. Béla Bartók, Zoltán Kodály, Alberto Ginastera and Heitor Villa-Lobos are among the many notable twentieth-century composers who have made use of such pentatonic series in their integration of native influences as their own markedly individual compositional styles evolved.

14. The middle C approach is my preference. But others include introduction of a five-note/finger position on middle C for the right hand simultaneously with one for the left hand on the C an octave below—a C position for each hand—encountered most frequently in elementary methods books for adults and older beginners. Another, increasingly promoted for beginners of the youngest age groups, uses a reduced staff without clefs. The intention is to better focus on note direction and intervals, rather than specific notes in specific clefs: the written line-space/space-line order of notes is emphasized rather than their fixed letter names in the treble or bass clefs.

15. Kleczyński, *Works of Frederic Chopin*, 30.

CHAPTER 13

1. One popular view, for example, holds that Chopin's use of the key of D-flat is a coded allusion to the Countess Delphine ("D") Potocka: his Valse, Opus 64 No. 1, the so-called Minute Waltz, is dedicated to her. In regard to the waltzes alone, only four of the seventeen (Paderewski Edition) have key signatures of fewer than three sharps or flats, and three of them are also written in their parallel majors of three or more sharps. Of the thirteen remaining, only two are in three flats, of which Opus 18 shares the key of D-flat, and the other *eleven* are in four or more sharps or flats!

2. "If the powerful autocrat of the North [the Tsar] knew what a dangerous enemy threatens him in the works of Chopin, in the simple melodies of those mazurkas, he would banish this music. The works of Chopin are like cannons hidden beneath flowers." *Neue Zeitschrift für Musik*, no. 33, 1836, in Adam Zamoyski's *Chopin* (New York: Doubleday, 1980), 140.

3. Eigeldinger, 100 n30.

4. Persichetti was a piano student of Alberto Jonás. In Book III (pp. 2–5) of his monumental *Master School of Modern Piano Playing and Virtuosity* Jonás extols the concept of symmetrical mirroring for its compositional potential: as "opposite" harmony.

5. Ernst Bacon, *Notes on the Piano* (Seattle and London: University of Washington Press, 1968), 47–49.

CHAPTER 14

1. In "The Well-Tempered Revolution," Anthony Burgess's contribution to *The Lives of the Piano* (New York: Holt, Rinehart and Winston, 1981), he goes so far as to write: "With equal temperament and new devices for getting from one key to another, the sonata was, within less than a century, able to convey the range and variety of the novel or the narrative poem" (11). In this regard it should be noted that, generally speaking, symphonies are in fact sonatas (from *sonare*, as opposed to *cantare* or even *toccare*) for orchestra, with string quartets, for example, being merely another instrumental combination for the same compositional form.

2. Jan Kleczyński, *The Works of Frederic Chopin and Their Proper Interpretation*, 29–31.

3. From the Jędrzejewicz (Chopin's sister Ludwika) copy of the *Projet de méthode*, as quoted by Eigeldinger in *Chopin—Pianist and Teacher*, 34.

EPILOGUE

1. Edward Rothstein, *Emblems of the Mind: The Inner Life of Music and Mathematics* (New York: Times Books/Random House, 1995), 168.

2. Ibid., 200.

GLOSSARY

A GUIDE TO NATURAL FINGERING

ANATOMICAL/MIDLINE/NEUTRAL POSITION OF ARM This is the fundamental position of the arm as determined by its natural spatial relationship to the upright torso at a position of rest at the side. If not distorted by chronic tension or habitual misuse, the humerus is found to be rotated inward, which results in the arm being slightly distanced from the rib cage (torso); the palm of the hand faces backward (Feldenkrais), not inward or upward. It is important for pianists as the "neutral" position from which the entire arm may move most easily forward and backward, unobstructed and without requiring further skeletal adjustment for position in space.

At the keyboard, pull of weight is least, relative to other positions of the arm in space, and movement from this position—in front, to the side, forward and back of the torso—results in elevation as a correlative action. Pull effectively increases in proportion to the distance that the arm abducts to the horizontal plane.

This midline represents the lowest point of the curvilinear path of the upper arm's movement—particularly its "swing" (see **Swing**)—in relationship to the torso and the keyboard.

ANTAGONISTS Muscles working in opposition or complementarily to those engaged in the principal coordinated action. They may be actively engaged (contracted) in opposition for dynamic reinforcement and stabilization, inactive (relaxed, inhibited) relative to the main action, or progressively disengaged for coordination and control.

ARM LOCATION PRINCIPLE (SCHMITZ) This is the fundamental principle regarding the kinesiological effect of the arm's location in keyboard space as it relates to well-coordinated application of vertical force throughout the entire keyboard range. Long fingers best neutralize the upper arm's natural elevation as it increasingly moves out of neutral position (from its midline) in movement toward the torso and then beyond it.

In these extreme ranges, the shoulder complex adjusts downward in conjunction with its dynamic stabilization in order to establish and maintain consistency of key depth (see **Shoulder Girdle/Shoulder Complex Depression**).

ARTICULATION A "touch" form. (1) In a musical context, common usage denotes the distinguishing emphasis of a particular note or group of notes relative to others within a motif, phrase group, or phrase. It is, in this sense, counterpart to any clarifying declamatory or rhetorical emphasis in speech, such as a stressed syllable or initial consonant.

(2) Technically, it is the physical means of a finger-to-finger, key-to-key "binding" (*legato*) of successive tones. As one of Schmitz's Fundamental Principles of Training (see Appendix 9), it corresponds to what is now known to be Liszt's directive for achieving a finger legato (Bertrand Ott) and may be accomplished with or without weight. It is also a chief technical means for implementing an expressive articulation within a phrase, as in (1) above.

AXIS A real or imagined line of action of a body, e.g., the length axis of the third finger as determined from the humeral "center," and the oblique (transverse) axis for the ulnar opposition of thumb and fourth/fifth fingers. Also, the real or imaginary point at which rotation occurs or conical movement takes place, e.g., forearm oscillation (pronosupination), inward-outward (medial-lateral) rotation of the humerus and the full curvilinear movement of the upper arm (circumduction).

BIOMECHANICAL As used here, the term denotes a unified interaction of anatomy, physiology and the laws of physics as they relate to operation of the pianist's playing mechanism and its role in transmission and application of force.

BIPLANAR This refers to the two horizontal planes of keyboard movement: one established by the position of the white keys, the other by that of the black keys.

CENTER OF AXIS The locus for maximally efficient movement at or along an axis; the primary orientation and locus for the most biomechanically efficient execution of a specific movement and application of its initial and motivating force.

CENTER OF CONTROL (PRIMARY CONTROL) This refers to the upper arm at the shoulder joint (a component of the shoulder complex) as the primary hub for any coordination of the playing mechanism's movement from center to periphery—essential for pianists. This does not disregard, but is not to be confused with, F. M. Alexander's "primary control" (the head) or the neurological "centers" residing in the brain and solar plexus.

CENTER OF GRAVITY The point at which the downward force of gravity (gravitational pull) effectively bears on the aggregate mass of a body or structure.

CENTER OF RADIUS OF ACTIVITY (WHITESIDE) The focal point for imparting movement manifest at the periphery. It is the point from which movement and force is generated, directed and controlled. See **Axis, Center of Axis, Center of Control** and **Conical**.

In *Indispensables of Piano Playing*, Abby Whiteside distinguishes it as follows: "For the full arm it is the shoulder joint. For the movements of fast articulation it is the elbow joint. For the finger it is the hand knuckle joint; for the thumb, the wrist joint."

COMPLEMENTARY (MOVEMENTS/MUSCLES) The dynamic interaction of *directionally* opposing muscular activity that has the potential for maximal efficiency in the balance of forces and distribution of effort as to degree, timing and direction of action. Although they may be outwardly static in appearance, internal forces are in dynamic opposition and *active* equilibrium.

Alternation of contraction and relaxation of the muscles engaged in any series of complementary or counteracting movements reflects and is an anatomical/physiological manifestation of the work-rest cycle: the basis of rhythm and all pulsation.

CONICAL Circular or elliptical movement that is cone-shaped as it proceeds from a central point (locus) to its periphery. Full rotation (circumduction) of the extended arm—fully outstretched or directed downward—in an ever-increasing range of curvilinear movement and, similarly, full rotation of the hand at the wrist are examples.

CORE PATTERNS The four-note/four-finger groups deriving from Chopin's Fundamental Pattern in which the shorter thumb is maintained on the long white key and the longer fourth finger on the shorter black key. Altered, transposed, or *translocated*, they determine the fingerings of all the fundamental forms. As five-finger patterns, they make up the primary groups for all double third diatonic scales and underlie those for all other diatonic double notes.

COUNTERACTION (COUNTERFORCE) An opposing action or force that may or may not result in movement in space; it may be active or reactive.

COUNTERBALANCE A dynamic equilibrium of opposing actions or forces manifest as maintaining a seemingly static position or spatial relationship of two or more masses or structures.

CROSS-TENSION Refers to the action dynamics of the development and control of the musculature of the hand and its architectural structure; the strengthening of the palmar bridge correlative with the flexibility of the knuckle joints. It is the fundamental means for developing the hand's innate capacity to receive and bear the weight of the torso, including any downward force generated by the shoulder complex and aided by torso flexion. Used specifically to connote isolated training of this fundamental aspect of the playing mechanism, as distinguished from its application to specific passagework (in contrast to **Modeling**, Schmitz's more comprehensive term).

CURVE The commonly applied generic term for kinematic representations of movement. Curves and semicurves represent direction, range and depth of the curvilinear paths for movements of circumduction and oscillation; useful as imagery as well as indispensable tools for movement analysis.

CURVILINEAR In contrast to linear: semi- or fully circular, elliptical, looped, "figure eight," or waved.

DEPRESSION OF SHOULDER GIRDLE/SHOULDER COMPLEX This is the vertical adjustment of the entire playing mechanism—from the (lower) tips of the shoulder blades to the tips of the fingers—for key depth; its source of application is the shoulder girdle/shoulder complex. The resulting downward action ensures a secure (keyed) base for continuous legato connection and weight transfer, as well as potentially generating an auxiliary force for tone production when dynamically applied—that is, on a continuum relevant to the upper arm's position in a specific keyboard range.

This downward application of weight/force is upwardly counteracted by the prehensile actions of the fingers or hand in conjunction with coordinated retraction of the forearm and upper arm. This counteracting retraction is felt as a "pull" upward and toward the torso; its control resides in the subtle balance of these complementary actions. (See Arm Release and Retraction in Appendix 9.)

DISTRIBUTIVE MOVEMENTS Horizontal and lateral movements serving to place the hand and fingers in position for key activation vertically.

DYNAMIC Refers to the action of forces on the motion of bodies in producing, altering, or maintaining their movement (or position) in time and space.

DYNAMIC EQUILIBRIUM Refers to counteracting or complementary forces in a state of dynamic balance.

DYNAMIC MOVEMENTS In piano playing, movements that both activate the key and act as agents in applying speed and force as it relates to key depression and release (retraction) in tone production. At their most efficient, these movements correlate with the key's own movement (descent and ascent) in its vertical plane.

DYNAMIC STABILIZATION As used here, it refers to that continuum of effort expended to aid in maintaining the optimal relationship of the upper arm (humerus) to the rest of the shoulder girdle/shoulder complex. The humerus (upper arm) is the primary base of the playing mechanism for the movements and stabilizing actions of the lower arm (secondary) with its hand and fingers (tertiary). Humeral stabilization enlists a continuously coordinated and reinforced equilibrium of opposing forces as required by specific movements and locations in keyboard space. Its goal is to facilitate optimal alignment throughout the playing mechanism for coordinate transmission of requisite force to the key(s).

Such stabilization manifests a dynamic equilibrium that is opposed to *fixation*, with its aim or sense of a fixed position or a rigid—even chronically rigid—muscular condition. In these terms, fixation is imprecise, incoordinate and inflexible in effectively gauging or adjusting to the ongoing demand for stabilization of the entire playing mechanism's movement in space, particularly at faster tempi and with more frequent directional change—for a balance of stability and mobility.

Natural stabilization, on the other hand, is the *inherent* stabilization of all joints that is naturally effected via an interconnecting network that includes connective tissue, ligaments, tendons and muscles, in their origins and attachments.

ELLIPSE A curvilinear movement path, or cycle, that is oval or similarly shaped (elliptical) but not circular.

ENHARMONIC In ancient Greek theory, the term refers to a scale construction containing intervals less than a semitone (half-step). In modern theory it refers to a pitch, scale/arpeggio, key or chord having an alternate spelling. Such reciprocal enharmonic relationships are, in fact, unique to the system of equal temperament and are of particular practical consequence in the course of pianism, its pedagogy and its repertoire.

As used herein, the enharmonic scales are those "overlapping" major keys (B/C♭, F♯/G♭, C♯/D♭) as represented by the Circle of Fifths and their relative minors (G♯/A♭, D♯/E♭, A♯/B♭). Although C-sharp and D-flat majors are enharmonic, there is not a D-flat minor scale, for example, since there is not a key or scale of F-flat major. The E major scale may be spelled enharmonically, but it would then be a purely theoretical construct, not within our system of twelve major and minor keys (equal temperament divides the octave into twelve equal semitones).

An *enharmonic modulation* to a new key or key "region" (a new tonality is implied or sensed, but not firmly established by a strong cadence) is effected by the enharmonic spelling of a single pitch, motif, other transitional figure, or "pivot" chord common to both keys. And the key scheme of entire sections may also be that of their related enharmonic "equivalents." Enharmonic spelling in some cases may be necessitated by a change of mode.

EPICYCLE A curve, or epicycloid, whose center is a point at the circumference of a larger circle. Such are the "curves within curves" of the movements of smaller relative to larger units of the playing mechanism.

FUNDAMENTAL FORMS Single and double note (thirds and sixths) chromatic and diatonic scales; arpeggios, as extensions of all triads and four-part chords. The whole-tone scale and chromatic and diatonic double note scales of seconds, fourths, fifths and sevenths may be included with these.

HUMERUS The bone of the upper arm. See **Dynamic Stabilization** and **Playing Mechanism**.

INTERPLANAR (BIPLANAR) Movement traversing the black and white key planes.

KEYBOARD SPACE Confines, parameters, dimensions, distinguishing attributes; vertical and horizontal planes and their oblique, intersecting planes of movement.

KINEMATIC As used here, any visual representation of motion in which movement timing and scope is depicted without causative factors.

KINEMATICS Movement study, but to the exclusion of causative factors and impacting or resultant forces.

KINESIOLOGY Physiology and physical laws as they are manifested dynamically as movement in space. It is distinguished as a discipline by muscular actions as they particularly influence application of force, the energy of momentum, effective movement planes, and the impact of gravity and time on all of these. An emphasis is on the generation of movement and the impact of outside forces.

KINETIC (KINEMATIC) CHAIN Groups of muscles whose complementary and overlapping actions and functions cooperate in series throughout or among larger units of smaller components, e.g. the shoulder complex, or the lower arm and hand.

KINETIC ENERGY The energy of, or as a result of, motion.

KINETICS Motion study and the dynamic forces of movement.

MIDLINE (OF THE ARM) see *Anatomical Position*

MODELING (SCHMITZ) Used herein to refer to application of the dynamics of *cross-tension* (see above) to the particular topology of a group or series of notes with the aim of intensifying the sensorial contact and further securing the physical orientation of the fingers and hand to the keys (see Appendix 9).

The term itself refers to the hand's innate plasticity, developing and maximizing its prehensile capabilities as they may apply to a specific group of notes—most valuably for those that are unusual or atypical.

MOTOR FINGERS (SCHMITZ) The "weight-bearing" fingers in *Articulation* (see Appendix 9) and the thumb-under pivoting action, in which the arm's mass/weight is displaced forward and upward via flexion of the first (terminal) joints of the fingers for subsequent release. This action also applies to all fingers to the extent that their role as "pivots" effects requisite alignment.

MUSCLE SPREAD (ORTMANN) The felt continuation of an intensified muscular activity or contraction to successively related muscle groups, somewhat similar to what occurs in shifting the gears of a bicycle or automobile, in which ratios of speed and power to mass are effected sequentially.

This sense of muscular spread—in which the total response is increasingly greater than the original response—is useful in determining appropriate levels of muscular activity, including the elimination of unnecessary "sympathetic" contraction. Ortmann refers to it as a "graded response" that is generated "either by gradations in the reaction of a single muscle or by a coordination between muscles."

NEUTRAL POSITION (OF THE ARM) see *Anatomical Position*

OBLIQUE (DIAGONAL) The transverse intersection of two movement planes at right angles to each other (vertical and horizontal: vertically oblique), and including the right angles of the keyboard surface (lateral and forward: laterally oblique). Also, movement in an arc that transects the space bounded by the right angle of those planes.

OPPOSITIONAL Flexing action of thumb and fourth/fifth fingers occurring along the hand's transverse axis (see Appendix 10).

ORIENTATION Relative position in space as regards skeletal alignment, weight distribution and potential for transmission of force.

PLAYING MECHANISM The total *ensemble* of the playing units from the tips of the shoulder blades to the tips of the fingers: the shoulder complex, which includes the shoulder girdle and upper arm (humerus); and the lower arm, which includes the forearm (ulna and radius) and the hand with its fingers.

PRIMARY CONTROL See *Center of Control*

PRIMARY PATTERNS These derive from the core groups of the Fundamental Pattern, in which their alterations or transpositions reflect and preserve the topographical advantage—*fourth on black, thumb on white*—for the thumb-under pivoting action. They are the primary determinants of the topographical fingerings for diatonic double thirds.

PRONOSUPINATION A more accurately descriptive and increasingly preferred term for what is commonly and misguidedly referred to simply as "rotation," by which is meant the side-to-side, oscillating action of the forearm. Also of the upper arm.

REPOSITION (OF THUMB) Given the varying and confusing terminology assigned to the thumb's complex movements, this is the term increasingly adopted by many to describe the thumb's return to its "neutral" position at its radial (metacarpal) base.

In the thumb-under pivoting action, this repositioning is the thumb's movement after ceasing its oppositional action along the hand's transverse axis; as it involves the fourth finger, the thumb's *playing* movement is initiated (obliquely) by the muscular release of its oppositional contraction.

RETRACTION Refers to withdrawal of a playing unit from the depressed key or keyboard surface. This withdrawal may be in the vertical plane, as in Arm Release and Retraction or Slap (Schmitz); horizontal as in finger flexion toward the palm of the hand (Schmitz: Articulation); or oblique, as in the opposition or reposition of thumb along its diagonal (transverse) axis and in the pronosupination of the forearm (see Appendices 9 and 10).

SECONDARY PATTERNS These reflect interval (harmonic, modal) alterations of a five-finger pattern, as do the primary patterns. The distinction here is that, in doing so, they do not afford the topographical advantage of a black-key fourth finger for the pivoting action of a white-key thumb. They are the secondary determinants of the topographical fingerings for diatonic double thirds.

SHOULDER JOINT/SHOULDER COMPLEX Essentially the "shoulder complex"—which includes the humerus and its glenohumeral joint (shoulder joint). Herein these terms are sometimes joined to specifically connote and emphasize the important stabilizing role of the shoulder joint, including dynamic inward (medial) rotation of the humerus, with that of the shoulder complex generally.

SUPINATION Oblique rotation of the forearm from the position of pronation. Ulna and radius are parallel to each other in the fully supinated position of approximately 90 degrees; lateral rotation of the upper arm (humerus) is engaged beyond this range.

SWING (OF ARM) Movement of the arm when released at the shoulder joint from a seemingly static but dynamically elevated position. Muscular contraction in elevation is disengaged, with the aim of releasing the arm's mass to the downward force of gravity. Its weight is best available for application to keyboard space when initially directed by the coordinated actions of inner humeral rotation and forearm pronation. The opposing forces of gravity and momentum are harnessed for horizontal distribution and vertical application of weight. Force is further augmented or diminished by muscular application.

It is a chief determinant of the playing mechanism's curvilinear path, kinematically represented as *curves* (see **Curve**).

TOPOLOGY An inclusive term, but specifically employed to connote spatial relationships (distances, intervals) in addition to the several topographical attributes.

TRANSLOCATE (FUNDAMENTAL PATTERN) This is a shift or transfer of the core WBBBW topographical arrangement, in which there are seen to be more than one group of three successive black keys as exemplified in the Fundamental Pattern. The three long fingers of the three black keys may therefore be shifted upward or downward. This extends the natural advantage of the long fingers on short keys in their neutralization of the two planes (white-key and black-key) of action. Because the interval arrangement is altered, it is not a "transposition" in the musical sense.

BIBLIOGRAPHY

Agay, Denes. *The Joy of First-Year Piano*. New York (?): Yorktown Music Press, 1972.

Andres, Robert. *Pianos and Pianism: Frederic Horace Clark and the Quest for Unity of Mind, Body and Universe*. Lanham, MD/London: Scarecrow Press, 2001.

Bach, C.P.E. *Essay on the True Art of Playing Keyboard Instruments*. Trans. and ed. by William J. Mitchell. New York/London: Norton, 1949.

Bacon, Ernst. *Notes on the Piano*. Seattle/London: University of Washington Press, 1968.

———. *Notes on the Piano*. Introduction by Sara Davis Buechner. New York: Dover, 2011.

Badura-Skoda, Eva, and Paul Badura-Skoda. *Interpreting Mozart* (2nd ed.). New York: Routledge, 2008.

Barrett, Mary Ellin. *Irving Berlin: A Daughter's Memoir*. New York: Simon and Schuster, 1994.

Berman, Boris. *Notes from the Pianist's Bench*. New Haven/London: Yale University Press, 2000.

Bernstein, Seymour. *With Your Own Two Hands*. New York: Schirmer Books, 1981.

Bolton, Hetty. *On Teaching the Piano*. Borough Green, Sevenoaks and Kent, UK: Novello, 1954.

Brée, Malwine. *The Leschetizky Method: A Guide to Fine and Correct Piano Playing*. Mineola, NY: Dover, 1997.

Breithaupt, Rudolf M. *Die natürliche Klaviertechnik*. Leipzig: C. F. Kahnt Nachfolger, 1905.

———. *Die natürliche Klaviertechnik*, Band I. Handbuch der modernen Methodik und Spielpraxis. Leipzig: C.F. Kahnt Nachfolger, 1912.

———. *Natural Piano Technic*. Vol. II: *School of Weight Touch*. English trans. by John Bernhoff. Leipzig: C. F. Kant Nachfolger, 1909.

Brower, Harriet. *Piano Mastery: The Harriet Brower Interviews*. Ed. and introduction by Jeffrey Johnson. Mineola, NY: Dover, 2003.

Burnett, Richard. *Company of Pianos*. Goudhurst, Kent: Finchcocks Press, 2004.

Busoni, Ferruccio. *A New Esthetic of Music*. Trans. by Theodore Baker. New York: Schirmer, 1911.

Chaffin, Roger, Mary Crawford and Gabriela Imreh. *Practicing Perfection: Memory and Piano Performance*. Mahwah, NJ/London: Lawrence Erlbaum, 2002.

Chase, Mary Wood. *Natural Laws in Piano Technic*. Boston: Oliver Ditson, 1910.

Ching, James. *Piano Playing*. New York: Bosworth, 1946.

The Complete Chopin: A New Critical Edition (Ballades, Preludes, Waltzes and Concerto No. 1 Op. 11). Series editors: John Rink, Jim Samson, Jean-Jacques Eigeldinger and Christophe Grabowski. Leipzig/London: Edition Peters, 2008.

Christiani, Adolph F. *The Principles of Expression in Pianoforte Playing*. Philadelphia: Theodore Presser, 1885.

Collester, Jeanne Colette. *Rudolf Ganz: A Musical Pioneer*. Metuchen, NJ, and London: Scarecrow Press, 1995.

Cooke, Charles. *Playing the Piano for Pleasure*. New York: Simon and Schuster, 1941, 1960.

Cooke, James Francis. *Great Pianists on Piano Playing*. Philadelphia: Theodore Presser, 1913.

Cortot, Alfred. *Rational Principles of Pianoforte Technique*. Paris: Editions Maurice Senart, 1928/1930 (U.S. distributor Ditson).

Coviello, Ambrose. *Foundations of Pianoforte Technique: Co-ordination Exercises*. London: Humphrey Milford, Oxford University Press, 1934.

Cramer, Jean Baptiste. *Fifty Selected Piano-Studies*. New York: G. Schirmer, 1899.

Creston, Paul. *Virtuoso Technique for the Piano*. New York: G. Schirmer, 1950.

Curcio, Louise. *The Single Note*. New Jersey: Rose Education, 1965.

———. *Space Playing*. Newark, NJ: Modern Pianistics, 1975.

Descaves, Lucette. *Un Nouvel Art du Piano*. Paris: Fayard, 1966.

Duffin, Ross W. *How Equal Temperament Ruined Harmony (and Why You Should Care)*. New York/London: Norton, 2007.

Edel, Theodore. *Piano Music for One Hand*. Bloomington and Indianapolis: Indiana University Press, 1994.

Eigeldinger, Jean-Jacques. *Chopin—pianist and teacher, as seen by his pupils*. Cambridge: Cambridge University Press, 1986.

Eschmann-Dumur, Charles. *Guide du Jeune Pianiste—Classification Méthodique et Graduée: Aperçus, Notes et Conseils* (Seconde édition, revue et augmentée). Zurich: Hug 1888.

Everhart, Powell. *The Pianist's Art*. Atlanta: Powell Everhart, 1958.

Fay, Amy. *Music-Study in Germany*. New York: Dover, 1965.

Ferguson, Howard. *Keyboard Interpretation*. New York/London: Oxford University Press, 1975.

Fielden, Thomas. *The Science of Pianoforte Technique*. Reprint. New York: St. Martin's Press, 1961. (Originally published 1927, 2nd ed. 1934.)

Fink, Seymour. *Mastering Piano Technique*. Portland, OR: Amadeus Press, 1992.

Fleischmann, Tilly. *Aspects of the Liszt Tradition*. Ed. by Michael O'Neill. Bryn Mawr, PA: Theodore Presser, 1991.

Fraser, Alan. *The Craft of Piano Playing*. Lanham, MD; and Oxford: Scarecrow Press, 2003.

Friedheim, Arthur. *Life and Liszt*. Edited by Theodore L. Bullock. New York: Taplinger, 1961.

Friskin, James. *The Principles of Pianoforte Practice*. New York: H. W. Gray, 1921.

Gaines, James R., ed. *The Lives of the Piano*. Essays by Anthony Burgess, Dominique Browning, Annalyn Swan, Anthony Liversidge, Ned Rorem, William Bolcom, Samuel Lipman and Richard Sennett. New York: Holt, Rinehart and Winston, 1981.

Ganz, Rudolf. *Exercises for Piano, Contemporary and Special*. Evanston, IL: Summy-Birchard, 1967.

Gardi, Nino. *Il Bianco e il Nero. Considerazione storico-critiche sulla tecnologia pianistica*. Varese, Italy: Zecchini Editore, 2008.

Garroway, Will. *Pianism*. New York: Carl Fischer, 1939.

Gát, József. *The Technique of Piano Playing* (4th ed.). Trans. by István Kleszky. London/Wellingborough: Collet's, 1974.

Gerig, Reginald R. *Famous Pianists & Their Technique*. Washington/New York: Luce, 1974.

———. *Famous Pianists & Their Technique (New Edition)*. Bloomington: Indiana University Press, 2007.

Gieseking, Walter, and Karl Leimer. *Piano Technique*. New York: Dover, 1972.

Glasford, Irene S. *Rhythm, Reason and Response*. New York: Exposition Press, 1970.

The Godowsky Collection, compilation and Introductory Notes by Millan Sachania. 4 vols. New York: Carl Fischer, 2002.

Goldman, Richard Franko. *Harmony in Western Music: A Study of the Principles of Tonal Harmony as One of the Great Accomplishments of Western Art*. New York: Norton, 1965.

Grabill, Ethelbert W. *The Mechanics of Piano Technic*. Boston: Boston Music, 1914.

Grindea, Carola. *Tensions in the Performance of Music*. New York: Alexander Broude, 1978.

Handbook for Piano Teachers: Collected Articles on Subjects Related to Piano Teaching. Evanston, IL: Summy-Brichard, 1958.

Hodgson, Percival. *Motion Study and Violin Bowing*. London: Lavender, 1934; Urbana, IL: American String Teachers Association, 1964.

Hofmann, Josef. *Piano Playing: With Piano Questions Answered*. New York: Dover, 1976.

Holcman, Jan. *The Legacy of Chopin*. New York: Philosophical Library, 1954.

Hummel, Jan (Johann) Nepomuk. *A Complete Theoretical and Practical Course of Instructions on the Art of Playing the Piano Forte . . . written and most humbly dedicated to His majesty George IV*. (Fingerings in English system.) London: T. Boosey & Co., 1829.

———. *Méthode Complète Théorique et Pratique pour le Piano-Forte . . . dédiée a Sa Majestié Nicolas 1er Empereur de Russie*. (Fingerings in Continental system.) Paris: A. Farrance, ca. 1828 and 1838/R.

Huneker, James. *Chopin, The Man and His Music*. New York: Dover, 1966.

Hutcheson, Ernst. *The Elements of Piano Technique*. Cincinnati, OH: Willis Music, 1967.

Isacoff, Stuart. *Temperament: How Music Became a Battleground for the Great Minds of Western Civilization*. New York: Knopf, 2003.

Jaëll, Marie. *Le Mécanisme du Toucher* (1897). Paris: Association Marie Jaëll, 2003.

———. *Le Toucher—Base sur la Physiologie*. Vol. I: A, B and C (1894). Paris: Association Marie Jaëll, 1983.

———. *Le Toucher—Base sur la Physiologie*. Vol. II (1894). Paris: Association Marie Jaëll, 1984.

———. *Le Toucher—Base sur la Physiologie*. Vol. III (1894). Paris: Costallat & Cie., 1899.

Jonás, Alberto. *Master School of Modern Piano Playing and Virtuosity* (seven books), in collaboration with Wilhelm Bachaus, Fannie Bloomfield-Zeisler, Ferruccio Busoni, Alfred Cortot, Ernst von Dohnányi, Arthur Friedheim, Ignaz Friedman, Ossip Gabrilowitsch,

Rudolf Ganz, Leopold Godowsky, Katherine Goodson, Josef Lhevinne, Isadore Philipp, Moriz Rosenthal, Emil von Sauer, Leopold Schmidt, and Sigismond Stojowski. New York: Carl Fischer, 1922–1929.

———. *Master School of Virtuoso Piano Playing*. Vol. I: *Finger Exercises*. Foreword by Reah Sadowsky, Introduction by Sara Davis Buechner. New York: Dover, 2011.

———. *Master School of Virtuoso Piano Playing*. Vol. II: *Scales*. Introduction by Sara Davis Buechner. New York: Dover, 2011.

Jones, George Thaddeus. *Music Theory*. New York: Barnes & Noble (Harper & Row), 1974.

Joseffy, Rafael. *School of Advanced Piano Playing*. New York: G. Schirmer, 1902.

Kaemper, Gerd. *Techniques Pianistiques*. Paris: Alphonse Leduc, 1968.

Kentner, Louis. *Piano* (Yehudi Menuhin Music Guides). New York: Schirmer Books, 1976.

Kentner: A Symposium Edited by Harold Taylor with a Foreword by Yehudi Menuhin. London: Kahn & Averill, 1987.

Kitson, C. H. *The Evolution of Harmony* (2nd ed.). Oxford: Clarendon Press, 1924.

Kleczyński, Jean (Jan). *The Works of Frederic Chopin and Their Proper Interpretation* (4th ed.). Trans. by Alfred Whittingham. London: William Reeves (undated).

Kline, Donna Staley. *Olga Samaroff Stokowski: An American Virtuoso on the World Stage*. College Station: Texas A&M University Press, 1996.

Kochevitsky, George. *The Art of Piano Playing: A Scientific Approach*. Princeton, NJ: Summy-Birchard, 1967.

Kocsár, Miklós. *Games with Intervals*. Budapest: Editio Musica Budapest, 2005.

Kummer, Corby. *Talking About Pianos*. New York: Steinway & Sons, 1982.

Landowska, Wanda. *Landowska on Music*. New York: Stein & Day, 1969.

Leimer, Karl. *Handbuch für den Klavierunterricht in den Unter- und Mittelstufen*. Hannover: Verlag von Louis Dertel, 1918.

Levinskaya, Maria. *The Levinskaya System of Pianoforte Technique and Tone-Colour*. London/Toronto: Dent, 1930.

Lhevinne, Josef. *Basic Principles in Pianoforte Playing*. New York: Musical Scope [undated].

Lyke, James, and Yvonne Enoch. *Creative Piano Teaching*. Champaign, IL: Stipes, 1977.

Mach, Elyse. *Great Pianists Speak for Themselves*. New York: Dodd, Mead, 1980.

Marcus, Adele. *Great Pianists Speak*. Neptune, NJ: T.F.H., 1979.

Mark, Thomas. *What Every Pianist Needs to Know About the Body*. (Supplementary Material for Organists by Roberta Gary and Thom Miles.) Chicago: GIA, 2003.

Martin, Jean (avec Barraud, Philippe). *Jouez avec Doigté . . . Deux Mains . . . Dix Doigts . . . Mais Tellement Plus—Traité sur les Doigtés*. Lyon: Aléas, 2005.

Mason, Daniel Gregory. *A Neglected Sense in Piano-Playing*. New York: G. Schirmer, 1912.

Mason, William. *Touch and Technic: Artistic Piano Playing*, 4 vols. Philadelphia: Theodore Presser, 1892.

Mason, William, and W.S.B. Matthews. *A System of Fundamental Technics for Modern Piano Playing*. Boston: Oliver Ditson, 1878/1905.

Matthay, Tobias. *The Act of Touch in All Its Diversity: An Analysis and Synthesis of Pianoforte Tone-Production*. London: Longman's, Green, 1903.

———. *Muscular Relaxation Studies, for Students, Artists and Teachers*. London: Bosworth, 1908.

———. *Musical Interpretation*. Boston: Boston Music, 1913.

———. *An Epitome of the Laws of Pianoforte Technic*. London: Humphrey Milford, Oxford University Press, 1931.

———. *The Visible and Invisible in Pianoforte Technique*. London: Oxford University Press, 1932.

Matthews, W.S.B. *Music: Its Ideals and Methods*. Philadelphia: Theodore Presser, 1897.

Merrick, Frank. *Practicing the Piano*. New York: Dover (3rd impression), 1965.

Methuen-Campbell, James. *Chopin Playing*. New York: Taplinger, 1981.

Mitchell, Mark, and Allen Evans. *Moriz Rosenthal: In Word and Music*. Preface by Charles Rosen. Bloomington and Indianapolis: Indiana University Press, 2006.

Monsaingeon, Bruno. *Sviatoslav Richter: Notebooks and Conversations*. Princeton/Oxford: Princeton University Press, 2001.

Napier, John. *Hands*. Revised by Russell H. Tuttle. Princeton, NJ: Princeton University Press, 1993.

Neuhaus, Heinrich. *The Art of Piano Playing*. Trans. by K. A. Leibovitch. New York: Praeger, 1973.

Newman, William S. *The Pianist's Problems*. New York: Harper & Row, 1950.

Niecks, Frederick. *Frederick Chopin, as a Man and Musician*. Two vols. Neptune City, NJ: Paganiniana (undated).

Orenstein, Arbie (comp. and ed.). *A Ravel Reader: Correspondence, Articles, Interviews*. Mineola, NY: Dover, 2003.

———. *Ravel, Man and Musician.* Mineola, NY: Dover, 1991.

Ortmann, Otto. *The Physical Basis of Piano Touch and Tone*. London: Kegan Paul, Trench, Trubner & Co., Ltd.; J. Curwen & Sons, Ltd.; New York: Dutton, 1925.

———. *The Physiological Mechanics of Piano Technique*. Reprint. New York: Dutton, 1962; Da Capo Press 1981. (Originally published 1929.)

———. *Theories of Synesthesia in the Light of a Case of Color-Hearing*. Reprint from *Human Biology: A Record of Research*. Baltimore: John Hopkins Press, 1933.

Ott, Bertrand. *Lisztian Keyboard Energy/Liszt et la Pedagogie du Piano*. Trans. by Donald H. Windham, Preface by Norbert Dufourcq. Lewiston, NY: Edwin Mellen Press, 1992.

Parrot, Jasper, with Vladimir Ashkenazy. *Ashkenazy: Beyond Frontiers*. New York: Atheneum, 1985.

Perlemuter, Vlado, and Hélène Jourdan-Morhange. *Ravel According to Ravel*. London: Kahn and Averill, 2005.

Persechetti, Vincent. *Little Mirror Book*. Bryn Mawr, PA: Elkan-Vogel, 1983.

Piano Lessons in the Grand Style: From the Golden Age of The Etude *Music Magazine (1913–1940)*. Edited by Jeffrey Johnson. Mineola, NY: Dover, 2003.

The Piano Master Classes of Hans von Bülow. Trans. and ed. by Richard Louis Zimdars. Bloomington: Indiana University Press, 1993.

Pichier, Paul. *The Pianist's Touch*. Edited by Walter Krause. Translated by Martha Ideler and Peter R. Wilson. Marshall, CA: Perelen, 1972.

Piston, Walter. *Harmony* (3rd ed.). New York: Norton, 1962.

———. *Harmony* (4th ed.). Revised and expanded by Mark DeVoto. New York: Norton, 1978.

Polnauer, Frederick F., and Morton Marks. *Senso-Motor Study and Its Application to Violin Playing*. Urbana, IL: American String Teachers Association, 1964.

Potamkin, Frank J. *Modern Piano Pedagogy*. Philadelphia: Elkin Vogel, 1936.

Potocka, Angèle. *Theodore Leschetizky*. New York: Century, 1903.

Rasmussen, Karl Aage. *Sviatoslav Richter, Pianist*, trans. Russell Dies. Hanover and London: University Press of New England, 2010.

Rattalino, Pierro. *Manuale Tecnico del Pianista Concertista*. Varese, Italy: Zecchini Editore, 2007.

Reubart, Dale. *Anxiety and Musical Performance*. New York: Da Capo Press, 1985.

Ristad, Eloise. *A Soprano on Her Head*. Moab, UT: Real People Press, 1982.

Robert, Walter. "In Defense of Scales." *Clavier*, 1(5), Nov.–Dec. 1962.

Roeder, Carl M. *Liberation & Deliberation in Piano Technique*. New York/London: Schroeder & Gunther, 1941 (revised 1981).

Rosen, Charles. *Piano Notes*. New York: Free Press/Simon and Schuster, 2002.

Rosenblum, Sandra P. *Performance Practices in Classic Piano Music*. Bloomington: Indiana University Press, 1991.

Roskell, Penelope. *The Art of Piano Fingering: a new approach to scales and arpeggios*. London: LCM, 1996.

Rothstein, Edward. *Emblems of the Mind: The Inner Life of Music and Mathematics*. New York: Times Books/Random House, 1995.

Rubinstein, Beryl. *Outline of Piano Pedagogy*. New York: Carl Fischer, 1929.

Safonoff, Wassili. *New Formula for the Piano Teacher and Piano Student*. London: J. & W. Chester, 1916.

Samson, Jim. *Chopin*. New York: Schirmer Books, 1997.

Sandor, Gyorgy. *On Piano Playing: Motion, Sound and Expression*. New York: Schirmer, 1981.

Schauffler, Lawrence. *Piano Technic: Myth or Science*. Chicago: Gamble Hinged Music, 1937.

Schick, Robert D. *The Vengerova System of Piano Playing*. University Park and London: Pennsylvania State University Press, 1982.

Schmitz, E. Robert. *The Robert Schmitz Editions of Modern Piano Classics*. New York: Associated Music, 1923.

———. *The Capture of Inspiration*. New York: E. Weyhe, and Carl Fischer, 1935.

———. *E. Robert Schmitz Edition of the Chopin Etudes* (Edited—Fingered—Explanatory Text). New York: Carl Fischer, 1938 (3rd printing, revised).

———. *Serge Prokofieff, Sonata No. 7*. Edited and fingered by E. Robert Schmitz. New York: Leeds, 1945.

———. *Virgil Thomson, Sonata No. 4 for Piano Solo*. Edited and Fingered by E. Robert Schmitz. [Place of publication unknown.] Southern Music, 1946.

———. *Virgil Thomson, Ten Etudes*. Edited and fingered by E. Robert Schmitz. New York: Carl Fischer, 1946.

———. *The Piano Works of Claude Debussy*, Foreword by Virgil Thomson. New York: Dover, 1966. (Originally published by Duell, Sloan & Pearce in 1950, no location given.)

Schnabel, Artur. *My Life and Music*. New York: Dover, 1988.

Schonberg, Harold C. *The Great Pianists, from Mozart to the Present*. New York: Simon and Schuster, 1963.

Schott, Howard. *Playing the Harpsichord*. New York: St. Martin's Press, 1971.

Schultz, Arnold. *The Riddle of the Pianist's Finger*. New York: Carl Fischer, 1936.

Selections from The Piano Teacher *1958–1963*. Ed. by Robert Savler. Evanston, IL: Summy-Brichard, 1964.

Seroff, Victor. *Common Sense in Piano Study*. New York: Funk & Wagnall's, 1970.

Sherman, Russell. *Piano Pieces*. New York: North Point Press, 1997.

Shir-Cliff, Justin, Jay Stephen, and Donald J Rauscher. *Chromatic Harmony*. New York: Free Press, 1965.

Simpson, Elizabeth. *Basic Pianoforte Technique*. London: Macmillan, 1933.

Smith, Macdonald. *From Brain to Keyboard*. Boston: Oliver Ditson, 1917.

Soderlund, Sandra. *How Did They Play? How Did They Teach? A History of Keyboard Technique*. Chapel Hill, NC: Hinshaw Music, 2006.

Speaking of Pianists with Adele Marcus. Neptune, NJ: Paganiniana, 1979.

Steinhausen, F. A. *Die Physiologischen Fehler and die Umgestaltung der Klaviertechnic*. Leipzig: Breitkopf & Hartel, 1913.

Storr, Anthony. *Music and the Mind*. New York: Free Press, 1992.

A Symposium for Pianists and Teachers: Strategies to Develop the Mind and Body for Optimal Performance. Contributors: Gail Berenson, Jacqueline Csurgai-Schmitt, William DeVan, Dr. Mitchell Elkiss, Seymour Fink, Phyllis Alpert Lehrer, Barbara Lister-Sink, Robert Mayerovitch, Dr. Norman Rosen and Dylan Savage. Dayton, OH: Heritage Music Press, 2002.

Szulc, Tad. *Chopin in Paris*. New York: Scribner, 1998.

Taylor, Franklin. *Primer of Pianoforte Playing*. Edited by George Grove. New York: Macmillan, 1890.

———. *Technique and Expression in Pianoforte Playing*. London: Novello [undated].

Taylor, Harold. *The Pianist's Talent*. New York: Taplinger, 1979.

Teichmuller, Robert. *Klavier Technik*. Leipzig: Verlag Franz Jost, 1937.

Timbrell, Charles. *French Pianism*. New York: Pro/Am Music Resources, 1992 (1st ed.). Portland, OR: Amadeus Press, 1999 (2nd ed.).

Tubiana, Raoul M.D., ed. *The Hand*. Vol. 1. Philadelphia: Saunders, 1981.

———. *The Hand*, Vol. 4. Philadelphia: Saunders, 1993.

Unschuld, Marie Von. *The Pianist's Hand*. New York: Carl Fischer, 1909.

Varró, Margit. *A Teacher in Two Worlds*, Edited by Mariann Abraham. Budapest: Abraham Mariann/Varró Gabriella, 1991.

Weir, Albert E. *The Piano*. London, New York, Toronto: Longman's, Green, 1940.

Wells, Howard. *The Pianist's Thumb*. Boston: Oliver Ditson, 1926.

Weybright, June. *Belwin Piano Method (Book One)*. Van Nuys, CA: Belwin, 1964.

Whiteside, Abby. *Indispensables of Piano Playing*. New York: Scribner, 1961. (Originally published 1955.)

———. *Mastering the Chopin Etudes and Other Essays*. New York: Scribner, 1969.

———. *The Pianist's Mechanism*. New York: G. Schirmer, 1929.

Wilson, Frank R. *The Hand*. New York: Vintage Books, 1999.

———. *Tone Deaf and All Thumbs*. New York: Vintage Books, 1986.

Winspur, Ian, and Parry, Christopher B Wynn. *The Musician's Hand: A Clinical Guide*. London: Martin Dunitz, 1998.

Wolff, Konrad. *Schnabel's Interpretation of Piano Music*. New York/London: Norton, 1972.

Woodhouse, George. *The Artist at the Piano*. London: William Reeves, 1925.

Zamoyski, Adam. *Chopin*. Garden City, NY: Doubleday, 1980.

Zilberquit, Mark. *Russia's Great Modern Pianists*. Neptune, NJ: T.F.H., 1983.

Zuschneid, Karl. *Methodischer Leitfaden für den Klavierunterricht*. Berlin—Lichterfelde: Chr. Friederich Vieweg, 1914.

KEYBOARD MANUALS, STUDIES
AND EXERCISES

Associated Board of the Royal Schools of Music. *The Manual of Scales, Broken Chords and Arpeggios for the Piano*. Introduction by Ruth Gerald. London: Associated Board of the Royal Schools of Music (Publishing), 2001.

Beringer, Oscar. *Daily Technical Studies for the Pianoforte* (Newly Revised and Enlarged). London: Bosworth, 1915.

Clementi, Muzio. *Gradus ad Parnassum (Complete in Three Volumes), Arranged in Progressive Order by Max Vogrich*. Kalmus, 1897. Melville, NY: Belwin Mills.

———. *Metodo Completo pel Piano-Forte*. Italy: Arnaldo Forni Editore.

Clementi-Tausig. *Gradus ad Parnassum (Twenty-Nine Selected Studies)*. New York: Kalmus [undated].

Cooke, James Francis. Mastering the Scales and Arpeggios. Philadelphia: Theodore Presser, 1913.

Creston, Paul. *Virtuoso Technique for the Piano*. New York: G. Schirmer, 1950.

Dohnányi, Ernst von. *Essential Finger Exercises (for obtaining a sure technique)*. Budapest: Editio Musica Budapest, 1950.

Hanon, C. L. *The Virtuoso Pianist*. New York: G. Schirmer, 1900.

Herz, Henri. *Collection of Studies, Scales and Passages*. Miami: Kalmus/Warner Bros., [undated].

Liszt Technical Exercises for the Piano, edited by Julio Esteban. Port Washington, New York: Alfred, 1971.

Mitchell, Mark, and Evans, Allan. *Moriz Rosenthal: In Word and Music*. Bloomington: Indiana University Press, 2006.

Moszkowski, Moritz. *15 Virtuosic Etudes, "Per Aspera," Op. 72*. Edited by Maurice Hinson. Van Nuys, CA: Alfred (undated).

———. *Écoles des Doubles-Notes pour Piano* (Nouvelle Édition, revue et augmentée). Paris: Enoch, 1901.

———. *School of Scales and Double Notes for the Pianoforte, Opus 64* (four books). London: Enoch, 1904.

Peskanov, Alexander. *The Russian Technical Regimen for the Piano. Exercise Volume V: Scales in Double Notes*. Florence, KY: Willis, 1991.

Philipp, Isidor. *Complete School of Technic for the Piano*. Bryn Mawr, PA: Theodore Presser, 1908.

Pischna, Joseph. *Sixty Progressive Etudes*. Miami: Kalmus/Warner Bros., [undated].

Slonimsky, Nicholas. *Thesaurus of Scales and Melodic Patterns*. New York: Scribner, 1947 and New York/London/Paris/Sidney: Amsco ("by arrangement with Schirmer"), [undated].

Wiehmayer, Theodore. *Die Etude für Klavier* (Band I–II). Wilhelmshaven, Germany: Heinrichshofens Verlag, 1914.

BODYWORK AND RELATED STUDIES

Alexander, F. Matthias. *The Use of the Self*. Downey, CA: Centerline Press, 1984.

Allport, Gordon W., and Philip E. Vernon. *Studies in Expressive Movement*. New York: Hafner, 1967.

Barlow, Wilfred. *The Alexander Technique*. New York: Warner Books edition published by arrangement with Knopf, 1973.

Calais-Germain, Blandine. *Anatomy of Movement*. Seattle: Eastland Press, 1993.

Clippinger, Karen. *Dance Anatomy and Kinesiology*. Champaign, IL: Human Kinetics, 2007.

Feldenkrais, Moshe. *The Potent Self: A Guide to Spontaneity*. San Francisco: Harper & Row, 1985.

Franklin, Eric. *Dynamic Alignment Through Imagery*. Champaign, IL: Human Kinetics, 1996.

———. *Relax Your Neck, Liberate Your Shoulders*. Hightstown, NJ: Princeton Book, 2002.

Gray, Henry. *Gray's Anatomy*. Classic Collector's Edition. New York: Bounty Books, 1978.

Jones, Frank Pierce. *Body Awareness in Action: A Study of the Alexander Technique*. New York: Schocken, 1976.

Juhan, Dean. *Job's Body: A Handbook for Bodywork.* Barrytown, NY: Station Hill Press, 1987.

Laws, Kenneth. *Physics and the Art of Dance: Understanding Movement.* New York: Oxford University Press, 2002.

Levitin, Daniel J. *This Is Your Brain on Music.* New York: Penguin Group, 2007.

Lowen, Alexander, M.D., and Leslie Lowen. *The Way to Vibrant Health: A Manual of Bioenergetic Exercises.* New York: Harper Colophon, Harper & Row, 1977.

Miller, Marjorie A., and Lutie C. Leavell. *Kimber-Gray-Stackpole's Anatomy and Physiology* (16th ed.). New York: Macmillan, 1972.

Murphy, Michael. *The Future of the Body: Explorations into the Further Evolution of Human Nature.* Los Angeles: Tarcher, 1992.

Myers, Thomas W. *Anatomy Trains.* New York: Churchill Livingston, 2008 (first published 2001 with subsequent reprints: 2001, 2002, 2003 twice, 2004, 2005, 2006, 2007 twice).

Norkin, Cynthia C., and Pamela K Levangie. *Joint Structure and Function: A Comprehensive Analysis.* Philadelphia: Davis, 1983, 1990.

Restak, Richard M. *The Brain: The Last Frontier.* New York: Warner Books, 1979.

Rose, Steven. *The Conscious Brain.* New York: Vintage Books, 1976.

Rossiter, Richard H., with Sue McDonald. *Overcoming Repetitive Motion Injuries the Rossiter Way.* Oakland, CA: New Harbinger, 1999.

Rywerant, Yochanan. *The Feldenkrais Method: Teaching by Handling.* San Francisco: Harper & Row, 1983.

Sacks, Oliver. *Musicophilia: Tales of Music and the Brain.* New York/Toronto: Knopf, 2007.

Sweigard, Lulu E. *Human Movement Potential: Its Ideokinetic Facilitation.* New York: Harper & Row, 1974.

Todd, Mabel E. *The Thinking Body: A Study of the Balancing Forces of Dynamic Man.* New York: Dance Horizons, 1937.

ARTICLES, JOURNALS AND MISCELLANEOUS SOURCES

Adler, Clarence. "Impact—Leopold Godowsky." In *Selections from* The Piano Teacher *1958–1963.* Evanston, IL: Summy-Birchard, 1964.

Ericourt, Daniel. "Master Class: A Lesson on Debussy's Claire de Lune." In *Selections from* The Piano Teacher *1958–1963.* Evanston, IL: Summy-Birchard, 1964.

Fletcher, Stanley. "Scale Fingerings for Facility." In *Selections from* The Piano Teacher *1958–1963.* Evanston, IL: Summy-Birchard, 1964.

Haven, Dale. "Notes from a Godowsky Master Class." In *Selections from* The Piano Teacher *1958–1963.* Evanston, IL: Summy-Birchard, 1964.

Isacoff, Stuart. "I, Claudio." *Keyboard Classics* 3(1), Jan./Feb. 1983.

Jordan, Krassimira. "Unveiling the Enigma: A Tête-a-tête with Marc-André Hamelin." *Clavier Companion,* July–Aug. 2009.

Kiorpes, George. "Cortot's Approach to Piano Technique." *Clavier,* December 2005.

The New Grove Dictionary of Music (2nd ed.), edited by Stanley Sadie; executive editor, John Tyrell. Entries "Enharmonic Keyboard," "Keyboard Fingering," "Moszkowski," "Temperaments." New York: Oxford University Press, 2001.

Newman, William S. "Beethoven's Fingerings as Interpretive Clues." *Journal of Musicology,* 1(2), Apr. 1982.

Scarton, Dana. "Get Along Without a Pinkie? It's Tougher Than You Might Think." *New York Times,* Jan. 12, 2008.

Scholes, Percy A. *The Oxford Companion to Music* (9th ed.). "Fingering of Keyboard Instruments" and "Temperament." London: Oxford University Press, 1965.

Schmitz, E. Robert. "The Arm and Its Relation to the Keyboard." *The Etude,* Apr. 1947.

Taruskin, Richard. "On Letting the Music Speak for Itself." *Journal of Musicology,* 1(3), July 1982.

von Bülow, Hans. Preface to *J. B. Cramer: Fifty Studies for the Piano.* New York: G. Schirmer, 1875.

INDEX